© 2006 Sienese Shredder Editions
ISBN: 0-9787108-0-0
Sienese Shredder Editions
344 West 23rd Street # 4D
New York, NY 10011
www.sienese-shredder.com

Printed in Verona, Italy at Trifolio
Designed at The Grenfell Press,
 New York, NY
CD assistance: Shaun Myles of
 Eyefullphotographics, NY

Cover collages by Don Joint
*Front:* Time is on his side *(2006)*
*Back:* Faith *(2006)*

*Submissions by invitation only*

# The Sienese Shredder

*#1*

Winter 2006 - 2007

Edited by Brice Brown and Trevor Winkfield

# CONTENTS

*History of Art Department 2002 Commencement Address*
*University of California, Berkeley, May 24, 2002*

The title of this talk is "History and Truth," which may sound beyond pre-posterous for a brief commencement chat, but what I mean to do to is lay out somewhat breezily some of my own diversity of purpose in the face of such enormous abstractions—and hopefully those will seem less daunting, more congenial by the time I've finished.

"Diversity"—because it can only be an allowance of diversity that got me here to address you today. I failed to ask Anne Wagner, when she called, if I was being invited to talk as a poet, a critic or an art-historian-without-portfolio (which is what I am, at best and gladly, in that department). So I don't know what she or Tim Clark or anyone may have had in mind by ask-ing me. It can't be that I am standing here as just, so to speak, my bare self, flagrantly denuded of any degree of official representation. In truth, I know myself to be representative of no official order. I also know I agreed to do this because when Anne said the date "May 24th" I immediately thought of the first book of poems by a favorite poet, James Schuyler's *May 24th or So*, and a line in that book that goes:

> *You can't get at a sunset naming colors.*

So, a pause here for naming oneself, for convenient identity control—just to get *me* out of the way: primarily, I am a writer—a poet who, as the art magazines say in their notes on contributors, "also writes about art." Early in my poet's life, 1960 or so, I slipped on a banana peel and began writing art criticism. The impetus was roughly that I wanted to avoid the fate then typical for American poets, which was to teach literature and/or creative writing in some small college far from where one wanted to be, which in my case was my hometown of New York. The working model for poets writing about contemporary art was conspicuous among New York poets like John Ashbery, Frank O'Hara, Barbara Guest and Jimmy Schuyler. (Could you tell that Schuyler was an art critic from his line about a sunset?) There was an honorable local tradition, and it seemed to fit; so, like several of my peer group in the second-generation New York School, I followed suit—until almost ten years later, with big changes in the art world (and particularly in the practice of criticism), the impetus wore thin. Moving to California in 1970, I abruptly left off, an art-world dropout. Then again, another fifteen years down the line, primarily on the strength of my New York background, I found myself hired to teach art history at the San Francisco Art Institute. As bananas go, this was stray peel number two—and as I was in dire need of steady employment at the time, I appreciated the chance to slip on it.

That takes care of my history to the extent that most of what I just told you is true. Is history an account of verifiable fact? The rest of this talk—in the form of ruminations (literally, grazing the topic)—follows from a set of epigraphs—two from Gertrude Stein, one from Robert Smithson.

The last line of Stein's "If I Told Him: A Completed Portrait of Picasso," completed in 1923, reads:

*"Let me recite what history teaches. History teaches."*

Joining this in my mind is the last line of Stein's 1929 opera libretto *Four Saints in Three Acts*, chanted emphatically by the full chorus in Virgil Thomson's setting. That line goes:

*"Which is a fact."*

(Which I've always felt to be the great, perfect exit line for just about *anything*.)

Lastly, Robert Smithson's admonition, written many years later, in the late 1960s:

*"All clear ideas tend to be wrong."*

As a poet, as an art writer and in my dippings into art history—in those activities altogether—I find I am nearly crazy about facts. A slide of a painting is a clear idea, photographically conveyed, and a poor—though teachable—representation of observable fact. (As Alex Katz likes to say, a slide of a painting gives you no scale, no surface, no light and the color's all wrong—so what you get is a graphic anomaly.) No slides today. Instead, I'll drop a poem or two in the slot. My poems are often the result of searching out facts regarding this or that name or word or thing—but I will also be the first to admit that I have an uncertain idea about what constitutes a fact beyond a fair notion of the possibility that something is, or has been, the case. An image of the case. A piece of Robert Creeley's goes: *"You want/ the fact/ of things/ in words/ of words."*

What is so appealing about a fact is often its inconsequentiality. Beyond the relief that somehow astonishingly there are words for what it tells you, there is the temptation to leave a fact at its own face value. Let the statement, observation or description, as the case may be, hang in the air as-is. Art historians know only too well how, and with what regularity, their eager colleagues' shrewd interpretations bring about sets of corrupted fact. Some facts, I believe, exhibit their true colors best by remaining beautifully, resolutely pointless. Authoritative history, however, has no appetite for pointless stories; thus, each fact is liable to be confronted with a preemptive glare or squint, the Muse of History's vast, groaning, imperious "So What?" Without that "what" there's nothing teachable.

Here is a poem that resulted from discovering in an otherwise dull book two or three things about the philosopher Denis Diderot and his family—facts rubbed together in a way that I think of as igniting a small, sly fire in the language. It's called "The Recital":

*The Recital*

*It is said that, late in life, Denis Diderot force-fed his wife Nanette a diet of R-rated poetry and fiction, including his own Jacques the Fatalist, as a cure for her feelings of moral superiority. Diderot read to Nanette morning, noon and night, and whenever the Diderots had company, Mrs. D. would recite to her visitors whatever she had just absorbed. Slowly but surely, the cure took. "Conversation doubles the effect of the dosage," in a letter to their daughter wrote Diderot.*

W.H. Auden wrote, "Culture is history which has become dormant or extinct, a second nature." Generally, the modern idea of history is a way of coping with, by accounting for, our tantalizingly unstable culture—to give events leading up to the present a look of logical development, where really there is none. Turnover, shock—or its corollary, resentment—is neither development nor revolt; it's our vernacular status quo. Logic masks a chaos which may be friendlier than the logic espoused to shield us from it. During his October 1986 talk on Hans Hofmann across campus at the Berkeley Art Museum, Clement Greenberg spoke of how "Hofmann's paintings…had the habit of faring better with time. His works never looked as bad, if they did look bad, as they did the first time you saw them. Ever after they got better."

This remark—a variety of dialectical upside-down cake, is in fact an accurate account of the average viewer's experience with Hofmann's work—and not so incidentally states a view of history as perfectly, sensibly unstable and illogical. Even better is the artist Joe Brainard's way of dispensing with Greenberg's hothouse problem over badness and getting straight to the point. In a letter to an older artist friend, Joe wrote, "What I like about Hans Hofmann is that he is hard to like." Such a remark appeals to the more open-air vicissitudes of art as a variety of social behavior, from which esthetic experience should never be thought to be exempt.

Art-historical logic, museological practice or the arguments of art critics are good as long as they direct us back to the works under discussion with their facts illuminated—and they are bad when they direct us away from the work in favor of an overarching—and sense-stultifying—idea. In 1966 the critic Gene Swenson remarked: "The theory of cubism is more visible than the paintings themselves." My daughter Siobhan, who never studied art history but who likes to look at pictures, visited the Museum of Modern Art in New York for the first time in her mid-twenties. There, standing flatfooted before a 1911 Picasso, she was nonplussed. Rushing to her aid, an older friend offered the conventional excuse that Picasso's Analytical Cubism was a way of painting objects as if seen from all sides at once, whereupon Siobhan shrugged, said "Bad idea!" and moved on.

"Bad idea!" covers a lot of territory. I love museums for what they permit me to see that otherwise I couldn't. But there is that type of museological thinking where art functions to flesh out only our "museum" idea of things—down the *enfilades*, as it were, phase by phase. Museums generally, for better or worse, are organized to help us see that way, to leave out what doesn't help maintain the perspective. (Presumably we would get lost without the logic.) Bad ideas enable you to move along. Good ones light up the occasion of seeing, often by contrast, but watch out, they might stop you in your tracks. Rudy Burckhardt's son Jacob is now himself a filmmaker like his late father. In Florence, at the age of two, he followed the prescribed route with his parents through the Uffizi. Seeing Botticelli's tall, blond Venus after nine galleries packed with Madonnas of various stripes, Jacob cried out in a fit of primal iconological ardor: *"Nice clean lady—no baby!"*

History is funny. Lately is it is full of what some recall as dearly departed afterlives. One day in the late 1980s David Antin said, "Depending on what you believe Modernism was, you get the Postmodernism you deserve." More recently, Hal Foster, one of the definers of Post-, wrote an essay called "Whatever Happened to Postmodernism?" Depending on what you believe Post- was, what now is our deservable present?—or more to the point, our *desirable* one? I was fascinated, gladdened to hear that Tim Clark was giving two seminars this year—one in the work of Paul Cézanne, and another in Nicolas Poussin, who exemplified for Cézanne what he called "the art of the museums." As it happened, just as Tim's classes were steaming along, the contemporary painter Vija Celmins was quoted as saying: "What we need now is less Duchamp and more Cézanne." As if a Cézanne-esque art of tirelessly plunging perceptual sincerity—earthiness mixed with rag-tag spiritual gropings—had a prayer amid today's otherwise laudable (and entirely Duchampian) skepticism and blitheness. If so, maybe we can now get back to our delicious chaos—our grand inconsequentiality.

"The ardent lover of history" proceeds toward knowing everything about a work of art even if all of the big original ideas about it get shredded in the process. One enjoys an art historian's tough—truly critical—love, wherein the work stays central and the historian's performance is a threading of her attentiveness—cultural, perceptual, lingual—around and through, making an orbit in kind. Frank O'Hara's most cogent political statement, "The only truth is face to face" serves by extension for the truth of art and poetry. Truth is face to face with every facet—or nuance—of fact. By nuance, every word of a poem gathers the poem's surface energy.

By the nuance of its surface a painting we might call "great" actualizes its place in the culture that bred it.

My last fact for today followed on the sad, unsociable events of last September. A very short prose poem, it proposes to be not much more than an accurate account of its moment, but it seemed to me after having written it that whatever urgency or pertinence it holds is all in the nuance, including the slip of mistaken identity that got me going. Bare ideology, needy and resentful, has little patience with nuance. But it is exactly the subtler aspects of this historical reality that must be faced, and deeply felt, or else we continue to suffer the extremities. I hope that, at one reading, this poem's anti- or *meta*-ideological stance is plain:

*Gloria*

*A large U.S. flag flaps loudly outside our dining room, suspended on a pole from the topmost balcony across the way. I keep taking it for some poor thug running through the late September night, sneakers smacking.*

Here are the two towers of Saint Leu d'Esserent, the village on the height, separated by the railway from the part that borders the Oise. You rise toward Chantilly while going alongside high, solemn sandstone hills, then there's a bit of the forest. La Nonette shines in the fields that edge the last houses of the town. La Nonette, one of those sweet little rivers where I used to go crayfishing. On the other side of the forest flows her sister, the Thève, where I almost drowned for not wanting to seem cowardly to little Célénie!

Célénie often appears in my dreams, like a water nymph, a naïve temptress, wildly inebriated by the scent of the fields and crowned with water parsley and water lilies, showing, in her childish laugh, between dimpled cheeks, the pearly teeth of an undine. And of course the hem of her dress was often wet, as befits girls like her. You had to pick flowers for her along the marly edges of the ponds of Commelle or among the rushes and osier beds that border the dairy farms of Coye. She liked the grottos lost in the woods, the ruins of old chateaux, the collapsed temples whose columns were festooned with ivy, the home of the woodcutters, where she sang and recounted the old legends of this area: Mme. de Montfort, a prisoner in her tower, who sometimes flew off as a swan, sometimes frisked about as a beautiful carp in the moat of her castle; the pastry chef's daughter who delivered cakes to the Count d'Ory and who, forced to spend the night with her lord, asked for his dagger to open the knot in her lacework and stabbed him in the heart; the red monks who carried off women and hurled them into underground caverns; the daughter of the Sire de Pontarmé, smitten with handsome Lautrec and locked up for seven years by her father, after which she died; and the knight, returning from the Crusade, who used a thin golden knife to unstitch her shroud of fine linen, and when she came back to life she turned out to be a vampire thirsting for blood... Henri IV and Gabrielle, Biron and Marie de Loches, and I don't know how many other tales that peopled Célénie's memory: Saint Rieul speaking to the frogs, Saint Nicolas reviving the three children chopped up like pâté by a butcher in Clermont-sur-Oise. Saint Leonard, Saint Loup, and Saint Guy have left in these regions a thousand examples of their sainthood and their miracles. Célénie climbed up onto the rocks or onto the druidic dolmens and told these stories to the young shepherds. From the old area of the Sylvanectes, that little Velléda left me memories that time revives. What became of her? I will find out around La Chapelle-en-Serval or Charlepont or Montméliant... She had aunts everywhere, endless numbers of cousins: so many dead among them, and no doubt many unhappy ones, in a land that was so happy back then!

At least Chantilly bears its poverty nobly; like these old gentlemen in white linen with their irreproachable bearing, it has this proud attitude that disguises the faded hat or the worn-out clothes… Everything is clean, organized, circumspect; the voices resonate harmoniously in the sonorous halls. One senses the habit of respect, and the ceremony that formerly reigned in the chateaux rules to some degree the relationships among the placid inhabitants. Chantilly is filled with very old retired servants, walking their limping dogs. Some of them have become masters, taking on the venerable look of the old lords that they served.

Chantilly is like a long street in Versailles. It must be seen in summer, in splendid sunlight, while passing loudly over the beautiful clattering cobblestones. Everything is readied there for the princely splendors and the privileged crowd of the hunts and the races. Nothing is as strange as that large gate that opens onto the lawn of the chateau like an arch of triumph, or the adjacent monument that looks like a basilica and is only a stable. In this there remains something of the struggle of the Condés against the older branch of the Bourbons. In the absence of war it is the hunt that triumphs, the hunt that restored that family's glory after Clio had torn out certain pages from the history of the warlike youth of the Great Condé, as expressed in the melancholy painting that he himself commissioned.

But what good is it to revisit this chateau now stripped bare, the only remaining things being the satirical Watteau room and the tragic shade of Vatel the cook stabbing himself in the heart in the orchard! I preferred hearing the sincere apologies of my hostess regarding this good Prince de Condé, who is still the subject of local conversation. In this type of village there is something akin to the circles in Dante's purgatory, circles immobilized in a single memory, where the actions of past lives are recreated in an even tighter center.

"And what has become of your daughter, who was so blond and so gay?" I asked her. "She must have gotten married."

"Goodness yes, but then she died, her chest…"

I daresay that this hit me with more force than the memories of the Prince of Condé. When I knew her she was quite young and of course I would have fallen in love with her had my heart not already been given to another… And now I suddenly think of the German ballad called *The Hostess' Daughter*, and of its three companions, one of whom said: "Oh! If I had known her, how I would have loved her!" And the second one said: "I knew you and I loved you tenderly!" And the third: "I did not know you… but I love you and I will love you throughout eternity!"

Again a face that grows pale, comes loose and falls, icy, on the horizon of these woods bathed in gray vapors… I took the carriage from Senlis that follows the course of the Nonette, passing through Saint Firmin and Courteuil; to our left was Saint Leonard and its old chapel, and already we noticed the high belltower of the cathedral. To the left is the field of

Raines, where Saint Rieul, interrupted by frogs while he was preaching, imposed silence on them and, when he finished, allowed a single one to make itself heard in the future. There is something oriental about this naïve legend and in this saint's goodness that allowed at least one frog to express the complaints of the others.

I found an unspeakable happiness in wandering up and down the streets and lanes of the old Roman city, once so renowned for its sieges and battles. "O poor city, how you are envied!" said Henri IV. Today it is forgotten, and its inhabitants seem to worry very little about the rest of the world. They live even further removed than the people of Saint Germain. That hill with its antique constructions proudly dominates its horizon of green fields bordered by four forests. In the distance Halatte, Apremont, Pontarmé, and Ermononville sketch out their shady masses, from which rise the ruins of abbeys and chateaux.

While going past the Reims Gate, I encountered one of those enormous carriages that carry from fair to fair an entire artistic family of saltimbanques, their props and household goods. It had begun to rain, and they kindly offered me shelter. The premises were huge, warmed by a stove and lit by eight windows, and six people seemed to live there rather comfortably. Two pretty girls were busy mending their spangled costumes, and a still beautiful woman was cooking while the head of the family was giving lessons in deportment to a handsome young man he was training to play the role of the lover. That is, these people do not limit themselves to gymnastics; they also put on plays. They are often invited to provincial chateaux, and they showed me several attestations of their talents, signed by illustrious names. One of the girls began declaiming some lines from a comedy that went back at least as far as Montfleury—the new repertory is forbidden them. They also put on improvised plays based on rough outlines, in the Italian style, with a great facility of inventiveness and repartee. While gazing at the two girls, one lively and dark, the other blonde and mirthful, I began to think of Mignon and Philine in *Wilhelm Meister*, and suddenly a Germanic dream came to me there between the prospect of the woods and the antique profile of Senlis. In the absence of a place to live in Paris, why not remain in this wandering house? But it was not the time to follow these fantasies of a youthful gypsy life, and I took leave of my hosts, because the rain had stopped.

*Translated from the French by Ron Padgett*

# Judith Stein

## AN INTERVIEW WITH RICHARD TUTTLE ON RICHARD BELLAMY AND THE NEW YORK ART WORLD

One afternoon in 1986 when I was on the curatorial staff at the Pennsylvania Academy of the Fine Arts, the guard at the front desk phoned. Three visitors from New York had come to see the Franz Kline show and wanted to consult the curator in charge. That was the day I first met the legendary art dealer Richard Bellamy, accompanied by his friends Mark di Suvero and Alfred Leslie.

At the time, I knew about Bellamy's Green Gallery, which had triggered the careers of di Suvero, Dan Flavin, Donald Judd, Robert Morris, Claes Oldenburg, Larry Poons, James Rosenquist, Lucas Samaras, George Segal and Tom Wesselmann between 1960-65. But the man himself was a cipher. Roy Lichtenstein had famously ribbed the dealer with a character whose thought balloon read: "I'm supposed to report to a Mr. Bellamy. I wonder what he's like."

Bellamy's appearance that day surprised me. Indistinguishable in dress from the men who queued for meals at the church mission nearby, his pant cuffs were frayed to a fringe. He wore two sets of eyeglasses, one tethered around his neck, the other—broken in half and taped—posed on his nose. He was exceedingly polite, socially awkward and immensely charming.

Our professional paths would cross intermittently over the years. With each encounter, his intrigue grew. To reconcile his legend with the modest man I was getting to know, I decided to write about him. I began by interviewing his contemporaries. The elderly Leo Castelli confided: "Although Dick was younger than I, he was my teacher." A mutual sense of play drew Oldenburg to Bellamy: he liked showing with a dealer who told people that he named his gallery after the color of money. To Richard Serra, Bellamy was less a dealer than a producer, seemingly immune to the profit motive. "Dick didn't sell art; he placed art," said Richard Nonas. For Bellamy, art alone had worth; artists were the true elite.

In the last decade I have talked with nearly two hundred people whose lives he touched. I discovered that Bellamy's decisive role in birthing the new American art that followed Abstract Expressionism was matched by his undocumented, behind-the-scenes activities as a facilitator and scout. He practiced acts of gratuitous kindness. My informants pointed to his egalitarian and subversive nature, and his penchant for sharing information and time with those whom others deemed nonentities—rare behavior in an often snooty art world.

I learned that Bellamy was the first Asian-American art dealer of influence, although few outside his close circle were aware of his ethnic background. Born in Cincinnati in 1927, he was the only child of a Chinese mother and Kentucky-born father who were both doctors. Bellamy came of age during WWII in the suburban Midwest, where the only people who looked like him were in newsreels or Charlie Chan movies. Throughout his five-decade career he was particularly supportive of Asian artists, championing Yoko Ono, Yayoi Kusama, Tadaaki Kuwayama, Kunié Sugiura and Tehching Hsieh.

Beloved by those he represented, Dick Bellamy would nonetheless exasperate them all; most would move on to work with other, more commercially-minded dealers. Unlike many of his artists, he would never become rich. Bedeviled by drugs, alcohol, hemorrhoids and bad teeth, he did not attain sobriety until his fifties. Mentioned only in passing in most histories of the period, this unassuming stoker of the star-maker machinery was nonetheless a major force in the post-war American art world.

For the past five decades, Richard Tuttle has rejoiced in what John Ashbery calls the "fun to be had in the gaps between ideas." In 1963 at the age of twenty-two, Tuttle arrived in New York during the height of the Green Gallery's authority. The following year he became an assistant at the Betty Parsons Gallery, located directly across W. 57th Street from the Green. Wordless communication characterized the early stages of Bellamy and Tuttle's friendship. They eyed each other on gallery visits, recognizing in the other a kindred sensibility.

Tuttle's tender, small-scale manipulations of unorthodox materials were inventive, subtle, elusive, playful and poetic, adjectives that apply as well to Bellamy's persona. The artist thought of asking Bellamy to show his work, but as a courtesy he first approached Parsons, who unexpectedly agreed. Tuttle's debut of constructed paintings in September 1965 launched his career. Although Bellamy never represented the artist, he did include his work in an unusual group exhibition after the Green Gallery closed.

During the summer of 1967, Bellamy mounted *Arp to Artschwager*, a wittily-titled selection of two dozen sculptors at the Noah Goldowsky Gallery. Tuttle showed alongside many of Bellamy's discoveries and friends, including John Chamberlain, Christo, Walter de Maria, Mark di Suvero, Dan Flavin, Donald Judd, Gary Kuehn, Robert Morris, Reuben Nakian, Bruce Nauman, Claes Oldenburg, Keith Sonnier, Michael Steiner, H.C. Westermann and Robert Whitman.

In my 2002 conversation with Tuttle about Bellamy, he talked about the tangencies of their lives, and the art world they mutually inhabited. After Bellamy's collaboration with Noah Goldowsky (1966-73), he operated the Oil and Steel Gallery on Chambers Street and then in Long Island City, from 1980 until his death in 1998.

*New York City, February 16, 2002*

**Judith Stein**: I thought you'd like to see a photocopy of a 1970 *Vogue* article on the New York art world that includes a picture of Dick Bellamy; he's the one down here with a shock of thick hair covering one eye.

**Richard Tuttle**: These were the hot young dealers of the moment?

**JS**: Yes, right.

**RT**: Oh, that's Paula [Cooper].

**JS**: Apropos of Paula, Richard Artschwager once told me he remembered the first time he ever saw her; she was so beautiful, she took his breath away.

**RT**: Paula had this Greek quality, the power and the dignity and the handsomeness, her beauty was a combination of that, the strength and character with the youth of her. I knew her when she had her first job at a gallery on La Guardia Place. Anyway, Dick liked her—he had an eye for the ladies.

**JS**: At the time, you were working for the Betty Parsons Gallery—when did you start there?

**RT**: In the fall of '64.

**JS**: That would have been the last season of the Green Gallery. Do you remember going to the Green?

**RT**: It was right across 57th Street from Betty Parsons. Normally I'd go to their openings. I remember the Larry Poons show [Feb '65] was a great show. Neil Williams I remember. Perhaps that was the season when Lucas Samaras lived in the gallery all summer long and recreated his studio/bedroom in his mother's house in New Jersey [Sept '65].

**JS**: Exactly.

**RT**: Yes that was terrific, very memorable. There were a lot of memorable shows—the Robert Morris show must have been that season too [Dec '64].

**JS**: Yes, he had two shows almost back to back, when he introduced the gray boxes.

**RT**: Minimal sculptures, yes.

**JS**: Later on that season—into the spring of 1965—the Green Gallery sponsored a Daniel Spoerri exhibition off-site at the Chelsea Hotel; although it's commonplace now for galleries to sponsor shows outside of their walls, Spoerri's was one of the first. Dick may well have been the pioneer—four years before the Green sponsored Claes Oldenburg's Store on the Lower East Side.

**RT**: I just read somewhere recently that Spoerri's work was not well-known in New York. I thought that was strange because, on the whole, he was definitely part of the Fluxus group. Fluxus work was known by some people and it was an important repository for certain kinds of aesthetic; I think that Dick's aesthetics were not antithetical to Fluxus in general and Spoerri in particular. But that would have been before what I think of as Spoerri's most famous works, where he would freeze tables after dinners. . . .

**JS**: In fact that *is* what he was showing at the Chelsea Hotel, "snare pictures" he called them, where he glued down the remains of a meal, food leavings, wine glasses and cigarette butts.

**RT**: Yes, which were totally wonderful, very aesthetically freeing, but, of course that's from Dusseldorf. So when I went to Dusseldorf, maybe two years later, I felt very comfortable with that kind of art. Spoerri is one of those very interesting artists who bridges, acts as a kind of a transitional personality. He had close ties with the Zero artists in Dusseldorf and then he was close to others. I guess the Zero artists could befriend Yves Klein and in turn reach others. There was almost a Pan-European communication at that time, the same kind as took place in the 1920s with Schwitters, Dadaists and early Surrealists.

You had Manzoni who traveled a lot through different capitals and connected artists with one another and Spoerri did that as well. It was kind of amazing that Dick's gallery—even to the degree that it sponsored a show in Spoerri's Chelsea Hotel room—would recognize that. Some people call that moment in European art New Realism which I think is actually a pretty good name. The destruction during the Second World War included a destruction of an old realism. The meaning of the new realism was that people were aware of this—a lot of the aesthetic does have to do with detritus.

I recently thought about Spoerri. I'm doing a book with a great poet in France, Anne-Marie Albiach[1] and I took the paper table cloths from the two square tables that we had at lunch and traced all the circles that were left behind from glasses and wine and plates and so on, and then folded the whole tablecloth together which produced exactly twelve images and twelve empty spaces because the back of the book of course had no drawings on it. That's where the poems will be going. In fact there turned out to be 48 stanzas in this poem so we just multiplied the table by four. For me, it brings a certain social relation and a warmth to the project. I think in the case of Spoerri's pieces, even though you're looking at cigarettes and ashes and leftover food and everything, there's the most wonderful social feeling that's created.

**JS**: How would you describe your relationship with Dick?

1. TUTTLE, RICHARD. *L'Exces: Cette Mesure. 48 poemes d'Anne-Marie Albiach & 48 dessins de Richard Tuttle*. Paris 2004.

**RT**: Perhaps even physically, he and I had a kind of similarity, or were similar types. When we looked at each other, there was a kind of a connection. And I'm not even sure if I ever spoke to him at that time; but for all the years afterward, I knew that whenever I came in his presence, there was instant recognition. It was more like two old souls, how they might recognize themselves in this world, or meet in this world. In a way I think our entire relationship was like that. It was never about anything in this life or this particular reincarnation. And we liked that, maybe, because at the very end, maybe even in the weeks before he died, we must have met 6 or 7 times just by accident in different places, waiting in line to buy tickets to concerts, or in museums, or on the street or wherever. I think of him as a bodhisattva, a lot of his work here was exactly what you'd expect a bodhisattva to do.

**JS**: In a way, he elected not to ascend to the nirvana of the other dealers.

**RT**: Well yes, that's the kind of move an artist knows very, very well. Just to carry on with the idea of earlier lives, he could be an example of someone who had been an artist in an earlier life, and he was one, in a way, here. He never seemed very comfortable being here although he loved helping artists. I think his greatest pleasure in life was helping artists. Certainly I felt that.

Whenever I met him I always felt he was asking, "Can I help you?" asking himself, "How could I help this person?" That's a wonderful recognition, especially when you're young and you don't know; that's why I worked with Betty Parsons—because she had been in the art world since the 1920s and knew so much about how an artist can survive, or take a position, or contribute in this world, because there are no rules, there are no patterns, and no concrete forms, as there are for doctors or lawyers.

But then it was also a question of, if he had been an artist, what is there after being an artist? A little bit, I think one of the things about Dick that was very elevated was his compassion. I mean you just took one look at him and you knew that this was a person who had enormous compassion, and that he was a higher being. It's almost like you could tell a higher being by the amount of compassion they have, but then if you have as much compassion as an artist does, then why do you come back?

There are some people who say that when you get maximum compassion then you can't read the object of your compassion. And I guess I felt a little bit about Dick that he liked to help people but he was also bound. His compassion for the artist bound him to the artist and I was a little uncomfortable with that. Also I kept a little distance.

A curious thing happened during the last talks I had with Dick. I had been to the University of Texas at Austin where the James Michener collection was located and there was this small group of extremely terrific artworks that Michener bought at the very end, before he gave his collection to the University of Texas. There's a Jo Baer, a Brice Marden, a work of mine, and so on. I had learned somehow that James Michener and Dick had been very close and so I thought the only explanation for the presence of these pieces was that Dick had just run him around town at a certain point and acquired these pieces for him. There's such an aesthetic leap— it's like light years between them and anything else Michener had collected. They are of such outstanding quality; it's awesome that such a high quality group had been acquired.

So I asked Dick pointedly, did you take Michener around town? He said that he had not, and that he in fact didn't know how Michener had done it. He also belittled his connection with Michener and said that they just liked to have a drink occasionally or something like that. I don't think it was like him to dissemble; this wouldn't come out of some extreme case of discreteness or self-deprecation. But on the other hand, I don't feel like committing myself to its truth either.

**JS**: In fact he *was* involved with shaping the Michener collection. The painter David Reed has been interviewing artists whom Michener collected and they speak about Dick as the liaison.

**RT**: In the introduction to his collection catalogue, Michener does mention Dick.

**JS**: But I found it peculiar that Michener refers to Dick as a "boy"—he was fifty years old at the time the two worked together. His take on Dick seems patronizing.

**RT**: Yes, I was thinking of Michener's rather laborious first steps into American art, visiting the Whitney Museum when it was on 8th Street, at lunch breaks, and really looking at what they collected. It would not have prepared him for a leap to the work Dick was showing, which was very much more self-realized, in a more leadership mode. It's a mystery.

**JS**: After Robert Scull pulled out his funding and the Green Gallery collapsed, Dick was working out of Noah Goldowsky's for several years. Did you track him informally in the post-Green years, or go to any of the shows that he did at Goldowsky's?

**RT**: Did he show the Japanese artist, Kusama? I remember seeing her at Goldowsky's.

**JS**: He showed Kusama at the Green. Donald Judd introduced him to her new work. Dick debuted her sculpture in a 1962 group show although he never gave her a solo show. During the Green's run, Dick brokered Yoko Ono's very first sale, to Robert Scull, although she didn't show with him. Dick had an extra sensitivity to women artists. He was also particularly receptive to Asian artists, likely because his mother was Chinese.

In the early '60s, there were not many women artists in a given gallery stable. Yet the percentage of women who were at the Green Gallery is above average. That didn't happen accidentally, although I don't credit him with a feminist consciousness per se.

**RT**: Yes, I wouldn't call it feminism either; but I think he had a particular, strong vision about where art can come from. It's very un-"PC" to say it, but you use a word like psyche. . . it seemed that Dick could distinguish it. Nowadays everybody will say that it just comes to the same place, but in some of these cases, it's good to go back to an emergence place and remember that. So, Dick would represent what was; there certainly had been examples of women, second-generation abstractionists, plenty of examples. But Dick really seemed to sense that art came from a very special place where cycles, physiognomy, the woman, without utilizing her, worshipping her even because of that special possibility but not, I guess the most important thing would be that he didn't feel it had to be defined.

He knew it, but defining would belittle it somehow or another, or wrap it up, encapsulate it some way or another and he didn't want to do that and that was great. I think that's what his treatment of Kusama was about. Sure there are dealers and there are artists and it's always a question of how a particular dealer will work with a certain artist, certain dealers. And it's wonderful these days to think about historic dealers and study them.

**JS**: What do you think made Dick special as a dealer?

**RT**: I think that another wonderful thing about Dick is that he tended to think artworks were living things, not dead things. That's both part of his greatness and part of why he wasn't among the best or the most successful dealers. Ultimately those people wind up thinking about art as a dead thing they're working with, dead.

**JS**: Well, they can have some distance. You were talking before about that. If I ask you about his least admirable traits, would you point to his lack of appropriate distance, or is there anything else?

**RT**: It's hard to say. My interest is to make my contribution, and so I would look at people in terms of how much help could I get from them, or what they were capable of doing.

Yes, I thought that he was more like an inspiration, or almost like a muse, a spirit. He had a beautiful spirit: it's wonderful in the art world to find somebody with that beauty of spirit among all the sort of dark, twisted, unattractive parts of the art world.

I remember visiting his Oil and Steel gallery on Chambers Street a couple of times, but it was too far out of the way for most people. I guess he also seemed to me to be somebody who must be like the sun, who would go behind the clouds, and then the cloud would go away and then he'd shine through.

It was curious that I met him so often in the last couple of weeks of his life. It was as if before he really did leave the world, he wanted to be present for me, more so than he ever had been before. Dick wasn't, what do you say, capable. For example, my wife and I would know the right way to get tickets, and avoid waiting in a long line only to find that they were all sold out.

Once we saw Dick at the end of such a line and went up to him to ask "why did you stay in the line?" He had a kind of funny dreaminess where he couldn't really take care of himself; he floated around but was also very present. I've spoken to other people who also said they saw him a lot in his last weeks; I'm not saying this had anything particularly to do with me.

**JS**: I have heard that in the weeks before he died, he went to a lot of concerts and would get tickets and invite many people to come with him.

**RT**: I went to his funeral and people mentioned things like that. It's interesting; everybody had a kind of a Dick Bellamy story, like seeing him on the other side of the street, him not coming over or something.

I think that art is a real thing. Sometimes I find it useful to personify art. There are people who seem to be closer or farther away from art at different times of their lives. Artists loved Dick because he was so close to art. He wasn't a threat because he wasn't an artist; but even if he were an artist, I don't think it would have made any difference. He had a wonderful presence and comfort for artists. A lot of times, artists will actually have a very difficult relationship with art. There's a lot of struggle involved, a lot of suffering. But somehow when we saw Dick, our suffering was placated and calmed and soothed because he had such a good relation to art. That's the way it seemed to me.

He did have a calming effect. It was marvelous during the Green Gallery days because the shows were anything but calm. That's another kind of anomaly. Dick was outstanding when around the anomalous. I feel now that the Pop moment was a reaction to the tremendous inward gaze that the abstract expressionists promoted. It had gone on for three decades and people were staring harder and harder at their navels, getting less and less out of it. It just suddenly hit everybody, "Why the hell don't we look at that chair?" Or look out for a second.

I know I'm drawing a picture of a collective, but I think it is a little bit more of that, a lot of people just looked out for that moment just because of this habitual introspection, which is another way of saying honing a criticism. But the moment they looked out, they not only had a great, fresh view, but they also had the benefit of the critical that was gained by this inward looking. Dick was very much an inward-looking person. So it's all the more anomalistic that he would be one of the chosen dealers behind Pop Art. In fact, he may have been the one who needed that more than anyone else, so it was more meaningful.

**JS**: Irving Sandler has called him "the eye of the sixties." And he was; he had such an important role in shaping that shift you've been talking about, and he helped invent the new art world canon of the '60s. He was right there at the key moment.

**RT**: I don't know if you've read the new book on Emily Hall Tremaine, *Collector on the Cusp*, which mentions Dick's relationship with Pop art—you should. What I'm saying about this moment is most directly coming from her. Classical Athens was overnight and the Renaissance was overnight too—these really terrific moments go by so fast. . . .

Bellamy was one of the first to see Pop, and he was the first to dump it. He dumped it far before his backer Robert Scull did; and he was right. The real energy didn't hold. Andy Warhol certainly had other reasons for existence; if you compare one of Andy's paintings from 1962 to his late ones, by my opinion, it's just not there. All the artists looked in the newspapers and just picked out things.

I just saw a Lichtenstein show in Miami. He's another case of someone who went on with the ingredients for a long time. But the great thing about Pop is you look at it and it just takes the words out of your mouth—you just can't believe your eyes. It's like the world stopped. It's curious for me to hear what you say because I find that dealers get connected with a specific moment in art. Every art has its idols, its dealers and its cultures. Why shouldn't Dick be a dealer of that moment? I think of him as being open to many moments. He also showed Minimal art—Robert Morris did his absolute best work with Dick. I know he appreciated Walter de Maria, and Kusama, who was not Pop. He really had something else that was outside the narrowness of one particular art movement.

**JS**: Dick was a great facilitator for many artists, particularly those he didn't actually represent. Are there specific points in your own career when he made introductions, or played a role in any way?

**RT**: I don't know of any examples. Every young artist—every young person—has a problem of being taken seriously. With Dick, he exuded information. Not only did he take *me* seriously but he took my art seriously, and that kind of support is incalculable in its meaning and its importance, not that it removed my doubts completely. I preferred not to know why he took my work seriously because I was scared it might be for the wrong reason. But you're not privileged to have the right reasons or maybe you can't handle reasons other than your own. There are hundreds of little interactions in the art world.

When I had attention given to my work, people thought it was time to make a show. Dick's Green Gallery was certainly one of the galleries that I thought to approach. But because I was working at Betty Parsons and I considered them friends, I thought it would be really insulting to go someplace else before I at least spoke to Betty, and so I never got to Dick.

**JS**: Ah, so you asked Betty first.

**RT**: Yes, she had already announced that she would never give a show to someone younger than 35 and I didn't have any hope; asking her was just a courtesy. But then she said to me, "Oh Richard, do you really want to get involved in all this?" She never said yes or no to the show. I said "yes," which I did in a very, very small voice, but that was our contract.

**JS**: Do you remember Dick coming in to see shows at the Betty Parsons Gallery?

**RT**: I do—they were carefully chosen, and that's another nice thing about him. He exercised his attentions with a lot of discrimination in general. He would come to see Ad Reinhardt's shows, for example.

And with Dick, it's also important to say that—what's that phrase, that he followed his own drummer? I can't tell you how encouraging that is. So many people follow their ears or they follow their art magazines. No one can be 100% right about art; there's always going to be mistakes—and serious mistakes too—but to find somebody who has the confidence to accept those risks rather than using some media service or something that promises to tell you 100%. Many services do make these outrageous promises to which a weaker person will fall victim. Dick was unbelievably sensitive, delicate and extremely refined  But he was strong—the strongest part of him was his belief in following his own way with art. In later years, I think he knew that he was on the wrong trail, but he still followed it and didn't give up on it. That's why people love him today.

**JS**: You had begun to tell me about a time you came to a show at the Green Gallery and said to Dick that you liked the art on view, and he said to you, "Oh, do you like that?" and that you found that a strange comment for a gallerist, who presumably liked it himself or he wouldn't be showing it.

**RT**: Yes, that gallery, that room was a place where I at least could have a true art response. It wasn't that I might assume *he* had the same art response—he put all of those things out in the room. What was more interesting for him was to make a room where other people could have an art response and that that was so permissible and signed with such permissibility as for him to be able to say, "Oh, do you like that?," a knowing, multi-dimensioned statement. It meant that he knew that I had responded, and that that was not only OK, but was in fact a wonderful thing.

He gave to this space, this room, a kind of freedom. If you're a person who needs art, who is desperate to have art in your life, there's hardly any place in this world where you can go to get it. In museums even now, I have to memorize and then run out and take a walk in a park and redigest them in order to have my art experience because, if you just feel that something terrible will happen to you because it is not permissible public behavior.

Dick with this humanity, he was a large enough person to make this room—just one room where people could go—they would be invited to have an art response, which means he knew what that was, and that it defined a gallery. It's not a boutique; it's not a shop; it's not a place where you're supposed to go through a code of behavior.

When you have such a room like that, it's a freedom, the most delicious freedom there is. It's what defines what freedom is. I say that art is an untamable natural force and to have it you have to accept that it's untamable. It goes back to the Greeks. Their definition in our culture is based on the definition of matter which is so all-inclusive as to allow an art response, for example. But we veer off from that definition this way and that way and when someone comes along who is large enough to define matter that allows, that's how Dick found his way into western culture.

Sassetta, *The Prophet Elijah*,
tempera and gold on wood,
7 1/2 x 21 1/2 inches,
Pinacoteca Nazionale, Siena.

Trevor Winkfield          THE EARLY SASSETTA

Sassetta was a painter of fragments. Or rather, as we perceive him today, he *is* a painter of fragments. The dismantling, dismembering and diaspora of his altarpieces, together with their physical abrasions, fadings, candle smoke stainings, restorations, excessive cleanings and varnishings have left us with an array of objects which can bear little relation to what people must have seen during Sassetta's lifetime. Posterity's paring of Uccello's oeuvre seems lenient by comparison.

Sassetta himself is a man of fragments, none of which add up to a solid portrait. We're in the position of those hapless archaeologists trying to reconstruct a vase based on slivers of crumbling handles. Sassetta is as lost to us as those anonymous craftsmen who erected cathedral towers. The few biographical facts to be garnered from the archives offer little more than a ghost of a profile: his body is missing, the personality remains a riddle. No temper tantrums with Popes or severed ears can be traced to him. Like reading shards, the profile has to be fleshed out using the surviving paintings. (Though we should keep in mind that in all instances not only is the painting more important than the painter, in a perfect fusion the painting *is* the painter.)

It should at the outset be observed that the painter we behold today differs considerably not only from the painter seen by his contemporaries, but also from the painter who was first extricated from historical obscurity a century ago. Fascination with his work has steadily increased in relation to the number of art movements his reputation has been subsequently filtered through. Transmitted via the distorting lens of Cubism, Surrealism, Abstraction, Pop Art and Minimalism (not forgetting comic strips and Technicolor), he now appears, along with Giovanni di Paolo and Paolo Uccello, as one of the most idiosyncratic and yet most profound painters of the Quattrocento period, one of those talents with most to offer present-day viewers and artists. (On the other hand, the cumulative effects of those very same movements which renewed interest in Sassetta have, by contrast, rendered Raphael's influence all but harmless.)

Quite literally, we see neither the spectrum nor space (let alone religion) as our predecessors saw them during the Dark Centuries preceding Impressionism. Sassetta has been one of the beneficiaries of the twentieth century's brightenings and flattenings—and, let's note, its parallel embracing, absorption and abandonment of the concept of "Primitive." As a result, he and his Sienese kin now feel closer to us than the Barbizon School.

"Could it be that at the center of Sassetta's art there lay no core of sodden sentimentalism but an original and virile mind?" So wrote John Pope-Hennessy somewhat uncertainly in his eximious 1939 disquisition on the artist. But just as there has been a pictorial revolution over the past century, so in the gap between Pope-Hennessy's query and our own time there has been a quickening aversion towards purely formal dissections of a painter's worth, a reaction to a clapped-out academic modernism, particularly in its abstract branches.

Without a hint of embarrassment, previously squirm-inducing designations such as "charm," "delightful," "mythopoeic," "lovely," "toylike," even Pope-Hennessy's "sentimentalism" have begun to vivify—or muddy, depending on one's stance—the aesthetic waters for the first time since Victorian days, adjectives no longer cast as epithets but as locations of interest. Not that Sassetta lacked classic skills in picture making: serenity, harmony and balance he had in abundance. No mere oddball he. But his career stands as one more riposte to the widespread belief that only formalists have long creative lives. Visionaries too can have longevity. Today, when individualism is a trait prized above all others, there's another point in Sassetta's favor: he looks as though he were painting for himself and not only for the clergy or wealthy patrons. He *was* painting for them, of course, but cleverly disguised this necessity. And it—the work—was all laid down before the aloof cleverness of the Renaissance stiffened bristles throughout Italy, at a time when fervid imaginations still granted improvisation a starring role in design.

The High Renaissance, that "ghastly mistake" as Georges Braque noted, was still a hundred years in the future when Sassetta was born, like his parents before him and according to deductive legend, in the Italian hill town of Cortona in 1392 (he died in Siena in 1450). No documents survive to confirm his arrival, nor why Stefano di Consolo was dubbed, for no apparent reason, with the moniker Sassetta sometime during the eighteenth century. Unless the label derived from the village of Sassetta to the west of Siena, which, according to some, was another possible site of his birth. Certainly the family must have moved to Siena or its environs in Sassetta's youth and established some kind of residency, since it was that city which commissioned his first known work, the Arte della Lana altarpiece in 1423. Financed by the city's guild of wool merchants, it was completed in 1426 and was destined for their guildhall and later their chapel, and was intended principally for use on the feast of Corpus Christi.

One of the joys and tribulations of exploring a long-lost artist is the often total evaporation of their juvenilia, vanished before fame accorded it some value. Particularly when that artist flourished in medieval times, what apprentice work may still survive is often subsumed anonymously within an older master's work, since the completed tableau would have been attributed to the master alone (though on occasion keen-eyed historians may now credit it to that master "and assistants"). A halo here, a sabot there, the fenestrations of towers in each and every painting over a five-year period—these pictorial plums would have been allocated to a prize pupil after they had mastered color grinding and floor sweeping. Perhaps the Virgin's eyelashes were Sassetta's specialty, who knows? Just who Sassetta's distinguished instructor was (and one can surmise his preceptor's distinction from the quality of his pupil's first known work, executed no doubt shortly after leaving his employ) remains unknown and unknowable. The name Benedetto di Bindo has been bandied about as one possibility; prior to him, Paolo di Giovanni Fei was a candidate. Whatever Sassetta's provenance, we can affirm that he must have demonstrated exceptional talent and mastered a variety of subjects to be deemed worthy of this first public commission, one intended to be visible in a public space and daily undergo close scrutiny from pious eyes. The worshipful would not have been disappointed: this epistolary polyptych was and remains not only sublime but infectious, providing a seminal quarry from which later Sienese painters could hack all the ideas they needed.

"Remains" is the operative word, since, like most of Sassetta's works still surviving, this one does so in bits and pieces. And to modern sensibilities, this dismemberment is all to the good. The individual panels of a medieval altarpiece, isolated and exhibited in a gallery setting against white walls, are now much more digestible than the original, cumbrous whole: our eyes scan a garden easier than a landscape. The dubious need only stand before a still-intact altarpiece, such as the one by Paolo Veneziano in the Accademia, Venice, to appreciate the difficulty of concentrating on the separate episodes. There are too many stories unfolding, there is too much to see. The intervening richness and profusion of gilded carpentry overwhelms everything. One cannot help but feel that the painted crucifix, a form that developed in tandem with the altarpiece, delivered its message much faster with a single iconic image. But no doubt the medieval eye was a much more patient scanner than our own.

These contemporary caveats aside, the altarpiece—broken down into its component parts—now constitutes something of a one-man exhibition unto itself, albeit an exhibition scattered over several venues. One could go even further, and make the claim that, given the richness of what remains, the Arte della Lana altarpiece could form a miniature retrospective: more or less all the Sassetta we need is here, or so it can seem. It isn't, of course, but each panel is so complex and so self-contained—this is, after all, the product of a genius and not a mere craftsman—that we eagerly accept the prospect. It appears that even at this early juncture Sassetta had embraced the old saw, "every picture tells a story." They were meant to be read as much as looked at. More or less all his paintings are narratives brought to life, and although all are free from literary overtones, each and every one can be explained and described as straightforwardly as Charles Perreault outlined his fairy tales. Though ultimately the panels veer closer to illustrations than to books.

The Arte della Lana altarpiece was essentially a triptych, comprising a central panel representing not the expected Madonna and Child, nor a Christ in Majesty, but a surrogate in the shape of a monstrance. It was a strange thing to draw attention to, this cosseted wafer, rather like emphasizing crucifixion nails without the cross, let alone disregarding the body of Christ. This hub was flanked on either side with panels depicting Saint Anthony Abbot and Thomas Aquinas. Surmounting these were pinnacles pairing the Virgin Annunciate with the Archangel Gabriel. Above the central monstrance panel, between the Virgin and the Archangel Gabriel, a Coronation of the Virgin was displayed. Two smaller dividers, in the shape of two half-length prophets, kept them company (now in the Pinacoteca Nazionale, Siena). Four narrow panels showing the patron saints of Siena, and another set of four Church fathers, perhaps acted as dividers between the three main panels (these eight figures are also housed in the Pinacoteca Nazionale, Siena). Down below, like so many footnotes, ran a line of seven predella pieces, showing—beginning on the left—two scenes from the life of Saint Thomas Aquinas (Vatican Museums and Museum of Fine Arts,

Sassetta, *Four Church Fathers*, tempera and gold on wood, 9 1/2 x 16 1/8 inches each, Pinacoteca Nazionale, Siena. Photo credit: Scala/Art Resource, NY

Budapest), an exorcism (Bowes Museum, Barnard Castle) and a Last Supper (Pinacoteca Nazionale, Siena) separating, on the right, two scenes relating to Saint Anthony (one lost, the other in the Pinacoteca Nazionale, Siena) and a seventh involving an anonymous monk (National Gallery of Victoria, Melbourne). All told, enough figures to populate a hamlet.

The focal portion of the Arte della Lana altarpiece—the lost central panel—was taken up with a topic so unusual, so outlandish, that we would tend to dismiss it as a figment of someone else's imagination if an eye-witness account from the eighteenth century describing its subject matter did not still exist. To wit, the aforementioned monstrance, that target-like sacred receptacle housing the sacrament. No doubt haloed with sunbeams, this monstrance was held aloft by floating angels playing musical instruments. Beneath, a sliver of landscape contained a duo of crenellated castles together with Gothic fortifications, towers and domes similar to those pastel-tinted toytowns familiar from other Sienese paintings. Two architectural landscape fragments in the Pinacoteca Nazionale, Siena—formerly attributed to Ambrogio Lorenzetti—are now more

Sassetta, *Landscape*, tempera on wood, 8 5/8 x 12 5/8 inches, Pinacoteca Nazionale, Siena. Photo credit: Scala/Art Resource, NY

Sassetta, *Landscape*, tempera on wood, 9 x 13 inches, Pinacoteca Nazionale, Siena. Photo credit: Scala/Art Resource, NY

comfortably assigned to Sassetta. With their anamorphic towers slotted into the deserted city, they provide us with some idea of how dazzling this lower stratum must have appeared. Provided, as we now suppose, that these are actual sawn-down extracts from that elusive central panel. Somewhere, hovering in the background, an inscription in semi-Gothic lettering read "Hinc opus ome. Patres. Stefanus construxit ad Aras. Senensis Iohannis. Agens citra lapsus adultos." What a strange apparition this aerial ballet must have presented to the congregation assembled before it, awaiting holy communion. It is (or was), so far as I know, unique in medieval art. At least nothing remotely resembling it has come down to us. But as a fitting emblem of Corpus Christi—Christ's body—whose feast day it was intended to commemorate, it could hardly be bettered.

Landscape occurs in other parts of the altarpiece, too. Indeed, it is a cardinal ingredient in Sassetta's mix, acting as an essential air vent, placed there to oxygenate the often overbearing atmosphere large religious polyptychs were prone to exude. They're like a welcome break in the weather. (Given the difference in climate, it's notable that most minglings of interior with exterior views occur in altarpieces from Southern rather than Northern Europe.) A couple of these sacral interiors suggest pop-up books, three-dimensional models of ventilation systems, with all their implications of coolness. Oddly, though Sassetta's skyscapes are often picturesque, they supply little clue as to the meteorological conditions within his paintings. Hot or cold, who can tell?

Individually, the panels rarely need airing. More or less all have a bright clarity which invariably carries over to their next-door neighbors like a beneficial domino effect, allowing even darker pigments to be ignited by association. A green wall in one panel takes on the pallor of glazed fruit through interaction with crimson copes in an adjacent panel; while the original ensemble must have been greatly enhanced by the gold-tinted borders separating and encasing each element. Some of the most aerated spaces in all of Sienese painting are the result.

In some ways Sassetta was an archaic painter, a throwback to an earlier time, a misapprehension which can be attributed to the intervention of the

Sassetta, *Saint Thomas Aquinas in Prayer*, tempera and gold on wood, 9 1/2 x 15 inches, Museum of Fine Arts, Budapest.

Black Death in 1348. Half the population of Siena perished, trade came to a standstill, the building of the new cathedral was abandoned and painting experienced a hiatus. When it began to flourish again fifty years later, it nostalgically resumed where it had left off: 1400 was now 1349. It's amusing to recollect that during the game of art-historical musical chairs which first credited Sassetta's two landscape fragments to Simone Martini's brush, they were dated 1310; when Ambrogio Lorenzetti was suspected as their author, 1340 was their presumed date. They fitted into either slot. And they look at home in 1423, too.

Though the central panel probably had the aura of fable or fairytale about it, its accompanying panels are closer to eye-witness accounts. It has little to do with any sense of realism, but rather a heightened sense of reportage. For perhaps the first time in Sienese painting we feel that an artist has seen these events rather than just heard about them. They tell their stories first hand. In *Saint Anthony Beaten by Devils* (Pinacoteca Nazionale, Siena), the panel portraying the hapless Saint Anthony assailed by devils at break of day, it appears that Sassetta has stumbled across this crime while out for a meditative stroll and set up his easel to capture it. It reveals Sassetta's filial piety for the landscape, his becoming a participant and not merely acting as an intermediary. He is *in* the landscape, recording not only what the landscape looks like, but also what it feels like. It has that kind of startled immediacy. Three devils, their feet armed with claws, (atrophied wings only emphasize earthbound rather than aerial origins) are splayed around the saint's fallen body in a hollow, cocooned by rocks

Sassetta, *Saint Anthony Beaten by Devils*,
tempera and gold on wood,
9 1/2 x 15 inches,
Pinacoteca Nazionale, Siena.
Photo credit: Scala/Art Resource, NY

resembling a child's conception of hills. Sparse vegetation dots the fore ground, while from the corner of the rock to the left a coppice crowds forward to act as witness. A grove of umbrella trees and a church cling to the distant upland. It looks every bit "the scene of the crime." Only the stoic Saint Anthony stares out at us, imploringly; the vicious fiends who are intent on beating him to a pulp wield clubs and a flexible scourge in the shape of two serpents. The general mucoid color scheme (grays, greens and browns) is relieved by mistake: a superstitious parishioner has scratched out the faces and genitals of the demons—no more progeny from those furry loins!—and inadvertently provided us with an x-ray view of the gilt undercoat, on which we can detect the exquisite stylus drawing lurking beneath the paint surface.

It's amusing to note that one defaced visage appears on the posterior of the right-hand devil: the anus as mouth. And from his psychological bag of tricks, Sassetta cleverly increases our horror by the white highlights on the crouching devil's fur, which subconsciously puts one in mind of maggots wriggling from a rotting corpse.

A further color accent is supplied by the band of red and blue nodules running along the wing vertebra of the devil to the left, as neatly aligned as a harlequin's waistcoat buttons. But overall the tone remains grimly vindictive. Sassetta knew exactly what color would infuse the desired minatory atmosphere. Close up, the microcosmic panel (not only an allegory of good and evil, but also a little elegy to wood) is limned with engravers' exactitude, nowhere allowed to lapse into finickiness. Evidence even at this early stage of his career as to why Sassetta's painstaking miniaturist's technique generated relatively few paintings. Even his ingenious (if overly prolific) contemporary Giovanni di Paolo looks coarse when the two are juxtaposed.

The composition is so riveting that, once seen, it is never forgotten. After all, one rarely forgets the mugging of an elderly person by vicious thugs. In purely formal terms however, it also reveals an abstract underpinning—probably unnoticed by Sassetta's contemporaries, but to ourselves equally as important as the subject. Thus the drama, though its action is hectic, is calmed and rendered contemplative by a strong flow of horizontals combing through the entire composition like a meteorological chart (horizontals which we first sense and only see later). Sandwiched between a sky striated with long flattened pancake clouds, and by footlights of parched plants, further horizontals can be detected in the chain of hills for instance, or the serpent scourge. Horizontals found in the strand of trees and the saint's prone body with its fallen staff find echoes in the lethal clubs; which incur other horizontals in the leftmost devil's stooped back and the three ailing plants aligned on the rock behind. Even the medieval graffiti gouged across its surface, SCS ATOGNO BASTONATO DA DIAVOIE, obliges us by obeying an invisible spirit level. And not for the last time does Sassetta play on our olfactory and aural senses: the shaggy

devil on the left positively reeks of old carpets, the air rustling with the unfurling of leathery wings.

Battered and disfigured though it may be, the panel nonetheless retains its magnetism. Proof of the truism which insists that a great painting, no matter what state of decay it falls into, retains its greatness even if only a portion remains. For that fragment has the status of "a chip off the old block," preserving the dominant aura of the whole intact.

A devil encompassed by geometry occupies another panel from the predella. This too depicts a tussle between good and evil (almost a superfluous description, since virtually all of Sassetta's compositions involve exposition of these two extremes). *A Miracle of the Sacrament* (Bowes Museum, Barnard Castle) portrays a story whose layout suggests a beginning, a middle and an end. Arrayed processionally across the picture plane, a group of fashionably attired males bunched on the left looms over a group of cowled women kneeling before them. Neither group seems concerned with what has just taken place further down the nave. Indeed, the composition resembles one of those before-and-after scenes so beloved of earlier Sienese painters, where two separate events are accommodated within the same temporal space. Both in terms of color and emotion, an invisible dividing line disrupts the narrative a little to the left of center. On the right, the main protagonists are gathered: a semicircle of Carmelite monks lean back in horror as one of its fellows catches the expiring body of another monk, struck dead (thanks to some latent and

Sassetta, *The Miracle of the Sacrament*,
tempera and gold on wood,
9 1/2 x 15 1/8 inches,
The Bowes Museum,
Barnard Castle, Durham.

unrepented sin) while receiving Eucharist from a priest. Like ectoplasm made visible, a nimble and very small demon extracts the hapless monk's soul via his open mouth (a gruesome extraction akin to pulling teeth). The gathering on the left is quotidian, that on the right hallucinatory, with the crimson and blue clothing of the earthly spectators standing in sharp contrast to the muted blacks and whites of the holy orders arrayed before them (monochromes which, when the altarpiece was intact, could have found echoes in the blacks and whites of the prophets' Carmelite habits elsewhere). Likewise, within the *Miracle* itself, color links to bind the surface are supplied by dabs of crimson from the bleeding Host on one side and crimson robes on the other, allowing the eyes to traverse the picture plane uninterrupted. There is rarely a "Stop" sign to interrupt Sassetta's movement, and though the invisible dividing line between the first two groups may give pause (and can be forgiven: it is, after all, a minor token of our painter's rapidly diminishing apprenticeship), nothing jars. The rises and dips of the assembled heads produce a flowing graph, a gentle undulation suggestive of waves. Sassetta gives us the sensation of looking into a cool aquarium, a reaction heightened by the aqueous green walls parading across this and the adjoining panels, where figures flit like some of the drabber species of tropical fish in and out of aquarium furniture, objects snagged in perspective (and where columns are used to partition and define space in the manner of Uccello's lances, often in later paintings to the extent of slicing through bodies).

It's in this panel, and the presumed central panel of the predella, *The Last Supper* (Pinacoteca Nazionale, Siena), that one of Sassetta's most characteristic trademarks comes to the fore. It first appeared in another of his early paintings, a *Crucifixion* (Musée Fabre, Montpellier) where the head of Saint John at the foot of the Cross tilts quizzically to one side. If this were its only occurrence, it could be dismissed as an aberration. However, in *The Last Supper* it is elevated to a fact of life. There, several of the apostles have their heads cocked at an angle, like boats keeling at low tide, or kernels nestled in shells, poses as psychologically appealing, as vulnerable and as inviting as a dog flat on its back with paws retracted. This characteristic vulnerability (a coyness which runs to sentiment rather than to sentimentality) helps differentiate Sassetta's hand from those of his followers, the group lumped together under the misleading rubric of the Osservanza Master (after a painting in the Church of the Osservanza, just outside Siena), a tag which would have made only slightly more sense if it had been in the plural, for if this were a single artist, he experienced as many periods as Picasso. Sassetta's heads are in fact as different from those of his followers as an Italian's head differs from a Russian's, both in shape and expression (a distinction which helped verify Sassetta's authorship of the early *Crucifixion*, whose origins had previously been steeped in dubiety). Shunning archetypes, the faces of Sassetta's apostles derive from a stock which he loved so

much he would paint them and their relatives again and again throughout his entire career, tokens of his belief in a serene humanism, a belief system which may have had its roots in religion but nonetheless remained mercifully free of cant. That's one reason why the portraits of Saint Thomas Aquinas register him less as a saint, and more as a saintly man. And why Sassetta's later series of paintings depicting the Madonna cradling Jesus simultaneously registers as Mother and Child—both icon and family portrait. The Virgin was, after all, a woman before she became a deity. This said, it has to be confessed that certain of his Madonnas contradict this stricture. In those depictions, bee-stung lips, waxen features and elongated fingers help lurch the model towards stylization. In fact most of the characters Sassetta painted double as both actors and next-door neighbors, participants in some medieval mystery play.

Though overblown operatics are noticeable by their absence, the modest hands assembled around the *Last Supper*'s white tablecloth already hint at the semaphoric signaling which becomes such a prominent theatrical feature in the later work. A curious muteness pervades the episode, a silence enhanced by the closed mouths of all the participants. It is as though open mouths and bare teeth had been banished from Sassetta's gatherings, to be replaced by a pantomime of gesticulations. Here we find hands used as pointers and indicators, raised in benediction, prayer and exclamation. Or, less expressively, put to use as head rests and balancers, all participating in some unfathomable vocabulary of signs, punctuations in a static world.

Before taking leave of this remarkable structure, a couple of further

Sassetta, *The Last Supper*, tempera and gold on wood, 9 1/2 x 15 inches, Pinacoteca Nazionale, Siena. Photo credit: Scala/Art Resource, NY

Sassetta, *The Burning of a Heretic*, tempera and gold on wood, 9 3/4 x 15 3/4 inches, National Gallery of Victoria, Melbourne.

points need to be stated. Firstly, it has been claimed that the Arte della Lana altarpiece proved influential to Sassetta's contemporaries and successors. I suspect it was. Probably it was unlike any other altarpiece executed prior to that date. But to play the devil's advocate, no subsequent artist left a written statement to that effect. (No surprise: artists' opinions only began to be recorded during the Renaissance.) This being the case, its influence is a matter of supposition, nothing more. That Sassetta's work as a whole was influential to the Tuscan school is, I think, beyond doubt. For artists and viewers alike it was (and is) very easy to like, to admire, and then to love. It must have been difficult not to fall under its spell. Helped, one suspects, by Sassetta's own amicability—for someone who painted such humanistic, accessible pictures can hardly have been a cold fish.

Secondly, the altarpiece's "immaturity" is often cited, if pardoned. Yet to my eyes it seems far from awkward—the chaos of *The Burning of a Heretic* panel excepted (National Gallery of Victoria, Melbourne). Indeed it shouldn't be, coming as it does from the squirrel hairs of a painter already in his thirties. Sassetta may have been a scavenger-cum-cuckoo, stealing from the Trecento what he needed in order to formulate a valid Quattrocento style, but here already we see the rudiments of his own style in place. His dexterous marshalling of oddments—bits of Martini and Masaccio here, some leftover Lorenzetti there—in no way detracts from the whole. Color in particular is perfectly pitched, paradoxically at once bright and muted: another of Sassetta's notable achievements. Light permeates from beneath each color. Cabbage greens, tomato reds, beet purples and orange golds add up to the painterly equivalent of a vegetable sonata. Nobody else in Siena was classifying colors in those poetic terms (Giovanni di Paolo's palette, though equally adventurous, was heading in a darker direction: carbonaceous rather than vegetal). We can already see Sassetta making the mental move from workshop to studio, a studio which would eventually double as a laboratory. Nothing is jolting under Sassetta's jurisdiction. Every hue is pinioned to its auxiliaries, and everywhere the brush defers to the paint, that magic medium here possessing a solidity which has nothing to do with thickness. Sassetta's technique may later have been perfected, but his vision rarely surpassed the level he attained in this altarpiece, a dossier where events are never allowed to stabilize into a ritual.

Talking crucifixes, toy forts, paintings within paintings, blood-spewing wafers, garden wells, serried ranks of books, horses as inoffensive as squirrels, and bonfires—these are just a few of the constructions to be found in Sassetta's first polyptych. What an imaginative factory he was!

Sassetta, *The Vision of Saint Thomas Aquinas*, tempera and gold on wood, 9 7/8 x 11 3/8 inches, Vatican Museums, Vatican City.
Photo credit: Scala/Art Resource, NY

## ON THE LINKS

In the margins of the fairway
A second-story man seeks the dark fantastic
That lurks within the contemplative life,
Rebounding with the strength of twelve men
To cajole the five iron to new highs.
Once the procession of the equinoxes
Comes back down to earth, jarring
The insane root that holds sway
In the minds of many, the autumn foliage
Sees you in the rough,
At sixes and sevens in the bright
If cloud-studded New England day.
This is no two-man show
Whose rich dualism cannot be missed—
An entire fleet of people are counting
On you to deliver the emotional Velcro,
A human thunderclap to shake the trees.
A vertigo in which the buzz is all around,
Reaching the dogleg, one must field
Many tough questions, the paranormal romance
Only ends to begin again, as it is the rotation
Of the ball that matters, the lip meeting the hook,
Hitting the ground to jog past the bean counters
Before fading to the left, relax the hips and shoulders,
Stop and breathe a moment,
This buzzard is a turkey shoot,
No thoughts of negative capability here
Or you may shank everything.
Instead, learn to be instrumental in the process,
Read the waters one at a time,
The bird is in your hand, think wood.

# TERMINUS

If we had only known what we know now
Things might have turned out differently,
But then again who knew the message
Was Sicilian in origin,
That they would sell the bear's skin
Before he was comfortable in it,
Or that the minister would come back
From vacation determined to recover
His lost credibility
In one last-ditch effort
To breathe new life
Into the ancient canard.
In that moment,
In which nothing seemed to change,
As fortune had it,
The cows were lying down in the field.

To visit the old chateau, kindly remain zen.
Grass makes the heart grow fonder.

Here at the institute we burn the candle at both ends
Because for some men, nothing is written;
Because prevailing wisdom tends to falter over water;
And sometimes the mind wanders,
And sometimes simply just because.

Misguided perhaps, I stayed in that station hotel
Many months believing as I did that I would
Never amount to much. Not knowing me then
As you do now, you never would have
Booked us passage on that packet boat,
Had it not been for the blessed missing variable.
A shadow of my former self,
You took me for one heck of guy.
The penny dropped, but turned up roses.
I owe you one for that, maybe everything.

# NO OTHER PEOPLE

The spreading lake and the low hills lent the chessman a noble oaken calm in their conical hats, and with it a sensibility of division wherein the winding river and the light paths disappeared into the trees, seemingly breathing in the generous darkness. Sea to land, night to sky, eye to hand, dog to cat—a calm of self-sufficiency blunting the contrasts, conspiring against those outward forms formerly aspired to, rendering the horses' hooves into straight grooves.

Utterly lacking in charm, his mien was remarkably casual for someone in his shoes.

Evening comes far more swiftly in the tropics than in the Mid-Atlantic states. In heated debate much of the great equation of facts may be lost or forgotten. One or two fingers extend as if the whole hand is about to enter into argument. Such is the life of one hand; the other daydreams alone in a maze lined with fine Corinthian leather, bleached and cracked by the equatorial sun.

At the sound of the bell, all mad cons went south.

In lieu of coin, a usurer offers a small phial to two young newlyweds. The mountebank, clad in red, is blurred in the double mirror, in which from a distance he appears as a school of apples plying the waters. In the phial, the Dark Ages lie sleeping. As the mirage fades and the music begins, our two newlyweds glean that this is no ordinary hunt.

Maybe I was more able then than I am now, if I understand your question correctly.

As the saying goes, one man's mickle is another man's muckle. And so it goes. The tranquil hamlet of Purview, whose neighbor is Hindsight, sleeps through the night even as the time of doves nears. But who can or will say, as a car drives by in the night rain, what might occur or may go unnoticed?

Mid-life obesity has its risks, particularly if you are light in your loafers.

The lack of tension was palpable, but on the forest floor photosynthesis as in fact occurring, as was spontaneous generation, however minute and often invisible to the human eye. Meanwhile, in Venice, blue held the east as nature tended to express itself in sky. The sinking sun, buckling under the rigors of life, knelt before the impending storm, which punctuated the drama with an affirmation of youth and the stimulus of lightning.

The unique thing she possessed was a sense of grace foreign to others.

In the time of the velour revolution, the lie of the land obsessed him in his soul-searching, as did the continuous thought of the Mistral and the parade of colors flashing through the *arrière pensée*. The first pale leaves moved him deeply, as did the fistfuls of moist autumn earth he clutched, and the long drinks he took to refresh himself from shallow brooks. But from time to time memories of Aix broke his nerve, and the emphasis on unbroken surface then in favor compromised his achievements. At such moments he would shake his clayey fists at the imagined adversaries, and vanish into the landscape.

## AT THE OLD SERAGLIO

*for Sacheverell Sitwell*

It was a sad relapse
To find the boathouse locked
And all that was left
Of the famous golden barge,
Last craft of its kind, gone,
Said the last of the White Eunuchs.
But life goes on in this pantomime court
With its multi-fingered hands outside the gateways,
The pashas find solace in wanton ways,
In the sublime port all edicts reach consensus,
And each day there is always
A ferryman to take you across
The harbor when you are banished,
As the Black Eunuchs were,
Said the sultan. Said I:
Now that the storm has subsided
And the private armies have been routed,
How strange it is to set foot
In this Chinese octagon
With its peculiar scents of familiarity
As if I no longer know the place.

El Greco, (Domenikos Theotopoulus, 1541-1614)
*View of Toledo*
oil on canvas, 47 3/4 x 42 3/4 inches
signed (lower right in Greek): Domenikos Theotokopoulus made this

"Self-lost, and in a moment will create
 Another World . . ."
                          — John Milton, *Paradise Lost*

El Greco's *The View of Toledo* at the Metropolitan Museum of Art is not a painting of the state of grace already fully realized, like Bellini's wondrous *St. Francis in Ecstasy*. Instead, we are in the middle of a hallucination, in the anxious peripheries of revelation. The sky is doubt, the landscape ambiguity, and the source of light a riddle.

As you travel through the painting, you realize the artist is taking you from the proximities of the shrub beneath your feet, sweeping past the stone architecture. You are at once pulled by the weight of weather, human events, history, botany, a familiar world—time-bound, color-bound, language-bound—up to the prospect of the skyline that is Toledo. The painting, at this point, abruptly stops. The skyline is a horizon. There is no beyond. There is only the above, leading the eye by way of the church spire. The church spire is a pointer, an indicator, to the light that creates the scene. The overall time of day is indeterminate—nighttime or day, twilight or dawn—but you do know that something supernatural is eclipsing the scene.

This is the spot of time in which the world of weather and human events stops. You have reached the terminus of earthly experience, even earthly potential. There is a potential for beyond, but here, the eye is held by the spot of time and cast skyward. El Greco takes the scene, arrests it, holds it, as if the totality of his vision of Toledo is ultimately being controlled from beyond itself. Then, through a series of silvery gleams of white light and the geography of billowy, downy clouds, he abstracts you from real time to the realm of timelessness. The approach to the realm of the spirit opens the only way it can: through the senses. The entire painting unfolds in a shadow, an overshadow, which confesses to the mystery of religious illumination, toward the opening in the sky, an oculus in the celestial dome. At this point, your whole being becomes absorbed in a sensorium of time and place. As Thoreau would say, it is a light to behold but to dwell not in.

You feel what El Greco must have felt: the radical sense of newness in this wild contrast of heaven and earth; the artist himself—ecstatic—intermediate in the divided union between determinism and free will. This state, fraught with the inadequacies of human comprehension, is put aside in the instant when the secular time of day is cancelled by the supernatural scene of the instantaneous second: the now, the radical awareness and the newness that comes with the shock of spiritual insight. The marker is the church spire, it punctuates the presence of God: here is God. Here is God's eye view of the sweep of the landscape with all the events of man and nature. All is held still for one instant, for one spot of time. And through the agency of the light of God and the direction of the pointing church spire, the eternal, in an instant spot of time, is apprehended.

You are in the exact spot where the ordinary is about to reach beyond itself to immanence. This hallucination in light and dark releases the gradations of secular time and distance into a supernatural hilltop and sublimity heaving upward and pointing sky beyond sky to receive God in an instant.

Denise Duhamel                    GHOST WEAVE

GHOST WEAVE is the story of three ghosts, or rather the story of one ghost told three different ways. After you read GHOST WEAVE, follow the scissor marks to cut the poem so that it hangs in three strips. To read WEAVE 1, cut horizontally along the scissor marks and weave the strips into the original poem, leaving the blank squares underneath the original GHOST WEAVE text, replacing the text of the original poem with new text. After reading WEAVE 1 remove the strips. To read WEAVE 2, cut horizontally along the scissor marks and weave the strips the same way into the original poem.

# GHOST WEAVE

Our ghost lived in the attic, above the trap door in the ceiling. He lived with our window fans and cooler in the winter, with our fake tree and Christmas ornaments in the summer.

He'd hung himself in the bedroom in which my sister and I now slept. He'd carved his initials in the banister we squeezed going downstairs to the living room. His initials were BR, the

beginning of brave, and his soul ascended out of his noose and rose like smoke into the attic my father could reach only with a ladder. Our boy ghost got stuck there, I guess, since he

wasn't allowed all the way to heaven. The floorboards creaked, even though our ghost weighed less than wind. He threw open the doors winter nights so we'd wake up to shut them, and

after do so, turn on a kettle for cocoa or tea, our middle-of-the-night presence, a way to keep him company. My mother wanted to move to a suburban development called "the plat," each brand

new house, devoid of history and sadness. Sure, displaced foxes ran through the yards there, but their furry maroon streaks were lovely brush strokes, not the pranks of a ghost boy wanting

attention. Whose fault was it that this boy killed himself? My father agreed we would buy a new place when we saved a down payment. My sister and I tried to contact our ghost with

a Ouija board, but BR kept strange hours and only came to us on his own terms. His family had moved away, to a different state, so all we knew about him were the rumors—a broken

heart, LSD, gambling debts he owed some junior bully. My sister and I made a pact we'd never let things get that bad, never wind up living in cobwebs, no one to help braid our hair.

# WEAVE 1

hadn't yet learned to drive and had nowhere to go. Our father had always favored our brother, and now nightmares made him pace. We'd wake, hearing our father's sights—then

Our ghost was once our flesh and blood older brother, the one teachers didn't believe was related to my sister and me. Our ghost scowled, even through jokes. Friends said his death was the

séances and prayers, and he'd sometimes answer back by hiding our homework or barrettes. In a dream he told me I had to be the strong one now and the reasons he died—a too tender

name refrigerator and stove—Amanda and Sears—a step towards forgetting. Chemical imbalance, the doctors had said and I saw our science lab. My father wish he'd paid his son more

# WEAVE 2

We lived in a small yellow rental, next to Terry's Variety, where we bought Pixy Styx, Chuckies, and bubblegum cigars. Terry told us about the frightful boy who'd set her box of wax lips on fire. to blame them and keep them from sleep. My sister and I couldn't help but be fascinated when we found BR's picture, his rebellious bangs zigzagging. We tried to contact him via

then pull pastel candy buttons from a strip of paper, looking up to the attic where our bad boy ghost practiced drum solos. Terry said the dead boy's parents took his sister away to live in a

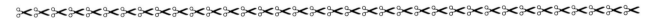

wood splintering so that the R of his last name looked like Rx, the symbol for prescriptions that doctors wrote for arthritis or colds. BR downed pills he bought in an alley, which is why he nose after a fistfight. A piano he took apart, lining up the silver innards like scalpels on the carpet. Potholders he wove for his mother in arts and crafts. Melting lips no girl would ever kiss.

# William Corbett        THREE GREAT TALKERS

I have known three epic talkers: Charles Olson, Philip Guston and Robert Creeley. (Had I known Ted Berrigan better he might have made a fourth.) I was in my mid-twenties when I knew Olson and had never met a person of such conversational force, like a waterfall or blizzard. Conversational is the totally wrong word for our relationship. There were those who conversed with Olson, but I was rarely one of them. He held court and I listened, awed by the leaps, twists and turns of his monologues. I could not always or, truth be told, often follow his references to mathematics, mythology, anthropology or Gloucester, Massachusetts history and geography. He delivered these in fragments as if his mind was on to a second or third thought before the first one had fully emerged. When he caught himself with too many incomplete thoughts in the air he laughed, shaking his head at the maze he'd gotten into but he moved on. It was exhilarating talk, exhilarating to be in the presence of someone for whom so much mattered, but had I taped Olson this may not come across today. Years after his death a tape surfaced of the legendary Bloomsbury talker, raconteur and wit Desmond McCarthy. A generation who had long heard of his prowess was all ears to experience it for themselves only to shrug, nonplused. You had to be there or McCarthy's talk, like Johnson's, needed a Boswell to help it travel. Olson left interviews, several recorded talks and some appearances on film. His reading of his poem "The Librarian" for WNET Television in, I think, 1966 captures his vitality and entertaining hamminess.

Guston and I did converse, on more than one occasion all night, from dinner through wine or beer for me, scotch and milk for him, several packs of Camel cigarettes, snacks to daybreak, breakfast and off to teach. He did need to be listened to, but he enjoyed the give and take of argument. And maddeningly, because he was a chronic doubter, he liked to argue with himself. The evening might begin with his taking one side of a question and arguing it with such lucidity and force that if you needed to be convinced, you were. But the worm of doubt was alive in his argument and soon he argued against himself—this is why Dore Ashton titled her book on Guston *Yes, but...*—until the merits of both sides were so clear it was impossible to embrace either one. Guston hated resolution. The concept of closure now in vogue would have driven him nuts. He liked a permanent tug-of-war, a frustrating chaos that he could achieve provisional treaties with in his studio. Often we became so straitjacketed in both sides there was no exit but laughter.

I knew Bob Creeley for thirty-eight years, far longer and more intimately than I knew Olson or Guston. Where they were old enough to be my father, Bob was an older brother. Before I met him I had read and reread his poetry and admired his craft, commitment and way of being a poet. He was someone I wanted to befriend and be accepted by. Accomplishing this could not have been easier. From the start, a dinner in Cambridge's Chez Dreyfus, certainly the poshest restaurant Bob and I ever dined in, we hit it off. Soon he either came for lunch or dinner or stayed with us when in Boston to read and I became initiated into the talk sessions he seemed to thrive on.

In the late 1960s and through the 1970s Bob's visits meant at least one all-nighter fueled by booze and grass. Where Olson's talk was airy, all lift-off and thrust, and Guston's grounded, Bob was elusive, a broken field runner, you had him in your grasp then he cut away. One listener and quiet conversation was sufficient for him. He had no celebrity radar and was without airs. At parties he preferred the kitchen. I came to see an element of shyness in him, his awkwardness in social situations expressing itself in talk, corkscrewing, burrowing talk. Yet he enjoyed an audience and no poet I know filled his reading with so many asides or gave such an up-to-the-minute account of what was on his mind. In his forties and fifties he was also a youngish man avid to exhaust an evening, wanting to hear if not deliver the last word.

Bob's talk had no beginning or end and was, if the word has meaning in this context, existential. He tirelessly parsed what he said, agreeing, drawing the subject to a fine point, qualifying, amending in his soft voice only to whittle away some more. What did he say? Poetry or art or a recent encounter with a friend were among his subjects or a story that evolved into an abstraction, but I remember little of the content of what he said. Bob was not an aphorist nor did he pause for jewel-like assertions or, in my experience, oft-repeated punch lines. His talk was a flow, one thread led to another with no point in sight. His mannerisms were unforgettable. He'd walk through our front door and after a kiss and hug start talking as if you were part of an ongoing conversation he had left suspended in the car on the way over or back home in Bolinas or Buffalo. "No, no, no, not that…" He entered our kitchen come down to breakfast in his signature cotton pajamas buttoned to the neck. "No, no, no…," reversing his field from where he'd been a few hours ago in the early a.m., his tone tender, adamant and full of concern. He had no small talk. He craved company and what began at breakfast could last, with a break to change from his pajamas, through lunch and if in his Maine house or on a day free of obligations into dinner and beyond. Once he followed me into the bathroom absorbed in refining his point, totally in the moment not wanting to reach a conclusion even the one implied by a break in the conversation. Perhaps this is what Olson had in mind when he named Bob "The Figure of Outward." (I can hear Bob say "not in some sense of pompous self-regard.") Bob's inner life talked itself ceaselessly rendering him active in the present to an unusual degree. His poetry, the first twenty years of it, balanced on saying only so much, on what was withheld, but his talk withheld little. In his case the clichés you know where you stand and what you see is what you get were true. It was generous of him, and I know in my case called forth equal attempts at self-revelation, at saying what really mattered. His listeners felt—I know that I did— in the midst of an important endeavor where talk itself accrued weight and meaning even if, or perhaps because, it spilled out untidily.

Given the duration and intensity of his talk Bob was a good listener with an exceptional memory. He had a gift for intimacy and an appetite for the experience of others. As he got older he adopted the pet phrase, "I hear you." He did and he remembered what he heard and other details of dinners, outings, readings and parties that would seem beyond one so absorbed in conversation. He was offhand about this and never one to flaunt the reach of his memory. As the years went by, when we didn't see one another for months at a time, Bob's memory made reunions feel like we had been constantly in touch. This may explain why so many felt so close to him and regarded him as a friend even though they saw him but once a year.

Bob has been and will continue to be remembered for his private language, words and phrases that, after a night, engraved themselves in your mind so that you might find yourself using them: "Dig it," "Not heavily, not absurdly," "company," "particular," "impeccable," "classic," "old-time" and, during the late sixties with memorable intensity after seemingly every fourth word—"viz," "e.g." and "i.e." It was easy to get thrown by these. Late one night Michael Palmer, Bob and I had reached a crossroads in our open-ended, never-to-be-closed three-way conversation when Bob said with some vehemence, "I went to my house i.e. home." We cracked up and fell out for a few hours' sleep.

# Mario Naves                                          SHIRLEY JAFFE

The abstract paintings of Shirley Jaffe delight not least because of the provocative question they entertain: What does it mean to be a Modernist painter in the twenty-first century?

How provocative you find Jaffe's bumptious arrays of clean, bold colors and quizzical cut-out shapes will depend on the value that is placed on continuity and reach—that is to say, on the acceptance of precedent and its ultimate transformation.

An American in Paris since 1949, Jaffe is unapologetic about divulging her artistic resources. The work is unimaginable without the brash angularity of Stuart Davis, the figurative impulses informing Jean Hélion's abstractions, and the stern and bracing hedonism of Henri Matisse and Piet Mondrian. Still, Jaffe is her own woman. Try to dissect one of the paintings. It's impossible. Integration, not appropriation, typifies her engagement with tradition. The paintings are fresh for all their borrowings or, rather, *because* of their borrowings. Individuality is made stronger through the (hardly reverent) assimilation of historical example.

Jaffe brings an oblique coherence to odd, fractured and what often seem to be ephemeral moments. The clatter of jutting boxes, wandering calligraphy and nestling rectangles in *Bruit d'ete* (2001) has an out-of-the-corner-of-one's-eye rush and spontaneity. *Four Squares Black* (1993) pictures an omnipresent entity, a banana-yellow splay of lines, hovering above a tumult of overlapping events.

The specificity—indeed, eccentricity—of Jaffe's cobbled shapes, crisp palette and loping, playful rhythms suggest sources outside the imagination. Jaffe's abstractions are elaborations on observed phenomena—among the items the artist has cited as visual stimulants are people, architecture and, of all things, pinball machines. Don't mistake the paintings for Utopian projects. Experience is Jaffe's true subject. The impurity of lived events is welcome even if it isn't necessarily presented in a forthright manner.

A Jaffe painting is like a conversation wherein pregnant pauses and knowing glances, rather than words or sentences, establish the drift. The internal logic of each composition is inferred rather than made plain. Somewhat mischievous in their allusiveness, the paintings are nonetheless decisive in painterly methodology and particular in pictorial form. As conundrums, Jaffe's canvases are crystal clear—a beguiling paradox only a painter of significant gifts could pull off.

How, then, do Jaffe's paintings provoke? They certainly don't propose an affront to art itself, the Dadaist's gambit. Jaffe insists on a past worth building upon, a present worth engaging with and a future worth striving for. Optimism is the order of the day; forward propulsion the rule. To put brush to canvas upon these principles requires a willingness to explore and, more important, relish uncertainty. A similar commitment is asked of the viewer, though without the struggle of having to locate a necessary equilibrium between material and vision. The artist's challenge is our pleasure.

Modernism is the engine that drives Jaffe's art but don't go pegging her as a throwback. The paintings are too resilient and wide-ranging in scope to settle for easy categorization. Pointing to possibilities yet to be imagined, Jaffe confirms the prospect of art itself even as she goes about re-imagining the world. The paintings are informed by a spirit of good will all too rare in contemporary culture. One gauge of an artist's worth is the extent to which her generosity is a component of aesthetic fact. In that regard, Jaffe has proved her worth innumerable times over.

Shirley Jaffe PAINTINGS

*Four Squares Black*, 1993
oil on canvas
84 1/2 x 70 3/4 inches
All images courtesy Tibor de Nagy Gallery, New York

*Towers*, 2003-4
oil on canvas
31 1/2 x 25 1/4 inches

*Bruit d'ete*, 2001
oil on canvas
87 x 67 1/4 inches

*Tiges et Grille*, 2001
oil on canvas
87 x 65 1/4 inches

*The Ferris Wheel*, 2001
oil on canvas
60 x 47 5/8 inches

*Riquet II*, 2001
oil on canvas
64 1/2 x 51 1/2 inches

*Opposite Yellows,* 2002
oil on canvas
52 x 64 inches

*The Door*, 2002
oil on canvas
51 1/4 x 31 3/4 inches

*Pink Mountain*, 2002
oil on canvas
28 3/4 x 23 5/8 inches

*Corners*, 2002
oil on canvas
29 x 24 inches

*Rings*, 2005
oil on canvas
31 1/2 x 25 1/4 inches

*Arc-en-Ciel*, 2002
oil on canvas
57 x 44 1/2 inches

## RINSO

The slight agitation
of pots and pans
and a few dishes
in sudsy water
into which hands
plunge and fingers
operate like in
a magic act in which
bubbles burst
into flowers presented
to the blonde girl
who rotates on
a wheel that flies
up through the
ceiling and
disappears.
The dishes
are sparkling.

## DEAD OR ALIVE IN BELGIUM

Somebody you think is dead is alive
and somebody you think is alive is dead

Sometimes it comes as a happy surprise
and sometimes you wonder

She was given a few days, hours perhaps
Now she looks stronger and even prettier

His chances of surviving were so-so
Now he's going to Belgium

which takes strength, just the thought
—Why do I say such things?

Because there's a Frenchman inside me
who jumps out every once in a while

Bonjour! Voilà, un bon café bien chaud!
Then he forgets to jump out

Or I jump out in front of him
I am much bigger than he is

He does not want to go to Belgium
or even say anything nice about Belgium

I don't want to go to Belgium
though I would like to go to Bruges

Ghent Antwerp and Brussels
and go inside the paintings there

and stand next to the Virgin
her forehead so large and pure

and be there alive with her again
oil on board in Belgium


# EVERYBODY AND HIS UNCLE

I was waiting to happen.
At a stoplight
the buildings curved up from my ears,
office buildings
with offices in them and people
doing office things, pencils
and paper clips, telephone rings—
Where is that report?
At Echo Lake the vacationers
have made the city only slightly
emptier, how did they get there?
By station wagon and dogsled
in the "old" days. The forest ranger
was Bob. He said we could spell his name
backwards if we wanted, then
our laughter vanished into his tallness.
I thought maybe he was not a forest ranger,
just a guy named Bob, but

it turned out he was part of the echo
of everything around there, which radiated
out a few short miles before the farmland set in.
The farmland had waited to happen
and then it did, just as it knew it would.
A farmhouse appeared and a front porch
and on it sat my Uncle Roy. He was very farmer.
Get on this horse, he said.
But the horse said, Don't.
I would prefer to play baseball, I said.
Later we took Rena Faye to the hospital.
Darn that horse, Roy said, when his ears
laid back I saw trouble. The light changed,
my shoes went across the street
while I rose straight up into the high part of the air
so as to form a right angle
with the dotted line that lit up behind my shoes
as they turned into pots of gold
receding into that smaller and smaller thing
we call distance. But I was already there
in the distance, I had been waiting my whole life
to be wherever I should be at any given moment,
a ring around not anything. Wake up, Rena Faye,
said Roy, we need to take you to the hospital.
She gave us the most beautiful smile
but it bounced off our faces and we forgot
to pick it up and put it somewhere safe.
It's probably still lying there on the road
in front of the house. Come to think
of it, I did pick mine up
as I looked out the back window of the car,
and as we skirted Echo Lake
everything got twice as big and then three times,
like laughter and hiccoughs flying among children
whose immortality has turned them
into temporary rubber statues of curvature in confusion
that slides into the appeasement of early evening.
That is, Rena Faye felt better, at least she was able
to know there was a bump on her head, and inside
the bump a small red devil running furiously in place.
Rena Faye is going to be okay, said Roy,
but I wasn't so sure, there was a doctor involved
and a hospital with a lot of white in it.
The house hadn't changed, but the barn

was gone and the land stretched out flat
to far away. The horse was still waiting, for what
who knows? I was waiting at the light, and when it changed
I went on across the street
to where another part of town was waiting,
it was Europe and I was in or on it,
I had Europe touching my foot, the train
was pointing its big nose toward the Gare St-Lazare,
where you wake up even if you aren't asleep.
Rena Faye opened her eyes and said, "I don't think . . ."
and then a funny look
came across the street toward me, the one big horrible face
of surging forward, but I was like whatever bends
but doesn't break because I didn't give a whit about any of it,
I was in the forest and my name was almost Bob and the trees
didn't care about any of it either because tallness can't care.
Roy wasn't really my uncle, we just called him that.
When the sun rose his new picture window could be seen through
to the lone mimosa tree, its pink blossoms smiling frizzily,
and a car went by, not a Chevrolet or a Ford,
not a green or blue car,
just a car, with a person driving it. My notebook
and its pencils were ready to go and I
moved toward them as if music had replaced the sludge
we call air. I.e., Swiss cheese had become gruyère.
The car started, then rolled back and stopped.
We got out and looked, then kicked ourselves. Moon,
is that what that is, that sliver? I was thinking,
the car was not thinking, my pencils were almost thinking,
all three of them, but they took too long and so
time went on ahead without them.
Then an angel from the side touched my head inside
and my head outside surrounded less and less.
His wristwatch is a street, green, yellow, blue, and open
as a meadow in which your parents are grazing
because the fodder and forage are stored away
in the kitchen cabinet too high for them to reach
with their muzzles. And lo the other parents are mooing
plaintively, tethered to an idea they like to dislike:
The fox is free. Silly old cows, the fox is never free,
he is just running, and with good reason, and with good legs,
from the ooga-ooga. Brrrrring!
Waterfall of afternoon!
And I left.

I went east three miles and then
fifteen hundred more, and then
three thousand five hundred more,
and then I turned around
and came back five thousand and no hundred.
My mother was still in the kitchen
standing on the yellow tiles
as dinner rose up out of the pots and pans
and hung in the air while she adjusted it.
Soon Dad came home and we dined
but he didn't and neither did Mother
and neither did I. We put the food
in our mouths and chewed and swallowed—
it tasted good—and we drank liquids
which also tasted good although
they were across the room and on the wall.
The phone rang. It was meaningless
like a proton, but Mother laughed
and said words that were exactly the words
she would have said, total illusion
and total reality at the same time, just as
Dad coughed fifty years later, it was me coughing,
which is why I left, heading east, and stopped
after fifteen hundred miles, and coughed again.
So this is Echo Lake? Sure looks nice.
Ice had once gone by.
High overhead was an iceberg just checking on things,
wings folded and in flames.
The soul materializes in the form of an echo and says
"I've been following you."
"But you are a shadow and only a shadow!"
"Only in the dark am I a shadow," the soul replies.
"In the light I am a very good light bulb!"
"You are a big nothing something," the soul says.
The light changes and I start across.

## WHIZ AND BANG

You hammer away on
the hills and braes of
bonny Scotland, where
oh the thrill of the thought
of it the heather
runs up like a girl all fresh
and wind-blown to shake
her head and wag a
finger at your naughty
naughty thoughts,
about her, of
course, and you
hammer those hills and braes
with all your might.


## METHOD, OR KENNETH KOCH

Sometimes Kenneth's method I guess you'd call it
was to have a general notion of the whole poem
before he started
such as the history of jazz or the boiling point of water
or talking to things that can't talk back
(as he put it) that is apostrophes
whereas my method I guess I'd call it
is to start and go
wherever the poem seems to lead

Sometimes it doesn't lead anywhere
other than to a dead end, and when I turn around
the street has disappeared and I find myself
sitting in a room.
Sometimes it leads somewhere
I have no interest in being
or the way I get there is contrived or silly

I have a face
that stays mostly on the front of my head
while inside my head wheels
are turning with a sound like music heard across water
over which a breeze rises and falls
cooling my face.

I should be nicer to my face

send it on vacation or just let it go relax

over there under that shady maple

Instead I let it carry all kinds of packages

back and forth from my brain to the world

though of course my brain is a part of the world

I should send my brain on vacation too

though it tells me now that I should consider the possibility that it has
    always been on vacation

Tricky brain! in which

the personality skates around

and the moral character rises and sits, rises and sits

and whose doorway at the bottom has a sign

that says . . . there's not enough light to read it.

I wish there were.

Kenneth said Write a poem in which each line begins with

"I wish . . ."

I wish gorilla

I wish squish

I wish deux-tiers

I wish onrushing cloudburst

and the hundred thousand one-second-old wishes came pouring forth

and still are pouring forth

like babies in trees and all over the place

in French postcards after World War I

like water streaming down Zeus

like the concept of optimism when it entered human history

like the simile when it said Do not end your poem with me

I am not like The End I am like a doorway

that leads from one thing

to Cincinnati, and who

am I to argue with a simile

I am a man of constant similes

that buzz and jumble as I walk

then shift and ramble as I buzz and jumble

At any moment the similes can line up

to form the log cabin Lincoln

is said to have built with his own similes

I am like a president

I am like a stove

I am President Stove I will chop down

the cherry tree over there on that page

But someone else is already chopping it down

a boy with a mad grin on his face
a glint of impish fire atop his head
Those cherries were too red!
So much for history
History that rolls above us like an onrushing stormcloud
while we below knit booties and adjust our earmuffs

Young Bentley bent over his microscope
and clicked the shutter of his box camera
thus taking the first photographic portrait of a snowflake
which is how he became known as "Snowflake" Bentley
Outside the blizzard came in sideways
like a wall of arrows
That is all you need to know about Snowflake Bentley

Who else would you like to know about?
Whom! Whom! not Who!
There actually was a great Chinese actor named Wang Whom
who immigrated to the United States in the mid-nineteenth century
and found fame and fortune in the theaters of San Francisco
due mainly to his ability to allow his head to detach
from his body and float up and disappear into the dark
The curtain would close to great applause
and when it opened his head was back
but his body was in two halves split right down the middle
Wang Whom never revealed his magic secrets
even to the beautiful young women who lined up toward him
like iron filings toward a magnet
powerful enough to lift President Stove out of his chair
and give him life again as a mountain
struck repeatedly by lightning
That is all you need to know about Wang Whom

Now for some commentary on things that are always horizontal
The earth is always lying down on itself
and whirling
It is totally relaxed and happy to let everything happen to it
as if it were the wisest person who ever lived
the one who never got up from bed
because the bed flew around everywhere anyone would want to go
and had arms and hands and legs and feet
that were those of the wise horizontal bed-person

Lines indicating very fast movement are horizontal
because the horizon is so fast it is just an idea:

Now you see it now you *are* it
and then 99 per cent of every beautiful thing you ever knew
escaped and went back out into the world
where you vaguely remembered it: your mother's smile
in the glint of sunlight on the chrome of a passing car,
her tears in a gust of wind, her apron in the evening air

as if she were a milkmaid standing in Holland
while those silver and gray clouds billow across the sky
over to scarlet and burning violet tinged with gold
just for her and that one moment.

You are next in line, which is exciting,
which is why life is exciting: every moment is another line
you're next in. Or maybe not, for what about when
you don't know what "line" is and "next"? A goat
comes up close and stares at your sleeping face.
The instant you wake up it turns into a statue
that starts out a goat and ends up a banjo,
something you can neither milk nor play.
But it doesn't matter because you started out a man
and ended up a pile of leaves in a different story.
In the library the other piles are saying Shush, they know
it is late autumn, they can tell by the ruddier cheeks
of the girls who come in and, when they see their books are overdue,
stamp their feet in a fit of pique.
They are so cute
that some of the leaf piles shamble across the floor toward their dresses,
but the girls laugh and throw their hair around and dash away.
If only you weren't a pile of leaves, you would run after them and throw
    yourself on them
like a miracle!

That's what it used to be like to be fourteen and surrounded
by miracles that never happened.
At fifteen the miracles started to crackle and at sixteen
they were positively scary—Look, a miracle on the ceiling!
By seventeen a miracle was a car you could ride in
and then one year later drive beyond the limits of consciousness.
The tapioca pudding was there.
You ate it.
The tapioca pudding was gone
but there too.
May I have some more anything?
Why, my fine young man, you can have anything

you want. Here, have this mountain!
Oof, it's too heavy! Do you have a smaller one?
No, only a larger one.
Then no mountain will I have today
and as for the future I cannot say
because I have no idea where I would ever put a mountain.
But, young man, you will become President Stove!
I will? But I don't want to be a president or a stove,
I want to glue a president to a stove.
Then go right ahead. Here is the glue.
Now go find a president and a stove.

## TOOTHBRUSH

As the whisk broom
is the child of the ordinary broom
which is cousin to the janitor's broom,
I am a toothbrush
when it comes to bristling,
insufficiently angry
or maybe too angry
to keep my bristles intact
since I know the debris
of the world is too great
for me to handle.
If I could save the world
by being crucified
I certainly would.
But who would nail
a toothbrush to a cross?

# THE ABSOLUTELY HUGE AND INCREDIBLE INJUSTICE IN THE WORLD

What makes us so mean?
We are meaner than gorillas,
the ones we like to blame our genetic aggression on.
It is in our nature to hide behind what Darwin said about survival,
as if survival is the most important thing on earth.
It isn't.
You know—surely it has occurred to you—
that there is no way that humankind will survive
another million years. We'll be lucky to be around
another five hundred. Why?
Because we are so mean
that we would rather kill everyone and everything on earth
than let anybody get the better of us:
"Give me liberty or give me death!"
Why didn't he just say "Grrr, let's kill each other!"?

A nosegay of pansies leans toward us in a glass of water
on a white tablecloth bright in the sunlight
at the ocean where children are frolicking,
then looking around and wondering—
about what we cannot say, for we are imagining
how we would kill the disgusting man and woman
at the next table. Tonight we could throw an electrical storm
into their bed. No more would they spit on the veranda!

Actually they aren't that bad, it's just
that I am talking mean in order to be more
like my fellow humans—it's lonely feeling like a saint,
which I do one second every five weeks,
but that one second is so intense I can't stand up
and then I figure out that it's ersatz, I can't be a saint,
I am not even a religious person, I am hardly a person at all
except when I look at you and think
that this life with you must go on forever
because it is so perfect, with all its imperfections,
like your waistline that exists a little too much,
like my hairline that doesn't exist at all!
Which means that my bald head feels good
on your soft round belly that feels good too.
If only everyone were us!

But sometimes we are everyone, we get mad
at the world and mean as all get-out,
which means we want to tell the world to get out
of this, our world. Who are all these awful people?
Why, it's your own grandma, who was so nice to you—
you mistook her for someone else. She actually was
someone else, but you had no way of knowing that,
just as you had no way of knowing that the taxi driver
saves his pennies all year
to go to Paris for Racine at the Comédie Française.
Now he is reciting a long speech in French from Andromache
and you arrive at the corner of This and That
and though *Andromache's* noble husband Hector has been killed
and his corpse has been dragged around the walls of Troy by an unusually
    mean Achilles,
although she is forced into slavery and a marriage
to save the life of her son, and then people around her
get killed, commit suicide, and go crazy, the driver is in paradise,
he has taken you back to his very mean teacher
in the unhappy school in Port-au-Prince and then
to Paris and back to the French language of the seventeenth century
and then to ancient Greece and then to the corner of This and That.
Only a mean world would have this man driving around in a city
where for no reason someone is going to fire a bullet into the back of
    his head!


It was an act of kindness
on the part of the person who placed both numbers and letters
on the dial of the phone so we could call WAverly,
ATwater, CAnareggio, BLenheim, and MAdison,
DUnbar and OCean, little worlds in themselves
we drift into as we dial, and an act of cruelty
to change everything into numbers only, not just phone numbers
that get longer and longer, but statistical analysis,
cost averaging, collateral damage, death by peanut,
inflation rates, personal identification numbers, access codes,
and the whole raving Raft of the Medusa
that drives out any thought of pleasantness
until you dial 1-800-MATTRES and in no time get a mattress
that is complete and comfy and almost under you,
even though you didn't need one! The men
come in and say Here's the mattress where's
the bedroom? And the bedroom realizes it can't run away.
You can't say that the people who invented the bedroom were mean,

only a bedroom could say that, if it could say anything.
It's a good thing that bedrooms can't talk!
They might keep you up all night telling you things
you don't want to know. "Many years ago,
in this very room . . ." Eeek, shut up! I mean,
please don't tell me anything, I'm sorry I shouted at you.
And the walls subside into their somewhat foreverness.
The wrecking ball will mash its grimace into the plaster and oof,
down they will come, lathe and layers of personal history,
but the ball is not mean, nor is the man who pulls the handle
that directs the ball on its pendulous course, but another man
—and now a woman strides into his office and slaps his face hard—
the man whose bottom line is changing its color
wants to change it back. So good-bye, building
where we made love, laughed, wept, ate, and watched TV
all at the same time! Where our dog waited by the door,
eyes fixed on the knob, where a runaway stream came whooshing
down the hallway, where I once expanded to fill the whole room
and then deflated, just to see what it would feel like,
where on Saturday mornings our infant son stood by the bedside
and sang, quietly, "Wa-a-a-ke up" to his snoozing parents.
I can never leave all the kindness I have felt in this apartment,
but if a big black iron wrecking ball comes flying toward me,
zoop, out I go! For there must be
kindness somewhere else in the world,
maybe even out of it, though I'm not crazy
about the emptiness of outer space. I have to live
here, with finite life and inner space and with
the horrible desire to love everything and be disappointed
the way my mother was until that moment
when she rolled her eyes toward me as best she could
and squeezed my hand when I asked, "Do you know who I am?"
then let go of life.

The other question was, Did I know who I was?

It is hard not to be appalled by existence.
The pointlessness of matter turns us into cornered animals
that otherwise are placid or indifferent,
we hiss and bare our fangs and attack.
But how many people have felt the terror of existence?
Was Gengis Khan horrified that he and everything else existed?
Was Hitler or Pol Pot?
Or any of the other charming figures of history?

*Je le doute.*
It was something else made them mean.
Something else made Napoleon think it glorious
to cover the frozen earth with a hundred thousand bloody corpses.
Something else made . . . oh, name your monster
and his penchant for destruction,
name your own period in history when a darkness swept over us
and made not existing seem like the better choice,
as if the solution to hunger is to hurl oneself
into a vat of boiling radioactive carrots!

Life is so awful!
I hope that lion tears me to pieces!
It is good that those men wearing black hoods
are going to strip off my skin and force me
to gape at my own intestines spilling down onto the floor!
Please drive spikes through not only my hands and feet
but through my eyes as well!
For this world is to be fled as soon as possible
via the purification of martyrdom.
This from the God of Christian Love.
Cupid hovers overhead, perplexed.
Long ago Zeus said he was tired
and went to bed: if you're not going to exist
it's best to be asleep.
The Christian God is like a cranky two-thousand-year-old baby
whose fatigue delivers him into an endless tantrum.
He will never grow up
because you can't grow up unless people listen to you,
and they can't listen because they are too busy being mean
or fearing the meanness of others.
How can I blame them?
I too am afraid. I can be jolted by an extremely violent movie,
but what is really scary is that someone *wanted* to make the film!
He is only a step away from the father
who took his eight-year-old daughter and her friend to the park
and beat and stabbed them to death. Uh-oh.
"He seemed like a normal guy," said his neighbor, Thelma,
who refused to divulge her last name to reporters.
She seemed like a normal gal, just as the reporters seemed like normal
    vampires.
In some cultures it is normal to eat bugs or people
or to smear placenta on your face at night, to buy
a car whose price would feed a village for thirty years,

to waste your life and, while you're at it, waste everyone else's too!
Hello, America. It is dawn,
wake up and smell yourselves.
You smell normal.

My father was not normal,
he was a criminal, a scuffler, a tough guy,
and though he did bad things
he was never mean.
He didn't like mean people, either.
Sometimes he would beat them up
or chop up their shoes!
I have never beaten anyone up,
but it might be fun to chop up some shoes.
Would you please hand me that cleaver, Thelma?

But Thelma is insulted by my request,
even though I said please, because she has the face of a cleaver
that flies through the air toward me and lodges
in my forehead. "Get it yourself,
lughead!" she spits, then twenty years later
she changes *lughead* to *fuckhead*.
I change my name to Jughead
and go into the poetry protection program
so my poems can go out and live under assumed names
in Utah and Muskogee.

Anna Chukhno looks up and sees me
through her violet Ukrainian eyes
and says Good morning most pleasantly inflected. Oh
to ride in a horse-drawn carriage with her at midnight
down the wide avenues of Kiev and erase
the ditch at Babi Yar from human history!
She looks up and asks How would you like that?
I say In twenties and she counts them out
as if the air around her were not shattered by her beauty
and my body thus divided into zones:
hands the place of metaphysics, shins the area of moo,
bones the cost of living, and so on.
Is it cruel that I cannot cover her with kisses?
No, it is beautiful that I cannot cover her with kisses,
it is better that I walk out into the sunlight
with the blessing of having spoken with an actual goddess
who gave me four hundred dollars!

And I am reassembled
as my car goes forward
into the oncoming rays of aggression
that bounce off my glasses and then
start penetrating, and soon my eyes
turn into abandoned coal mines
whose canaries explode into an evil song
that echoes exactly nowhere.

At least I am not in Rwanda in 1994 or The Sudan in '05
or Guantanamo or the Tombs, or in a ditch outside Rio,
clubbed to death and mutilated. No Cossack
bears down on me with sword raised and gleaming
at my Jewish neck and no time for me
to cry out "It is only my neck that is Jewish!
The rest is Russian Orthodox!" No smiling man tips back
his hat and says to his buddies, "Let's teach
this nigguh a lesson." I don't need a lesson, sir,
I am Ethiopiian, this is my first time in your country!
But you gentlemen are joking . . .

Prepare my cave and then kindly forget where it was.
A crust of bread will suffice and a stream nearby,
the chill of evening filtering in with the blind god
who is the chill of evening and who touches us
though we can't raise our hands to stroke his misty beard in which
two hundred million stars have wink and glimmer needles.

I had better go back to the bank, we have
only three hundred and eighty-five dollars left.
Those fifteen units of beauty went fast.

As does everything.
But meanness comes back right away
while kindness takes its own sweet time
and compassion is busy shimmering always a little above us and behind,
swooping down and tranfusing us only when we don't expect it
and then only for a moment.
How can I trap it?
Allow it in and then
turn my body into steel? No.
The exit holes will still be there and besides
compassion doesn't need an exit it is an exit—
from the prison that each moment is,
and just as each moment replaces the one before it

each jolt of meanness replaces the one before it
and pretty soon you get to like those jolts,
you and millions of other dolts who like to be electrocuted
by their own feelings. The hippopotamus
sits on you with no sense of pleasure, he doesn't
even know you are there, any more than he takes notice
of the little white bird atop his head, and when
he sees you flattened against the ground
he doesn't even think Uh-oh he just trots away
with the bird still up there looking around.
Saint Augustine stole the apples from his neighbor's tree
and didn't apologize for thirty years, by which time
his neighbor was probably dead and in no mood
for apologies. Augustine's mother became a saint
and then a city in California—Santa Monica,
where everything exists so it can be driven past,
except the hippopotamus that stands on the freeway
in the early dawn and yawns into your high beams.
"Hello," he seems to grunt, "I can't be your friend
and I can't be your enemy, I am like compassion,
I go on just beyond you, no matter how many times
you crash into me and die because you never learned
to crash and live." Then he ambles away.
Could Saint Augustine have put on that much weight?
I thought compassion makes you light
or at least have light, the way it has light around it
in paintings, like the one of the screwdriver
that appeared just when the screw was coming loose
from the wing of the airplane in which Santa Monica was riding
    into heaven,
smiling as if she had just imagined how to smile
the first smile of any saint, a promise toward the perfection
of everything that is and isn't.

# David Carbone        ON SEEING NADLEMAN'S
                       *STANDING MALE NUDE*

"One never stops discovering unexpected details in a masterpiece."

— Jean Cocteau

How often do we allow ourselves to truly see a work of art? After all, looking at art is not a passive experience, like watching television; it requires focused mental effort, a playful openness, and a willingness to stay with a work until it reveals something of itself. Often when we turn, momentarily, from an art work, to watch others move through an exhibition, their goal seems rather different: it's as if touring the room without breaking one's stride was the sure mark of an aesthetic sensibility. The slight bobbing of heads as they pass each exhibit is a sign to anyone in the room that they have recognized each object, as if it were an answer to a simple quiz.

All of us are susceptible to this kind of response in a museum or gallery exhibition. Modern and contemporary shows tend to promote spectacle in an effort to entertain. Successful blockbuster exhibitions have, for some time now, re-oriented the thinking of curators. By carefully channeling traffic patterns to increase flow through museum galleries, curators suppress opportunities for viewers to linger before an object. Aesthetic experience, interpretive contemplation, have been largely cast aside in the pursuit of attendance and money.

One symptomatic factor in all this is the treatment of sculpture as if it were an image rather than a spatial experience. The classic way to achieve this reduction is to place a sculpture against a wall, so that you can't move around it, allowing one unified view of an object over those qualities which only reveal themselves in our continuous perceptions around it. This is further reinforced by photographic representation in books and catalogues, where the view selected, through repeated viewing, gradually imposes itself on our memories as the essential view and truth about the work depicted. This proved to be especially so of a mostly unremarked-upon bronze masterpiece by Eli Nadleman, called *Standing Male Nude*, traditionally dated 1908-09, and recently re-dated 1912-13. In its appearances, in the MoMA catalogue of 1948, the Whitney catalogue of 1975, and the catalogue for the Jewish Museum's exhibit of 2000, *Paris in New York*, the

figure is shown from the right in a three-quarter frontal view. The full frontal views in the Sidney Janis catalogue of 1987, and the recent Whitney monograph of 2003, don't vary significantly. These photographic conceptions reinforce the work's title and have succeeded in suppressing its real subject and achievement.

I first became aware of the magnitude of Nadleman's achievement in the first Whitney retrospective. The bronze figure was there, but I don't remember noticing it, until I attended an exhibition of Nadleman's work at the Sidney Janis Gallery, twelve years later. In the large central gallery, ten bronze works were set out, beginning with four large figures and moving back toward the wall with earlier, smaller works, three forbidding layers deep. *The Standing Male Nude*, almost twenty-six inches high, stood on a tall pedestal, flush against the wall. Positioned to display a full frontal view, it is anything but a frontal figure.

Remembering my first impression, the dark brown bronze silhouetted the elegant mannerist figure against the bright white wall; the resulting contrast emphasized the extreme contrapposto of the figure's pelvis and the elaborate play of serpentine rhythms in every detail of the body's gestures. Stepping back a bit, I was struck by the extravagant theatricality embedded in what seemed to be a declamatory pantomime. With its extremely elongated proportions (ten heads high), open twisting movements, and smooth surface, this figure immediately recalls the work of Giambologna to me. Yet the forms are proto-biomorphic: all the anatomical details have been interpreted as continuous curved swellings that pulsate with energy. It is, all at once, coolly intellectual and slyly erotic. At the time, it seemed the most fey figure I had ever seen in all twentieth century sculpture. Yet unable to move about it, I turned my attention to the other works on view.

———————◆•◆———————

Thirteen years later, on a hot June day in 2000, I found myself at the Jewish Museum, looking at a show of Jewish artists who worked in Paris in the first decades of the twentieth century. The installation was a cacophonous clutter of works by Kisling, Weber, Modigliani and others. But stationed at various places, untypically away from the walls, were various moderate-sized sculptures, four Nadlemans among them. As I glanced across to the other end of the room, two elderly women were having a lively exchange as they stood regarding Nadleman's *Standing Male Nude* from the back. What could have excited them, I wondered, as I moved in their direction hoping to catch the drift of their remarks. I advanced toward the figure's right, its head and extended arm gesturing to the left. How confidently masculine the figure appeared, it was like watching a principle dancer in a momentary pause before a dance.

"Gertrude, it still disturbs me, it's not right," said the little lady who continued to stare at the figure's back. Her slightly taller companion had moved farther around the statue and was looking almost directly into its face. "Darling, it's abstract, you just have to accept it." "No," replied the former emphatically, "there's something wrong, but I can't say what." I paused at the figure, delighted with their exchange and a little giddy in anticipation.

As I gazed at the bronze, its taut swellings seemed full of energy and as I began to move toward the figure's back, the play of light on the body's musculature produced a distinct rippling sensation. And there it was. Lying hidden, the profile perdue had shifted from a man's body into a woman's. Against the tilt of the pelvis two hugely round buttocks projected, the center of the body's coiled energy. If the front felt Florentine mannerist, the back was distinctly Hellenistic and something more. Flowing down the back of the right leg, the muscle bundles rippled as if liquid, flaring out in the calf like a wave crashing into shore, as they rolled on toward the heel. Pushing up from the hips, the spinal muscles shot up into the neck, which moved in a perversely serpentine counterpoint to the calf. The skull-capped head and long tumescent neck were emphatically phallic. What I was looking at was a continuous metamorphosis, executed at least sixteen years before Picasso's and Arp's hybrid concretions of the late twenties and thirties. The full back view pulsed like a fountain, its twisting movement drawing me forward and around to the left as the body regained some of its masculinity.

My eyes were drawn up to the left side of the face. And there I saw, as if from a Greek coin, a wry Archaic smile of a Kore, and on the other side, almost the same, an idealized self-portrait. With a high forehead, aquiline nose and a forceful chin, Nadleman appeared much as he did in other of his works and in whimsical paintings by Florine Stettheimer. I wonder if Stettheimer's friend, the art critic Henry McBride, had this bronze figure in mind when he wrote of Nadleman's work, in 1917, "It's Greek, it's Italian, it's yesterday in Paris, the past and the present are blended almost cruelly."

———◆———

Clearly the figure is not a man at all, it's a hermaphrodite. And not a traditional one with breasts and a penis, Nadleman had made several of those. This one appears to be an evocation of the Ovidian Hermaphroditus fused with the water nymph Salmacis. Like some of the poem's images, we see the glint in her eye, the snake-like movement of his/her head, and everywhere the movement of flesh-like water merging as the two run together. It is rare for a sculpture to echo a poem; often it is the other way around. In this Hermaphroditus, movement creates an ironic theatricality that deliberately lacks naturalism. Instead of a cry from the heart, Nadleman creates an assemblage of quotations held in an unstable equilibrium which, as I've related, can knock the viewer off balance. What we see is a vision of a subjective reality, a shifting self, where the efforts of passion are presented playfully.

An early reader of Freud, Nadleman brought a new understanding of sexuality and the role of the unconscious to the reading of myth, long before the Surrealists. As a sculpture that presents interior states of feeling through metamorphic form movements and quotations, it is unprecedented. All earlier depictions either show Salmacis in ardent pursuit of Hermaphroditus, and/or the two combined as a two-headed freak with four shoulders and four arms. In these, the conception of self remains discrete, male or female, and an emblem of marriage. Nadleman's unique version presents us with a self-conscious integration of selves. There is also a witty correlation between the metamorphosis of Hermaphroditus, and the distinct form ideas of the sculpture itself, providing an analogy with conflicting aesthetic impulses in the artist, hinted at by the self-portrait. This idealized profile is a synthesis of the parts; it looks forward to Nadleman's society portraits and circus figures.

Sculptural space is ideally suited for the shape-shifting of a sexual transformation. Each passage of quotation avoids pastiche by being assimilated into Nadleman's rhythmically driven simplifications. Two previous examples of the metaphoric use of contrasting forms in sculpture immediately come to mind: Michelangelo's Rondanini Pietà, and in Ovid's time, the Augustus of Primaporta. Nadleman stripped the figure of the pedestrian imitation of nature, while reasserting a canon of beauty based on abstract form. He joined four models: his interpretation of Greek antecedents, Rodin's use of movement, Rosso's use of light, and the animating curves of Jugenstil.

As Nadleman wrote: "To interpret the charm of life, often at its most fragile and shifting—by inflexible and solid physical laws—here is the definition of art." Presented at a modest scale, as is the case with most of his work, the Hermaphroditus has been misunderstood and overlooked by curators and writers on the history of modern sculpture (it was, at one time, in the collection of MoMA). Of all his bronze figures of this period, it is the most complex. It is a summing up of the past and a forward leap. Not at all a sexual confession, as some might have it who misconstrue his late work, but a complex expression of his intellectual and spiritual culture. Looking at this dazzling example of plastic expression, one question continues to nag, "Who titled the bronze, Nadleman or his dealer?"

1.

A worm was so fond of his Young Man that at length, seeing with insolent contempt base traps to ensnare the harmless, one day he would marry *his* constant companion. A SpiderCat, weaving her web with the greatest SILK, became a woman working at her shroud much quicker than a young bride. "Yes," said the Silk, "but your labours, which are at first Venus, sprang from the room, the nature of a Cat. AND the Cat determined that there were no longer the half finished arms of her husband and, only this morning, caught the Mouse, and it was very fine and transparent; and it is still down here HIS YOUNG MAN, hearing you acknowledge that I work behaviour with the greatest care, and seeing that I began it, changed the Cat into a blooming woman. They swept the princes away as dirt, and under the form of a woman she married and killed it; but at night my web is changed and worse than useless, whilst his wishes, as soon as they are seen, are preserved on and in her affection. THE worm and her form and accordingly, mine are made slow and swiftness is hidden." SPIDERCAT used to declare that if she were back again, the Silk should see how large and how sincere was nature become. "what do you think of her and his gratified ornaments?" disagrees THE SILK; "AND Venus angry at her neighbour designed only as a Mouse of my lady, destroyed the young, although beautiful, WORM." See this in time: and he looked to THE WORM for labour cries.

2.

An Ape sat looking at a Carpenter who was cleaving a Snail, who had fixed himself beneath the moulding of the piece of wood with two wedges, which he put into the cleft sacred to beauty and the fine arts. Its nudest attitude, its pedestal, beheld with an evil eye the admiration it excited. one after another as the split opened. The Carpenter at his dirty work took the freedom to assure him that he leaving his work half done, the Ape must needs try his elegant proportions, assisted by the situation in which it pulled out the wedge that was in it without knocking in THE SNAIL AND THE STATUE. Accordingly, watching his opportunity, he strove, by trailing hands at log-splitting, and coming to the piece of wood which he could not endure to hear so for meddling with his work. A STATUE of the Medicean Venus was erected in a grove by its fore paws so fast that, not being able to get away, the moody Carpenter, when he returned, knocked his brains out so that the wood closing again held the poor Monkey of this finished piece, yet a more accurate and close inspector would infallibly lose his labour. "For although," said he, applauded. An honest Linnet, however, who observed his filthy slime over *every* limb and feature, to obliterate those beauties, much attracted the regard of every delicate observer. THE disguise thou mayest CARP AND APE him "to the perfection through all the blemishes with which thou hast endeavoured to ENTER an injudicious eye, will sully a beauty, discover its other THE was placed, the it."

# Adrian Stokes     THE BODY-EMBLEM AND ART

## I.

What is the essence of the aesthetic mode in recording experience, in reconstituting or restoring the object or—to use the terms of the earliest psycho-analytic investigation—in stabilising the day-dream?

Following the example of the Berenson of even some fifty years ago, many visual art critics speak of formal qualities as 'life-enhancing;' the stimulus of art has been attributed primarily to the formal qualities: aestheticians, such as Roger Fry, proclaimed them to be the focus of interest in art whether from the side of the creator or of the spectator. Whatever we think of this judgement, we all know that meaningful suggestions of mass, movement, repose, texture, volume as we find them harmoniously inter-related and magnified in an economic manner by painter or sculptor at the service of the subject-matter, are 'life-enhancing.' Such attributes combine in what we call a composition whereby each interacts with others and with further aspects of itself. I have used the word 'economic' because of the need for a prodigal relevance in the detail, for generative potentiality, for nuances that bring in their train precise effects owing to their power within the context. The use of the word makes a link with the aesthetic means employed by dramatist and novelist, who must convey character and situation through the inter-acting of a few evocative confrontations, just as in ballet a story may be told by means of a string of movements and gestures. Poetry suggests a great deal more than it says. But I will not labour the starting-point of much aesthetic discussion since the time of Aristotle: we all know that the work of art, more especially when we contemplate the mighty inter-action between formal values and subject-matter, suggests an organism whereby the whole is more than the sum of the parts. Constructions outside art can often claim this virtue, and thereby suggest aesthetic quality.

I tried to show in a recent paper[1] that many simple words and clichés contain a corporeal meaning the ages do not stamp out. The effect of even so cursory an examination of popular expressions was, and always will be, whatever the extent of collection and research, the unavoidable corporeal reference. Words are symbols, all our mental constructions are symbols based in the last analysis, as we well know, upon parts of the body. Now, in the previous study of words, my main point was concerned with implied judgements concerning the conscious ego whose situation, I found, was

1. 'Listening to Clichés and Individual Words,' collected posthumously in *A Game That Must Be Lost* (Carcanet, 1973).

described in references to balance, position, substance, tension, shape, in sum, to a degree of *stability* and indeed to those very formal elements that are considered to be 'life-enhancing' in art; I myself would add, in all art. Thus, discussion of poetry is centred today on what is called the texture of words: it means the suggestiveness of the composite sounds and rhythm of several words in enhancing their composite senses; it means the provocation in the process of abstract as well as particular images, images of substance and of stress recognised not only by the eye or ear but by touch and kinaesthetic or haptic sensations. Obviously a very complicated subject: yet where such analysis is successful and the fragments may be amassed, a figure emerges, the 'organic' line which has already said it all. We speak of the texture, the feel, the shape of this line, using words that should not be judged fanciful if in the poetry we are confronted by a representation of the body, a framework by whose closeness the sense and series of particular images have been communicated. I do not think the matter differs in regard to the texture of music: furbishing every cry from the heart is the sculptured pulse of the body's fabric. Perhaps we come near to hallucinating an aspect of the body wherever we look, more distinctly in the case of art. There would be no other general framework for post-infantile experience, just as there are no prime experiences which are not concerned with parts of the body.

Are we dealing with only one mode by which systematic symbolisation through substance takes place, or will the material to be adduced call for an invariable image, for a body-image as has sometimes been suggested in other, and predominantly physiological, contexts? My contention in regard to art will be for a body-image, though I shall not call it that, since I pay far more attention to tactile and kinaesthetic attributes, as did J.O. Wisdom in *The Concept of the Phantom-Body*, than to the visual. I shall use the term 'body-emblem,' ignoring entirely the alleged physiological aspect. Briefly, I think the ego's ceaseless desire for reassurance in regard to stability involves the projection, the enlargement by means of projection, of a primitive image of itself (compacted also from the incorporated mother's body and other internal objects), a primitive emblem, tactile, kinaesthetic, inseparable from the function of the body-ego which can be contemplated only in this way, in the terms of a construction.

Freud wrote in *The Ego and the Id*: "The ego is first and foremost a body-ego." I shall not be treating the body-ego merely as a construction based upon the perception of our own bodies and their sensations, though the activity is the ground. I regard the body-ego as also a pre-conscious amalgam fed selectively by unconscious fantasy, a fabrication in tune with the holistic character of perception. Freud tells us in the same book that "perception consciousness alone can be regarded as the nucleus of the Ego;" and that "anything arising from within (apart from feelings) that seeks to become conscious must try to transform itself into external perceptions." I submit that the contemplation of a pre conscious body-ego must rely upon a projection (body-emblem) whereby it is perceived, providing, in terms of art particularly, an enhanced feeling of ego-stability. This projection is more succinct as well as more 'real' than the pre-conscious material.

It has not been thought that the ego's task is easy: it would not appear unlikely, therefore, if a general activity, namely art (among many others less single of largely identical aim), should attempt to impose corporeal stability upon feeling of every kind and especially upon those ambivalent feelings concerned with the so corporeal inner objects such as the mother's body; if the formal values in a work of art should communicate to us through the senses by means of a gloss upon an emotional content often of a dire or confused nature (and only later tragic when harnessed to this form), the sense of a construction equated with the body emblem that thereby subsumes, for the moment rules, even hidden experience. Since I make the point that with whatever sense we perceive, the work of art provides a stimulus of tactile and kinaesthetic value, it will be worth remarking that in *The Ego and the Id* Freud wrote: "The body itself, and above all its surfaces, is a place from which both external and internal perceptions may spring. It is seen in the same way as any other object, but to the touch it yields two kinds of sensations, one of which is equivalent to an internal perception." Freud is pointing to the fact that when we touch our own body—it seems to me the remark is applicable to the touching of *any* object in a lesser degree—we are aware not only of the object, we experience also an inner sensation in the touching. The other senses do not provide this dual effect. In eating we touch with our mouths and tongues: the experience of tasting, if it may be isolated from the touching, is an external perception only, as in seeing and hearing and smelling. If we leave subject matter and sublimation of the id on one side for the moment, aesthetic appreciation appears to be an exercise in the perception of an outside structure that elicits strongly and pleasurably a perception of an inner structure, the ego and the helpful objects incorporated in the ego. Since these provide the basics of developed object-relationship, the work of art invokes in us a heightened sense of its own object-nature, self-sufficient and single, together with a sphere of communion, of non-differentiation, that corresponds to very early experiences at the mother's breast. In terms of an emotional structure attributed to the outside world and thence to his completed work, the artist tests or reconstructs his ego, his body-emblem, thereby re-asserts and re-creates those introjected good objects that are the ego's citadel in all encounters. These introjected objects are regarded here as the spirit or soul of the body-ego whose reconstruction in a work of art provides a not unrecognisable emblem of the body.

I would now introduce another consideration. In many cases we would prefer to contemplate aesthetically the painting rather than the subject that the artist has painted. As well as what the artist has 'put into it,' we know there has been careful selection—he could not have represented everything even if he had wanted to—and that in poem and drama no less than in painting the artist tries to distil the essence of a situation as he feels it to be. So it comes about that the artist sometimes claims his world to be 'more real' than nature, or that he has distilled the essence of nature. This Platonic claim will remind us of an attitude in some primitive societies— we preserve other echoes of it—wherein the sign is as significant as the entity for which the sign stands and his name is perhaps more than the man; it is his essence. Such a line of thought is not entirely removed from what is called concrete thinking; and, indeed, I at any rate have found in reading case histories that schizophrenic utterances are sometimes extremely poetic in virtue of a parallel to the equations by which the poet extends imagery. A less exalted use of words throws light here, namely obscene terms which particularly in a few perversions may be uttered as the near equivalent of a sexual act. The poetry of words is sometimes enhanced, sometimes denied, by such a magical and concrete function of language, observable not only in obscenities but also to some extent in slang: for a split second the word possesses more than the mere aura of the thing; hence the juiciness of words, and indeed very often, of things in virtue of a word that equals up to them. Plainly the artist in words must obtain for his effect something of this juiciness; he does so, I think, more often through the manipulation of sound and rhythm than by the blatant invoking of symbolic equivalence—I use Dr Segal's term—at the expense of metaphor. Yet, though art be the exemplar of the full extension of mean- ing through symbolisation, an element of concrete thinking is unlikely to be altogether absent. In the first place the work of art, the symbol, is put on an equality, in regard to essence, with the phenomena thereby symbolised, an unwarranted assumption in regard to the content deriving from the id. Moreover this 'reality' is regarded as super-real in virtue of the first aim in art, to represent by imagery or concretely, as direct objects of the senses, mental structures as well as physical structures.

But it seems to me that the mechanism is explained if we accept, by and large, that art projects by means of form the body-emblem as well as symbolising in the subject-matter an id content. The unconscious ego, unlike an id content, becomes less, rather than more, diffused when pro- jected. We perceive in virtue of form, the essence, the desired stability, of the body-ego insofar as we find the building or painting to be 'life-enhanc- ing.' This is a conclusion that fits in well with the constructive yet simpli- fying activity attributed by Gestalt theory to the perceiving of shape or vol- ume; art entails the ego's perceiving of itself by means of its own root activity; ego and its emblem are partly identical; super-ego value becomes largely physical value, 'good' becomes 'stable.' But I hope the stress I put on the form in art will not cause you to consider that I intend to underes- timate the manifold compulsion in subject-matter, the symbolisation of every experience and state of mind, the pressure of the content or subject-matter which interacts with, and largely determines, the character of formal presentation.

Now it seems to me that modern art, the art typical of our day, is the slang, so to speak, of art as a whole, standing in relation to the Old Masters as does slang to ordinary language. There are many beside myself who consider the work of the painter Braque to be the most perfected of our time. Let us see what he has to say about his own art and about art in general. He has written: "I am no longer concerned with metaphors but with metamorphoses... To define a thing is to substitute the definition for the thing itself." I will interrupt to mention that that is considered by Braque to be unaesthetic: painting should not provide a substitute for the object: better to appear as a metamorphosis of the object than as a metaphor for the object. "It is wrong to imitate what one wants to create," writes Braque. "One does not imitate appearances; appearances are results. In order to achieve pure imitation, painting must disregard appearances... It is not sufficient to make people see what one has painted, one must also make them touch it." In viewing, it should be as if one were touching the painting. "I care much more for being in unison with nature than for copying it."[2]

Some of these remarks will suggest a very primitive state of mind: indeed, one function of art may be to rebuild the world with adult strength around the primitive core of the ego, the primitive vision, not entirely lost, whereby objects are extensions of one's flesh, one's own organs, objects whose absence will be overcome by hallucinating them. Braque has written: "I am extremely sensitive to the atmosphere around me, and if I had to try and describe how my pictures happen, I would say that first there is an impregnation, then hallucination—a word I do not like, though it is not far from the truth—which turns into an obsession: and in order to free myself from this obsession I have to paint the picture as a matter of life and death." (ibid).

The phantasy of metamorphosis, particularly in connection with the art of painting, must derive in part from the translation of food into faecal matter. Cubism required fragmentation of the object and a rebuilding by means of facets, many more facets than could have been seen in looking at the object, by means of combinations of facets so that there is evolved from the subject-matter a so-called metamorphosis extremely evocative for the sense of touch in virtue of the multiplicity of planes. Texture—and texture will be represented by many means other than the actual textures of the pigment—plays an enormous part in the effect. The paintings are indeed constructions or reconstructions of the most palpable kind.

We will view these works largely, but not entirely, for their abstract or generalised content. But we know, and we may finally feel, that their

2. Georges Braque, quoted in the Introduction by D. Cooper to the Catalogue of the Arts Council Exhibition (1956).

manifest subject-matter, a portrait, a still-life, was of first importance to the Cubist painter: he cannot let the subject go: he dissolves it in order to appropriate it, and we are able to follow him in this to varying extent. The object must be preserved as well as re-created, as well as joined to the ego in an oceanic union. But the framework, the indispensable carrier of this passionate process (and of a degree in symbolic equivalence) resides in the whole construction being seen as the near-equivalent to the body-ego itself: hence our feeling of well-being, of health, before the successful painting: with the help of good inner objects the command of the ego, the command of the ego over id, has been demonstrated.

To restore the ego is simultaneously to restore the object, and vice versa. I have contended that part-objects will be drawn into whole objects if they shall contribute to the structures in which the ego delights, no less than for art the depressive position during which the mother was seen originally as whole and self-sufficient, provides in this presentation the nodal stage of the ego's development. The work of art is esteemed for its otherness, as a self-sufficient object, no less than as the body-emblem.

I have said that modern painting is the slang of the Old Masters. Let me remind you what slang implies. Many slang words seem to partake somewhat of the action they designate though in a less powerful way than obscene words. I have already indicated that I think that this quality is retained in the vivid, that is, poetic, use of words, and in art as a whole. By calling modern art the slang of the Old Masters, I wish to point to a near-concrete type of thought now overtly displayed. We have as well in much modern art a process of fragmentation, also usually identified with schizoid states. I do not think that those who accept Melanie Klein's infantile paranoid-schizoid position preceding the depressive, would have difficulty in supposing that schizoid nuclei remain intact or easily resuscitated, and that they may be put to work especially in the more narrowly compulsive ranges of ego activity (art) dominated by the depressive position. On the other hand, whereas the schizophrenic allows no separate existence to the objects in the outside world upon which the image of his psyche has been cast, an emphasis on separate existence provides the means by which projected emotions are transfigured in art. The modern painter, as we have seen through the words of Braque who speaks in this respect for many others, insists on the separateness particularly of the object he himself creates, as well as on oceanic feeling; indeed, according to this theory, the otherness of the outside world can only be represented by the separateness and wholeness of the work of art. Yet it is a means also for realising the structure, the stability, of the body-ego in the very terms of object otherness. I think that the near-identity of body-ego with the perceived body-emblem facilitates concrete thinking, increases the projective identification that tends in a schizoid state to cause loss both of the ego and of the sense of object-otherness; whereas in art, possibly richly to compensate for a certain amount of undue concrete thinking, wholeness, self-sufficiency, object character, the restoration of the independent object, are prime concerns. There is a sense whereby a moderating of schizoid projective identification through the adoption of depressive attitudes will be re-enacted and recorded by every work of art.

## II.

Works of art have no taste or smell, that is to say, that their taste or smell, should they have them, are entirely excluded from the aesthetic aim and the aesthetic result. This is the more remarkable because we know that the strength, and even the direction, of reaction-formation has greatly varied in different societies. It would seem that even apart from the interference of reaction-formation, taste and smell are impossible experiences for wakeful, rather than dream-like, contemplation: they would suffer in their constancy, whereas the body-emblem must suggest a bright and compact permanence. Whatever the history of reaction-formation, feelings about the body will always have fluctuated violently, so violently, that there will even have been the need of a stable emblem to serve as the reference not only for love but for distaste, stable not in the sense of an unchanging fashion but in virtue of an unalterable tactile and kinaesthetic nexus that culture moulds afresh.

It may be relevant to remark that previously—that is, in the near, not the distant, European past—the emblem was idealised by art more weightily than now, by a manner often far removed from succulence and prettiness, in ages in which artists were more concerned with beauty, when all, or nearly all persons were filthy, when deformities and suppurations could not be corrected nor assuaged, when, too, there was rarely accessible the water supply, and never the detergents or chemicals, with which to clean clothes. We find it difficult to hold the conditions of the recent past in mind largely because no art has reflected them, unless the frank nobility of so much old art may be seen as sometimes supporting, but more often repudiating, the smell evaluation which was common then as now, and then as now preponderant in the judgements of social life. Contra-wise, with the early days of developing sanitation the artist, guardian of the body-ego, became more bohemian, that is, non-conformist in regard to the vulgar testimony that a clean body, a head with a recent haircut, a body dressed in smart or neat clothes, was in virtue of these precautions to be deemed to provide an acceptable body-emblem. Similarly, it is not as a rule the artist who cares one way or the other about the cosmetics used by his mistress, the cut of her clothes or her tidiness; I mean insofar as he is pure artist; whereas for many people even everyday clothes marmorealize the body-emblem: they serve an important aspect of what should be called popular art. The artist's depression is here the all-important point, his melancholy which will not be banished by burnished fingernails and a pot of flowers on the piano. Integration must be wider, must to some degree include as well as vanquish filth. The anal drive is of use to many an artist: he employs the sublimation in order to work his material, his medium and even perhaps to build up images of substance: excretory products and prime part-objects will, in a similar way, have helped to construct the emblem of the body-ego. As I have said, it is the generalised body-emblem with which the formal side of art is concerned, rather than the ever-changing accretions and the particular adaptation, best termed the personality, reflected very often both by the artist's subject-matter as well as by his handling. Subject-matter, epitomising a fixation-point, may provide the immediate compulsion and inspiration to art. We are concerned now with the form the spur takes, the mode by which the ego masters it.

Particularly since Schopenhauer, aestheticians have underlined the contemplative nature of art, that is to say, a quality of enjoyment sufficient to itself, unrelated to an immediate call to action, erotic or otherwise, a way for viewing or enjoying a presentation of experience that in virtue of its pattern may symbolise the contemplation of far wider patterns of experience. One recognises the distinctive otherness of the aesthetic object in the character of the contemplative state incorporating it, an oral engrossment that leaves the cake miraculously intact; a breast feeding and a simultaneous contemplation of the self-sufficient mother of the depressive position; also, the perusing by the senses of a stable figure from which the body-ego takes new life. And so we identify ourselves not only with hero or heroine of drama and novel, with tender or supernal music, but with the strong entanglement of the forms that convey this character; we identify ourselves with the very manner of telling, inseparable from what is told. That is why, it seems to me, the buildings construed from a ruthless hotel porch of outworn pretensions as we see them everywhere in London, especially in the non-prosperous parts, may stimulate a greater depression than any confusion due to natural forces. Just because they are made by men, these buildings become the far stranger symbols of lack of identity, of the dissipation of good things.

Let us now visit a life-class. The student must summon a degree of contemplative attitude towards the model, towards attractiveness, towards repulsiveness. Should we speak of his working there as a sublimation of genital and other erotic aims? They are held in suspension though by no means necessarily banished from his feelings, nor from his work if it be of merit. Thus, his drawing may suggest that he burrows into the model's belly with his pencil as he represents the contours, the folds of flesh. When his drawing is examined, the student will complain to the teacher that the model has moved her head and put his drawing 'wrong.' The teacher does not appear to have the slightest interest as to whether the lines drawn on the paper look like a head. His corrections and suggestions may be conccrncd with proportion, but much more eagerly with matters of the pose, the distribution of weight, the angle of arms to trunk, the exact shape of the space between the legs. A contemplative attitude to the body is introduced and reflected in the drawing *through the essential matter of visualising flat pattern.* Command over pattern will be extended to the tactile and kinaesthetic matters of weight, density, space, mass, movement, rhythm, at the service, as vehicles, of a particular model, a particular expressiveness, a particular emotive state. The image was grasped, then spilt, as it were, upon the paper, yet the aim is to preserve so palpable an image, to build up this girl's body, doubtless in fantasy to own her genitally thereby, but also to make her absorbable, and yet in both cases to leave her intact. Drawing is a meaningful circumscription of an object so as to make it not only absorbable but memorable. Our own value, our egos will be enhanced by the uniqueness of the object; values attributed to this object are of a general as well as of a particular kind. Those naturally good at drawing have strongly developed the power, perhaps in the interest of prime part-objects dissociated from their function, to see a hand, or indeed the body in general, as shape pure and simple in concurrence with all other apprehensions that this body stimulates, and as a result of them. Not technique only but also the transmission's emotional value depends in part upon a degree of impersonal or contemplative attitude. A good drawing conveys palpability in the vivid terms of a particular pose. Such corporeal generalities that serve a particular context bring health to our good inner objects, to our egos. Like steel girders built into the basement of a period house, they underpin the structure. In much western art, an erotic content is often manifest, genital and scopophilic. Even so, our touch rather than sight, our whole bodies take possession of the object whose desirability is enjoyed in terms of mass, weight, proportion, represented movement or repose, texture, as well as in the terms of naked erotic elements if such there be.

We in Europe inherit the phantom of an idealised body, invented by the Greeks, a body innocent of messy insides, solid marble all through, polished without. Maybe we sometimes expect of any nakedness, however hoary, a smooth and marble verve that corresponds with the fantasy of brightness attributed to the flesh, and thence each sagging and blemish seem unusual. We are often under erotic compulsion to idealise the body, but this need is clarified by another, the need of the ego for a stable body-emblem, an eternity for the body, be it the mother's or our own. As well as through idealism the artist seeks this eternal substance even through ugliness by allowing us to contemplate a body re-formed in terms of pattern, a pattern of experience expressed plastically which can be of any kind that is deeply felt. I think the description covers the products of every form of non-decorative art in any period. "What is the Nude," asks Sir Kenneth Clark in his book of that name. "It is an art-form," he answers, "invented by the Greeks... The nude is not the subject of art, but a form of art...the image it projects into the mind is not a huddled and defenceless body, but of a balanced, prosperous and confident body: the body re-formed." And again: "We recognise how necessary it is for the naked body to be clothed by a consistent style...the Antique scheme has involved so complete a fusion of the sensual and the geometric as to provide a kind of armour." I think we understand that the armour is not confined to the nude, that it is the mode of fashioning a durable object for contemplation and absorption, a smoothing out of the actual world into an eternal cast that nourishes. Not an armour against genital interest: on the contrary, genital appeal will assume something of the oral cast. All the same, as Sir Kenneth wisely remarks: "The amount of erotic content (genital interest) which a work of art can hold in solution is very high... To scrutinize a naked girl as if she were a loaf of bread or a piece of rustic pottery is surely to exclude one of the human emotions of which a work of art is composed; and, as a matter of history, the Victorian moralists who alleged that painting the nude usually ended in fornication were not far from the mark." It is, however, even more to the point when in connection with a Titian nude the same author remarks: "This passage (a detail of the painting) of violent sensuous attachment into the realm of non-attachment where nothing of the first compulsion is lost...thus Titian could maintain that balance between intense participation and absolute detachment which distinguishes art from other forms of human activity."

You will remember that I have already associated aesthetic detachment and contemplation with oral engrossment, though, at the same time, the object remains, intact, unconsumed; with the recognition also in the object of the body-emblem so that subject and object join in oceanic communion under the aegis of the good breast. It is not surprising that the quality often demanded of a work of art concerns 'vitality.' The artist feels he bestows life and thereby receives it. In all works of art there is an imagined or actual or represented surface, a communication to the senses of touch and position. The image is in our arms, in our hands, as well as present to our eyes or ears. This cannot be said primarily of the subject-matter; and in view of the generalised attributes of the body-emblem, it cannot cause surprise that much, even of the visual, art of the world, is extremely conventionalised and often abstract, sometimes strongly geometric. Hence, as I think, the fear of all the ages, the fear of a mechanical body that has delayed the invention, or at any rate the exploitation, of machines for so long, a fear that our own time has partly, but only partly, overcome. The dynamic machine is an ego-less body. The body-ego is easily bent or dissolved by id forces, by the direction of the ego's attention from moment to moment. The generalised emblem of the body-ego is of supreme importance to us, if only as measuring departure from it. For contemplative purposes we desire to think of a leg neither as a limb leading to the genitals, nor as a congery of muscle and bone only, nor as ulcerated, nor shapely as a harp. A leg means each of these things and very many more, from time to time; yet it seems to me that for contemplative or aesthetic purposes that enhance the sense of ego, there is to hand a composite leg-image from which every impression departs, though the image will have absorbed each of them. Does the composite image, or the word, come first? I think the image, the body-emblem, inspires the word, and so language. This composite image, largely the fruit of repression, fed libidinally like a neurotic symptom, every moment influenced or bent but recorded by language, is a primitive construction, as old as the ego. Freud's famous phrase about the aim of psycho-analysis: 'Where id was, ego shall be,' should, in my view, be applied as lens to the aim of art, an activity that strengthens the body-emblem through diverse experience, the deeper, the more hidden experience the better. We are nearer to id sources in art than in any other kind of communication outside analysis; to a content, however, subject of aesthetic form, that is to say, of the body-emblem. Whereas id drive may be more apparent in romantic and in what has been called primitive art, in all art of a content freely illimitable, the imposed power of the ego, of the body-emblem, comes to us most strongly from the moments of a classical art, still fresh and lyrical, wherein form and content attain their happiest equilibrium.

Without the body-emblem of a Hellenic cast whereby the spirit is marble flesh, we would be even harder put to it to suffer disease, disfigurement, disablement, decay and old age, in a word, to preserve some brightness for the flesh, in view of guilt, anxiety and aggression. Most disciplines, philosophies, all civilised religions have deprecated the value of the body of which disaster and death are in constant search. They do so in favour of a transcendental body-emblem. But though the super-ego deprecates, it will not always defeat, the ways in which the ego thrives. Except for art, only psychoanalysis, as if it were a Hellenic discipline, encourages us to hold the urges of the body, and thus the body itself, in constant view without the gloss of transcendental disfigurement. If I am justified in appropriating Freud's dictum for art, the alleged therapeutic value of aesthetic activity will lie in direct encouragement for the ego through the enlargement of the body-emblem, a reconstruction that may have a bearing on the disposition of tensions that are sometimes stressed as an outcome.

The possibility of durable love, it seems to me, postulates a consistent image held partly in common by lovers. Attachment needs the medium of constant touch, the fantasy of attachment feeds on a constant phantom-tactility, on a generalised corporeality, including the mother's body, that the ego contemplates. When the ego fades in sleep, so does this structured body-emblem. It is possible that all our working mental structures are in reference to this norm. The word 'structure' indicates here the 'feel' of a train of thought, the come-and-go of argument, the reservations which are like indentations on a surface. A statement of fact denotes an object or records an event, but any argument involves pattern.

Pornographic photographs are sometimes advertised as 'art photographs.' Similarly, though no one believes that the visitors to nude reviews go there for aesthetic reasons, the authorities allow the nude upon the stage if there be no walking, no moving, if statue-esque poses are held. The body, the train of thought was, will then be mistaken for a statue. In cases of extreme beauty it may be possible to view the figure thus; hence the story of the Greek girl, Phryne, which as well as to direct sexual interests refers to an interest or seizure of the whole in a generalised way, an oral-derived experience without need for exploitation of the flesh. The flesh, in fact, is somewhat at a discount; it becomes a texture evoking many other textures, fruit, flowers, and all the paraphernalia of lyric poems. A schema, a system of stresses and proportion, has partly usurped the place of female vulnerability; as far as the sculptor is concerned, weight, mass, the air displaced, the nude, are now the weighty robes of mere allure. Praxiteles was reported to have been Phryne's lover: he will have valued her also as such an ego-idol, an inspiration fed by genital activity that reinforces the capacity to allow full figuration to objects and thereby to love them. On the other hand it may well be that genital acts performed without undressing, sometimes regarded as indecent in the context, are in this respect the more severely genital.

I have said that art is sometimes centred on the projection of individual organs in the guise of whole bodies. It is a remarkable fact, however, that in divergence from the habit of everyday perception, faces in visual art are at some discount. As part of the head, the face of course is a prominent theme but not, except for masks, the face alone, nor the eye, disembodied and all-seeing, hallucinatory, often the dire super-ego representative in the drawings of psychotics. Yet all through life we are reading faces for what they could display of intention and mental structure. Art notes but cannot fully transcribe the theme. In art it is as if character was revealed to us in a way more primitive, through the sense of touch, through the exploration of tension in all the body, or in clothed attitudes. For we are concerned in art with the primitive and unconscious part of the ego more directly than with the id. There are many beautiful sculpted masks, particularly African and Mexican; beautiful, though, because extremely stylized and therefore linked with the primitive body-emblem. The fate of amorous adventure at a masked ball will depend almost entirely on the later moment of unmasking: the painter, however, even in portraiture, should try to convey the psychological effect of features to our hands as well as to our eyes.

I have referred aesthetic pattern and incisiveness to the body-emblem in the belief that there is no other as capacious to provide a form for other images. I fully admit that it is impossible to strengthen my point by referring *per se* to manifest representations of the body in art: they are no more representative than many other themes. I have not based my argument at all on the mere fact of figuration. Indeed, what impresses me most is the prevalence, the dominance, of the theme of texture in *all* the arts, of bone and flesh, as it were, of rough and smooth, wider considerations than the expression of any mood or subject. No one will deny many references to the body in architectural art scale, of course, refers to ourselves and the alternations of architectural features have suggested to many the rhythm of breathing. Buildings are giants of ourselves as well as symbols of the mother and of the womb. I have made elsewhere a generalisation concerning the alternations of wall with aperture, the recession and protuberance of architectural members and the constant interchange of surfaces which are smooth or suggest smoothness with those which are rough or suggest roughness, an antithesis that in my opinion provides the key to all the other alternations, including dark and light and even void and the objects that surround it. I have tried to show also that the same alternation, so sensible to kinaesthetic feeling and to touch, underlies further the process of the graphic arts which so often in our history have been servants of building, until we come down to modern Europe when the graphic arts have won an independence entailing a larger use of manifest texture by means of brush-stroke (as in the case of Oriental painting, an art independent of architecture) or by the contrast of broken with homogenous surfaces and, indeed, as in the case of Braque already mentioned, by the breaking up and reconstitution of every plane.

To consider just one detail, that which was for so long considered picturesque, that is to say, picture-like, namely ruins or other architectural bric-à-brac, moulded, decayed but the more durable and obstinate since their brick and stone emit a structure, pulsating still with a projected life that intensifies our own, a world inhabited by eternal bodies of which column and pediment are giant emblems. There have been great styles of graphic art wherein the representing of dramatic events relied necessarily on an architectural *mise-en-scène*; or when theatrical décor possessed no other theme by which to show off each qualification made on them by human action on the stage. It is decorative, rather than figurative art, I submit, that requires the supposition of a prevalent body-emblem. The pulse of rhythm, too, another life-giving theme of the arts, cannot be isolated from structure; that is to say, rhythm is movement of or in something, of or in mass. Though it be a metaphor we are driven to speak of the texture of sound, even of an individual sound.

This, and most of what I have said, may indicate only that thought and projected feeling and, above all, words, must employ the terms of substance; and that the body is the most significant of substances; rather than that there is a pre-conscious and unconscious body-emblem inseparable from the stability of the ego and the use of language. The projections discussed in this paper may be interpreted in either manner.

NOTE

'The Body-Emblem and Art,' which I have edited from the original manuscript, was composed between 1956-57, contemporaneously with the essay referred to in paragraph three, 'Listening to Clichés and Individual Words,' and with the writing of the book *Greek Culture and the Ego* (1958). Certain paragraphs of 'The Body-Emblem' re-appear in *Greek Culture*, and the essay at hand can be read partly as an abstract or condensation of that book's various ideas on corporeality and art production.

In *Greek Culture*, however, the less compelling expression "ego-figure" replaces "body-emblem." By this substitution Stokes may have intended to avoid any connotation with his earlier consideration of 'the emblematic' in regard to sculpture, in chapter two of *The Quattro Cento* (1932), although these are fairly synonymous usages, at least insofar as both conceive of art-making as an activity of corporeally projected *outwardness*. With Stokes' increasing affinity for the psychoanalytic theory of Melanie Klein (subsequent to *The Quattro Cento* and first explicit in *Smooth and Rough* [1951]), the conceptual addition to this theme is that of reparation.

The term "ego-figure" does not recur in Stokes' later writings, whereas "body-image," rejected in the course of the above essay, is briefly retrieved for the great lecture 'The Image in Form' that closes *Reflections on the Nude* (1967). Even the manuscript of 'Body-Emblem' (at the Stokes archive in the Tate Gallery) proposes two alternate titles, 'The Body-Image and Art' and 'The Body-Ego and Art.' In view of this variance the final title is chosen for its consistent deployment in the text of the manuscript, and for its greater pungency as characteristic Stokes terminology.

Thanks to The Estate of Adrian Stokes (Ian Angus, Ann Stokes and Telfer Stokes) for permission to publish this essay.

THOMAS EVANS

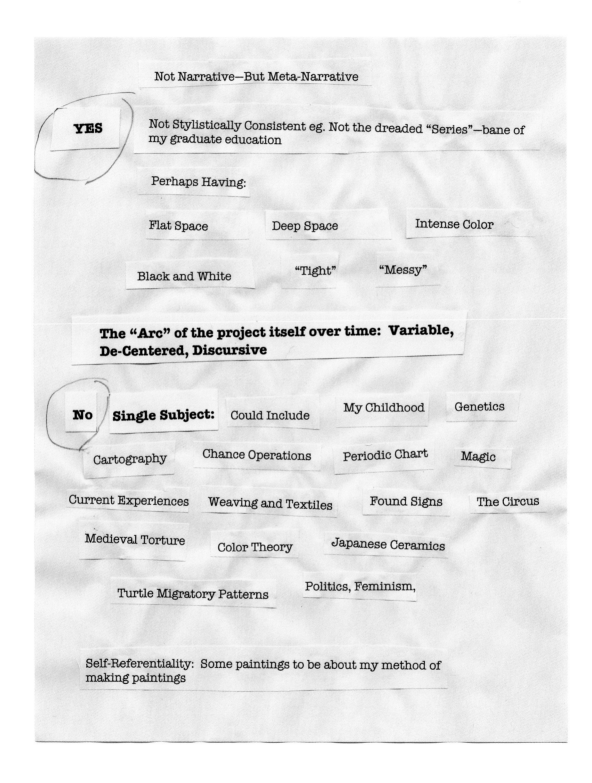

Not Narrative—But Meta-Narrative

**YES**

Not Stylistically Consistent eg. Not the dreaded "Series"—bane of my graduate education

Perhaps Having:

Flat Space          Deep Space                    Intense Color

Black and White          "Tight"          "Messy"

**The "Arc" of the project itself over time:  Variable, De-Centered, Discursive**

**No**  **Single Subject:**  Could Include          My Childhood          Genetics

Cartography          Chance Operations          Periodic Chart          Magic

Current Experiences          Weaving and Textiles          Found Signs          The Circus

Medieval Torture          Color Theory          Japanese Ceramics

Turtle Migratory Patterns          Politics, Feminism,

Self-Referentiality:  Some paintings to be about my method of making paintings

Process Totally Creating Image, eg> the Pontillist Fly Painting
as Marriage of Xerox Break-up and Pontillism

Semiotic Consonances between found images of the same and
different things

**Again:  Variable, DeCentered, Wandering, May Loop
Back, but doesn't have to.**

**THINGS WHICH ARE IMPORTANT TO ME:**

Individual pieces of information—that wishbone from that
English boys book from that Skipjack diagram, ie particularity
not genre

**"Jamming"**—that each individual piece of information is a bit
freighted with the particularities of its origin, eg, fashion
illustration of the 40's, Japanese drawing from the 1880s.
Keeping that and not homogenizing things, yields some friction,
some tension that mitigates against the sameness of oil paint as
one medium, or any other.  The "collage" which is not physical.

**Making Fiction of Facts** —taking found pieces of information
(facts) and combining them to create new realities, mine,
fictional.

Not appropriation, not about the death or originality, death of the author, blah, blah, blah.

**Re-Assigning**, Re-Purposing, Robinson Crusoe—making new things from other things.

The "Mash-Up"

**Collaboration—** Behind my voice is the chorus of all the other people who made all the other things and all the other people they made them for. All the work is a collaboration. The photos contain the eyes of other photographers. I know Im collaborating with them, but they don't know about this collaboration...vs. say, John Ashbery

**Translations**     cf. Jess but more varied sources.

**Fragments**

Point beyond yourself, beyond the diaristic, beyond the artist as solo flyer. Collaborate with your "Self".

Paintings take time and in that time they slip into being something else, other than your idea for them. I still embrace that.

*Untitled (240, 34)*, 1989
oil on linen
76 x 70 inches
All images courtesy of Galerie Lelong, New York

*A Parliament of Refrigerator Magnets,* 1994
oil on canvas
73 x 87 1/2 inches

*And God Created Tunisia*, 2002
oil on wood panel
52 1/2 x 89 x 6 inches

*Heavenly Puppeteer*, 2003
mixed media on heavy rag paper
60 x 79 x 2 inches

114

*Keeping the Orphan*, 1997
oil on canvas with mixed media
114 x 137 inches

*Midwife to Gargoyles*, 1996
oil and mixed media on canvas
74 x 98 inches

*Scrapbook (Paper Lantern)*, 2003
mixed media
25 x 43 x 2 1/2 inches

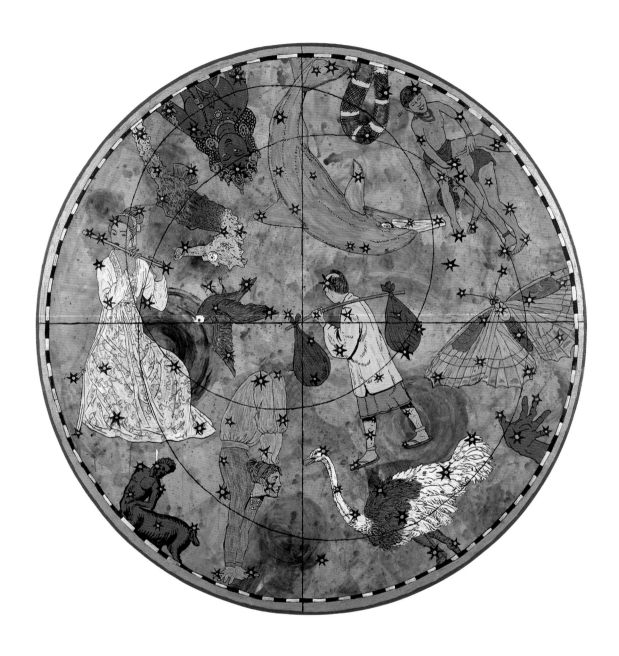

*Happiest on Your Hands*, 2003
oil and mixed media on canvas
70 inches in diameter

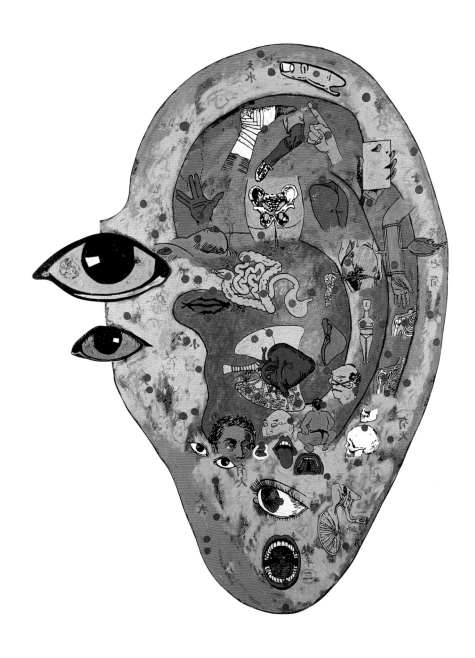

*Sore Models #5*, 1995
oil and mixed media on canvas
84 x 58 inches (1 part of a 3 piece panel)

*Untitled (156, 251, 121, 116, 55, 227, 231)*, 1992
oil on canvas
70 x 76 inches

*Shanghai Costumes* #7, 2003
oil on wood panels
57 x 92 x 3 3/4 inches (overall)

## UNPLANNED ACCOUNT

Everybody has a story. The mountain threw rocks at me. I stood up to it. At
the top I built a shelf for my record. There was enough sky for another life,
an abutment of air. Science itself authorizes blue, whoever comes along may
have some. Up here one can appreciate the eye as an exposed part of the
brain. That's Helga, the chick who shares my pad. She's not really orange,
it's the picture. We're moving the aerial into the hall. I'm an emotional guy
who lacks a cohesive point of view, and Helga has an eating disorder. She's
a monist. I can dig it. I mean, why did the universe go to all that bother?
Bears drunk on honey wrestling with monkeys, electric burgundy odd-toed
ungulates, and the two-headed snake—one head for eating and drinking,
the other just for thinking.

## POETRY INFORMATION

Rain with a sour smell. Not to worry, though you might wind up with it—
primarily a race against your own skin. The skull is showing. The jerking
horses in the old footage, bound to end badly. Psychic hardening, I suppose.
Poetry is arranged by sound. I can say no more. A beloved relative from out
of town was arriving the next day with a brand new infant who would be
tense, disoriented and distraught at discovering herself uprooted from her
familiar bassinet and plunged into a great metropolis seething with cut-
throats and cheap chiselers. People ought to get out more, play cards more,
fight more, fall down more. But we don't need each other to watch a film,
streaming overhead. At your behest, I stood behind the statue, peeking over
its shoulder at live persons, catching something of their tenderness.
They've been marinating, the young and the tough. Meanwhile you should
all have live blood cell analysis.

## BUS EXPLOSION

Another bespoke poem, written while I wrote! Freddy the Newsboy sees
trees and water for the first time thanks to the Fresh Air Fund. What if that
were you—a prince with large pie hat? My petunia fairies took me out in
an automatic boat. We sailed to the sun, where else could we go? Not back

to grandmother with Jim Beam and a whip! Other children were seen under the ice, tallywhacking jellyfish with a rusted bracket, the pouring of time and trouble to junior levels. But I have questions three. What is your favorite cholera? Prince Pointy wuz his name, resided in a cottage wedge. June fairies are free. They lay their eggs under his skin. (That can't be right.) But stay, they'll give you the carbon off their backs. And their heads would have to smoke. All corn fairies wear overalls. One is called Spink, a little girl. She took command of the Lady Schick, not caught up in hope and fear. We sailed to Tortola, where else could we go? Flat nudes were mitered like planks. Stabbed in the chest by my own pencil! After death they move with ease. The wind never lets the rain touch the ground. But now we're traveling in opposite directions, trumpet battles of gold-gold collisions, and thick glorious fields of jewels.

# FRANZ K.

The moon belongs to everyone, a scared mirror. Mahoning spoke of free things, invoked a state of *nunc stans*, or eternal present. He was right, but be alive in all periods, all bodies, living and dead, etc. Allow three to five business days. You are aware of what's lost yet measure no loss. For example, rabbit disappears in briar patch, a slow business. A new story might spoil the old ones. Black is the color, more luminous than my true love's hair. The best things in life are black. Or buried reds. Inside the bulldog's mind, it's a different it. Old and free, understand? Buffoon did it illogically (horizontal) to himself. Once on board, down on your bended knee. He had a long association with Wingy Manone, who could paint. Beginning and end of fishlike emoting.

# COMPLETE FRAGMENTS  *(Portrait of Jessica Dessner)*

The grass came with the snake. She moved like a walking beam, perusing enchantments among the hay mazes, risking and losing with additions. Perhaps her poems shocked because you found in them only talk and no style, bits hammered and stacked. Discipline and personality—these are the limits of style as I understand it. Yet she is not a snot nose. A liver fluke of sheep agrees. She sensed and listened and observed the kind of language that would manifest in contained or absolute space, to its outermost tip. Toes too short, hips too slim, what's that on her elbow? She who never spoke would speak: "I have that swarming vision," and she fainted among her flowers. "Merely emotional" (whatever that is), not an idea "wrapped in emotion." Her fall broken by the acacia bushes, she shook her curls amiably, rummaging in the shed for her watering can.

## JOANNE HATES THE CURTAINS IN THE KITCHEN

What's the name of this in this language? Virgil would write in the morning and spend the evening struggling to put it into hexameters. But Ovid lay it out straight into verse. Brodey's flashing bolt. Yellow-pink-red-blue-green-black rhomboids with little sprays of paisley. I understand well enough resistance to words. The birds is coming, that's what they used to say. Now they say. . .the truth is. . .transubstantiate. Time briefly lengthens, bleeding a little, so we have history to live out, the naturalness of melting. Everyone is hungry for this collation. Why are we in this world? Why does it have to be us? I don't know, kids, I'm just a little Dutch girl holding my pitcher of milk. Change here for all points, many times in future.

## FOLLOW ME QUIETLY

Story I told the kids about the guy in the basement with a head the size of a grape. How then the imagined darkness blazed with slapstick and death. Assortment of mile-long phrases. They boarded up the screen doors on the submarine and left on their vacation. An end to supposing, one supposes. Just being here feels like a dangerous parenthesis. But no forms, no models may speak. Let's have it quiet for a moment, the words will understand. Yes, I think language is sacred, it made a man out of me, the cherry on top of time and space. I grew up, moved off into, continued until the interruption. Somebody (Ebbe?) taught me all about the holidays, and how to build a boat. They called me The Boy Named Billy. I paid a visit to an old oversoul, a graduate of Bard. We stood together in the dirt. I wouldn't mind trading tasks for awhile, he said, you sting, I moisten. There was a fire here a few years ago and things are always being moved around a bit, which explains Simon Pettet standing next to Robespierre. A large marsh of pitch boiling. Are you in there? Are you coming out?

## DIG & DELVE

No strict pattern holds. We had to let go of rule of thumb. I can't explain but you understand. A need to internalize the chief's words, creating animated mental models of the chief and his sayings. Mix our blood with the Indians. Then he sets out and we fall in behind him. The little crust of blood appeared in many places at once. Molecules stood on their heads, constituting a scene: the view that life was something happening to us. Ink-accepting. Its only claim to be was that it was happening without us, a hair wound around a nail. That's enough truth. When the meaning becomes clear, I'll be able to say what it's about. (It's impossible to get pictures from the cops.) He had a way of running all his sentences together into one shout. He never looked for anything he found, reality of outer objects belonging only to appearance. As king, he couldn't run around too much. He decided what opened and closed, in which names mean nothing. It was one of those lady or tiger deals. Now we object to everything as it occurs, but whatever we think and feel, we're left with what he does. It is no pink tea. We're not working with a human perspective, none of the talking nose-tips are related. Cold snakes came. Once they're out you can't put them back in. It's all string theory to me. I'm not creative enough to think of another way other than resignation. Well, there's always summer school. Deaf & Dumb. As a post, as paint. Couldn't dent the cuticle of a custard pie. Yet if my whole security system is based on myself, then I have to be perfect. Doily on the organ. I'll just sit here and read the paper. No more funny stuff. Make believe this piece of toilet paper is the picture of a saint. And it's in the book, the one with several spines. If you don't cut it in half it'll be all down your arm. Everything everywhere. I didn't mind. The sticks were already straight when we picked them up. I just happened to be out that way, string in my leg. Something crawling on my arm. It's only my breath. Big fat hen was crazy, too, but in the wrong way. Her smile fooled her brain so she "became" happy for a minute. The hum was coming from her. Then we noticed the dent in the credenza. Silent tick. The chief split the scene, not even leaving. We followed him through the opening where they have to let you in. Return with us now. The page will take your duster. But it will not speed up when you put your foot down. Like I told the cat, you have to stop living in your own world. One more of those sneak attacks and you'll be back in the manufactory, bolting curved plates onto rotary cylinders. Sorry but that's the way it is. Abandon all thoughts of fruition. Avoid the grand piano. Beware of pattern books. Never trust anyone you don't have something on. What's the longest unbroken melody you can play? Lungs like a freight train, dried up, then slaked. Anytime you go into a park you'll find an elf. Its only competition is reality. Dig no deeper. You'll be given a gnomic name unless your own is guttural enough. Suppose it were all true, the mind couldn't break it down. Verily, intruders were here looking for us, not tungsten. Oozing out of their claspers only to meet your own edge and freeze: the Dummheit of escape. You never saw them in anything after that. When I returned to the eyebrow house it had collapsed flat. I'm no smart apple but I can smell a screwy setup. Then… nothing happened. The pig could not greenlight anything. He just worked there and never thought about it, unconscious even when alert. Having nothing isn't much of a pose. Fluffy tore at his throat. What of it? Then the chief appeared on a beam. I marveled at the unknown that he had become. The way out was a slanting line passing downward through a horizontal fluid plane. Mice of time entered my heart by surprise. Tell them there is nothing for them to do. We went back to our chore, shoveling fleas across the barnyard. The child-master blue with hate. The simple mouth, everything written in it. In his lean-to the shelves held only what sagged them: the open book. They (doctors) tell us to turn the page but it weighs a ton. Bits of matter, enduring self-identically in space, which is otherwise empty. In the passing sky, we sleep or we are stunned. Ring for the wagon. And yet it is the same person who recovers consciousness. I'm only repeating his words, begun before forming. Itchy, watery eyes, when I am huge among the stars. The owl sleeps, the lark jogs with a neighbor. Looks like I've rewritten an old standard again.

## THE MUD BATH

I look at melody as rhythm. No, I rescind the day. I love the night, stripped of extraneous content. Checkerboard stutter. Do you have the stuff to make the rug? When pestering flowers do you act according to a principle? No reiteration because I am wrong, not by living poorly, not by shaking the box (crackers). I differ only in form, in glasses and vest (cartridge). I will play for you, who have an extra ear. Pentimento. I begin with a barcarole. The blind offer darkness. They hold their instruments but seldom play them, creating a silence as present as space. They love getting high on their way downstairs. I wind my way to the bridge, wait for what washes up on the steps. This is a sawing piece. Meloday.

## NOTE TO PORTER FOX

Your pursuit must be a type based on research from which every pretension or individual vanity is excluded. Helpless isn't hopeful. Go after her, or go before her. Frieze of a dream. It requires an unsentimental composure, knowing how and when to withdraw, like a good valet. Love's brick for Ignatz. Then it's finished. Get on your bike. But how you gon' get respect when you ain't cut your process yet? Rollers have messed up your brain. Nevertheless step lively. "By now," she said, "I know who I want to sleep with, but lending my equipment is something else." Look at the highlights on her fingernails. Walk across her like a fly.

## FURIOUS HANDICRAFT

The Naxos Sphinx had broken a wing. I'm sure it can be glued, she said, nursing a Rob Roy, a Rusty Nail and an Apricot Sour. Who'll know the difference? She would conceal it. The dog was dead. I'm so hungry I could eat a dog, she said, wagging her head and chewing. How about an omelet, potatoes and toast? It stood nearby, glacial as a great white whatsis. When he saw her with cards he said, "The man who invented the little wrapper for the sugar cube would never have done that if he'd been playing with cards."

Reduce the picture, she becomes a statue, looking out on the one view. It's an oryx with its hoof on her shoulder. Stuff everybody goes through, crying in the bathtub, wasting the expensive lavender. These articles can't be easily parsed. Too much chingwa. Presently knowing. And so on to the paranoiac, maintain a facial expression that comes off as interested. Derelict wit, no end to it.

## ARTIST'S TRICK

You can fool me some of the time. I have other plans, another art. A little snip/of potato chip/and a trifle of the Eiffel Tower. To know the difference between those things. Red petals, jar of pennies. Remove the limited criteria, something your eye can't do on its own. Their collection outperformed ours. It's all tidbits anyway. Half-cocked billy goat. On my 11th birthday, Gorky hung himself. I took off all my clothes and got into bed. Look let's just do it, I mean next Monday. Investigate how our bodies became mineral. She's right, it's too much work. Everything is. "I'm going to the Louvre—anything you need?" Be careful there, you don't like fun. When it's over there isn't any more. I made my decision in the bar last night, told them I wanted a single bed in the gallery. Find something useful in this that's no good anywhere else. Explain what it means. Comet vapors. We talked all night, went home, made green with mummy brown.

## ACID ROCK

It looked human, no one I knew. I tried talking to it, it went *eek*. They put us in the same room, we must have dreamt something. In the morning they said go. Later I followed it around in the flat light, kept going right off the pier and under the sea like a bathysphere. Once I fell in a hole, it was interesting. But for now my education consists of standing still. A wire might catch on fire. The week had a good late beginning and a moderate fade. Wandering in the pitch black, put a little beret on my head, a little blue bagel. Something a-whirring up from the floor, only the magazines reposed, and a box of cards. A new theory created to contain it. What could help me in my wool business? I'd go abroad but they're always shutting down the displays, and nothing works, have you noticed? Nothing mechanical, anyway, or electrical, with or without transformers. Poor bobbins. Well it's tough. I have one leg, as do you. But if we can just hang on to each other. . . A little mistake was made. In trying to fix it, it got worse, bigger and so forth. It was always there, always will be. Other than that we know nothing. I spent most of my childhood alone. Being liked is important to me. Remember when I said I was going to be honest with you? Those were the days. Am I the pretty one? We seem to be happy doing things sadly. A moment ago you stood in the garderobe holding your pillow like a sacrament. Funny we're up in the air again, sky actually, looping through warm spots. Good destiny accomplished. Is it really necessary to smile to prevent frostbite? Another finding was you were in the lead, thrusting upwards. I held on tight, falling on my knees in the clouds. They're coming, bringing their memory movies, some piece of work to take with us to the moon, this long overdue blotch.

*for Jerome Hiler*

## THREE MOODS

Scraping sound. I've come down with a case of some kind of -itis. In any case, *It Is*. Crazy bastard thinks he's Napoleon. Still he has convinced me that I can just let go, the way they come back from first-half deficits. A little throat culture, maestro, or Monstro, if you please. What is the verb of this music? "Think bed, not pedestal." (Konitz) Now you know.

Brown and gray wash, gum and pencil. Drew the sound of eyewitness poem. Slowly the poison the whole blood stream fills. Yet it all passes, how about that?

One cannot use the cat for something. Whiskers caught in watch gears. Let her out, let her back in. If she has no fiddle, shows no musical ability, give her to Beatrice of Aragon, who never opens her eyes.

## BALKAN HOSPITALITY SPOONS

In the middle of the book was a hairpin, which I could take and double back to the known world. I couldn't get to the end anyway because there was always an extra page or two blocking the way. Having to conserve oneself while utterly absorbed in at least six other characters. It's cold out tonight, mediated by valuation juice. Now they're nothing. "Cookie the Blow" has vanished, possibly inkblots to Bowling Green. But I'm glad to be near you. Inaction available to all goers, 'long as they've left a leg on the tracks for allegorical futures.

# chapman's homer

is scored for solo violin, with the G string tuned down to Eb (the other three strings are tuned as usual). All notes are notated at pitch. Throughout, rhythms are to be interpreted freely, though I have indicated a rough scale of durations for notes and for silences:

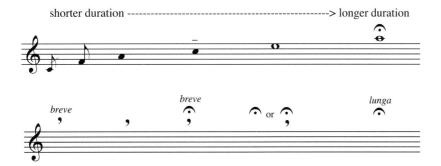

Any traditionally notated rhythms (other than the single, flagged eighth notes from the scale above) may be played as approximate proportions (any notated 16ths, or any dotted eighths for example). Starting soon after the change of mood beginning in the middle of the second page of score some eighth rests appear. These are always paired with stemless filled noteheads, and each of these pairs may be played as approximately equal—each pair equivalent to a bright and bouncy dotted quarter. Any sections marked with repeat signs may be repeated any number of times.

This brief single-movement work for solo violin requires the retuning of the lowest string of the instrument, from its usual G, to a rather flabby Eb. I wrote the piece over the course of a couple of afternoons in Chapman Studio at the MacDowell Colony in May 2005. The title came first from a melding of Keats' poetic reference to George Chapman's translation of Homer's *Odyssey* and the studio where I was working at the time. As I repeated this phrase in my mind I realized that "Chapman's homer" could just as easily refer to baseball: "Red Sox Beat Yanks 5-4 / On Chapman's Homer." Since I felt the conclusion of the piece had a decidedly American sound, and since I was working in a studio previously inhabited by such luminaries as Aaron Copland, Marc Blitzstein, and others, it felt right to make that punning reference. *Chapman's homer* was written for violinist Roger Zahab—Pittsburgh's champion of new music!

# chapman's homer

### for Roger Zahab

alan shockley

2        chapman's homer

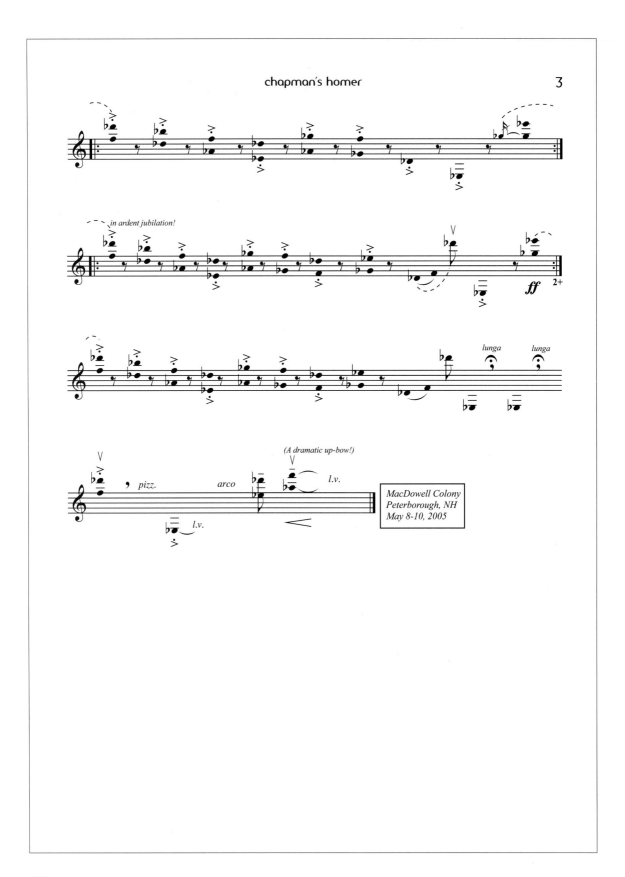

# wndhm (1785)
## [i]

*for Benjamin Binder*

alan shockley

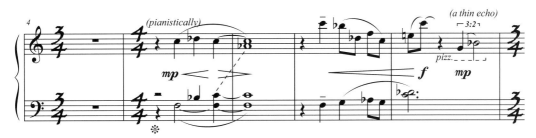

133

**wndhm (1785): [i]**

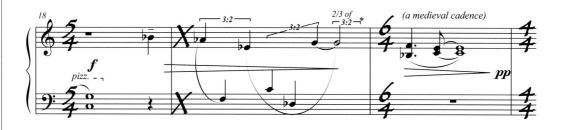

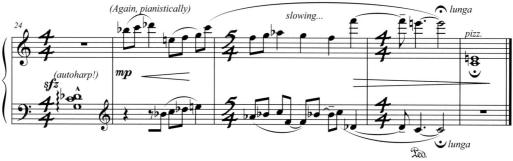

* An X time signature is used in place of an
otherwise irrational time signature. In this
measure, there are two complete sets of quarter
note triplets, and one incomplete set. (This solution
is used rather than a metric modulation for a single
measure, or a time signature of 5+1/3.)

4

# [ii]

**after Daniel Read**
*for John Cage*

My father was a cheese grater
My mother was a stair
I'm a no-nonsense escalator
Less I couldn't care
I'm a slick machine but I turn mean
When from inside my parts that glide
I smell the fetor of a musky sneaker
Taking an upward ride
I grab the toes as my slabs close
I grate my steel
On feet that feel
Tom felt that grab
In his sneaker's toe
Click-clack
He can't pull it back
Ilzich-zack
The monster won't let go
The danger peaks
He nearly freaks
Untie the shoe lace, Tom!
He did.
Free the foot slid.
The escalator foiled,
Tore the sneaker, and ate it oiled.

THE RESEARCH STUDIO
MAITLAND, FLORIDA

THE MAIL
IN
GERMANY

THE MAIL
IN
TUNIS

White Head, Cushings Island, Portland Harbor

901.    A CLUSTERED SAHUARO. (GIANT CACTUS).

A-5718

143

Wishing Well, Ramona's Marriage Place, San Diego, Cal.

144

## ROMANTIC POEM

*for L. S.*

In the dead of night
In the dead of the past
The landscape of mathematical bats
With inviting slate-lined troughs sunk in gravel
Can you think of me
Can you think of us
Armorially intricated like a bunch of bananas
In wastelands of utopian desire
Can you think
How can real things if lovable be so uncomfortable
Sloth, nevermindness, sweetish pus
Excuses worse than astrological babble
Tomorrow was another day
With vicious sunlight
Not even room enough to moralize
Just get down and stay down
I can't remember but then you
Are not to be forgotten
Putting myself out of your reach
Backing towards immobility
So sluggishly attained
Then as now

# IN PRAISE OF HEINRICH HEINE

In longing, the underage seaman veered from the drift,
Elsewhere, out of the wind, scuppered his stone desire.
Unluck cleaving to him made him no schadenfreuder—
What was plus or minus? He loved the least cat.

Starbursts should light up this moment, the child
Be jealous of nighttime and its laughing yellow listener!
The red doe of the prince of studies sunders,
Shedding her likeness. Her undimmed luster fits him.


# SUSSEX DAYS

Singing has shed its sound,
Soundless song articulates itself
In mauve fevers
That sting the unopened nose.

Halal lamb is distributed
Like goose on Christmas afternoon.
You likewise will be cut into pieces of deliberation:
Relics sufficient for passionate sleepiness.

Emboldened by their Dada apprenticeship, the Surrealists were not shy about publicizing their views. From the splash of Tzara's surprise Paris debut at the First Friday of *Littérature* in 1920 to the group's presence on the barricades in May '68, these boys liked shouting it from the rooftops and taking it to the streets—the streets that, said Breton, "could test like nowhere else the winds of possibility."

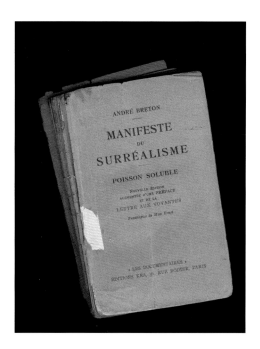

In the fall of 1924, as Breton and a knot of like-minded malcontents tried to give a name to the (as they termed it) "vague" current that had been preoccupying them for several years, the question of publicity became paramount. Surrealism, whatever else one might say about it, was also a product, a concept to be marketed to as many receptive consumers as it could reach. And, as with most products, its launch was threatened by an assortment of obstacles: limited media access, the public's resistance to novelty, even a rival creation—specifically, the Apollinaire-tinted brand of Surrealism promoted by Yvan Goll and Paul Dermée. In this light, the flurry of activity that accompanied the movement's premiere, including the broadside *A Corpse* and the first issue of *La Révolution surréaliste*, stands as nothing so much as a vast advertising campaign, with the *Manifesto of Surrealism* as its lead press release. Like Tzara before him, who had pushed Dada to the front of the avant-garde pack just after the war, Breton intended both to spread the word far and wide and to knock the competition on its ear.

Breton's works abound in references to the attention-grabbing artifacts and slogans of the modern world, as purveyors of the marvelous: the huge billboard for Mazda light bulbs (not simply because of its consonance with Nadja), the "modern mannequin" evoked in the *Manifesto*, and the humble painted signs for wood and coal are only a few examples. Since the beginning of his poetic adulthood, he had looked for ways to break language out of the cloister into which it had been shut by literary preciousness, and he saw advertising as one such means. "What is it that poetry and art do?" he had written to Louis Aragon in April 1919. "They extol. Extolling is also the aim of advertising." And that same month: "Naturally, we must take the word advertising in the widest sense…Christianity is an advertisement for heaven." Like dream condensation, Isidore Ducasse's reworking of old maxims, or the surprise detours of automatic writing, the best advertisements reconfigure the familiar into something recognizable but different, revivifying both language and its object and making them new. Breton later remarked that he'd wanted to compose "an advertisement for heaven" (in the *Manifesto* he added: "or for hell") that would be "striking enough, convincing enough" to make everyone commit suicide.

So it is not surprising to find the *Manifesto of Surrealism* borrowing tone and tactics from the publicist's arsenal. A manifesto by definition is an exercise in persuasion—in extolling. In this case, the *Manifesto* became the primary announcement, mission statement, and poster for the nascent Surrealist movement, and perhaps even more importantly, a kind of patent application for moral claim to the term "Surrealism" itself. Had Breton been a less skillful copy writer, our use and understanding of the word today would no doubt be quite different—assuming it would still have any currency at all.

The origins of the *Manifesto* go back to 1919 (the same year Breton lectured Aragon about poetry and advertising) and the Breton-Philippe Soupault co-production *The Magnetic Fields*. Convinced that this inaugural volume of automatic writing constituted a true revolution, Breton had sent copies to book critics and to Sigmund Freud, its patron saint, but had been severely disheartened by the scant response. In the five intervening years, he had practiced various other kinds of non-composition, such as dialogues obtained during seances and poems generated "from the most random assemblage possible of scraps of headlines." He had also returned to automatic writing proper, producing, among others, the poems of *Earthlight* in 1923 and the "short anecdotes" of *Soluble Fish*, written between March and May 1924. Wanting to publish these anecdotes in book form, but hoping to avoid the neglect that had greeted *The Magnetic Fields*, Breton thought to arm *Soluble Fish* with a preface, an explanation and presentation of automatic prose that, this time around, would clue the reader in to its radical significance.

The reason for the preface was clear; its exact nature less so. Breton's first idea was to draft a short, basic introduction. Then a fifteen-page collective letter, addressed "to the Dawn," in collaboration with his faithful mainstays Aragon and Soupault. But Soupault, evidently figuring that his co-authorship of *The Magnetic Fields* and its two spin-offs, *If You Please* and *You'll Forget Me*, was collaboration enough, soon begged off. As for Aragon, who had been absent for the earlier experiments with automatic writing, he now decided to plant his flag in the Surrealist terrain and strike out with a preface of his own, an elliptical celebration of delirium entitled "Une Vague de rêves." Breton, flying solo once more, extended his introduction from a fifteen-page letter into its final form, a full-fledged theoretical program nearly five times that length.

In addition to presenting *Soluble Fish*, the *Manifesto* served another strategic purpose. Twenty-eight years old at the time of its composition, Breton was widely considered a young writer on the rise, though one who had not yet "broken through." He had received some favorable notices for his essay collection *The Lost Steps*, published by the prestigious house of Gallimard in early 1924, but his other books, all poetry, had garnered the kind of attention one could expect for small-press poetry volumes. Though Breton did not truly reach a wider public until *Nadja* (1928), it was the *Manifesto* that put him on the literary map—which his publisher noted by crowing in an ad for the book: "The whole younger literary generation is talking about the *Manifesto of Surrealism* by André Breton."

And perhaps more than any of these, Breton's very claim to the label itself, which he and his friends had been using with regard to a particular form of mental and written activity, was being challenged by a rival faction of poets. Yvan Goll and Paul Dermée had been members of Apollinaire's circle, and were eager to further the magus's words—particularly the word "Surrealism," which he had famously coined in 1917. It was to Dermée that Apollinaire had justified his adoption of this term "rather than Supernaturalism, which I had initially used. Surrealism does not yet exist in the dictionaries, and it will be easier to manipulate than Supernaturalism, which is already used by the Philosophers." Although Apollinaire's understanding of Surrealism was a far cry from Breton's, it was he who had launched the brand, and according to Goll and Dermée, it was he (or rather, now that the poet was assassinated, they) who held the copyright.

The battle—a tempest in a teapot, but a tempest nonetheless—began in May 1924, at around the time Breton started writing the *Manifesto*, and lasted through October of the same year, when he published it. The first strike was Dermée's remark in a newspaper article that "Surrealism" was synonymous with "literary Cubism," in other words the kind of literature practiced by Apollinaire, Pierre Reverdy, Max Jacob, and (surprise!) himself. Breton answered that, although coined by Apollinaire, the word had now outstripped its vague original usage and more properly designated such precursors as Lautréamont, Rimbaud, and (surprise!) *The Magnetic Fields*. The tone quickly escalated, becoming more pointed and more personal, each side accusing the other of bad faith. Goll and Co. charged Breton with misappropriating of Apollinaire's original invention. Breton responded by ridiculing them as mere literary bit-players, which history has in fact shown them to be, and by publishing his now-famous definition ("SURREALISM, *n.* Psychic automatism in its pure state…"), lifted from his manifesto-in-progress. The situation became so confusing, especially from the outside, that the bemused newspapers often reversed the two factions' viewpoints, or reported them as one and the same. Finally, hoping to score a winning blow, Goll founded a new magazine in late October, provocatively titled *Surréalisme,* in which he reproduced Apollinaire's letter to Dermée as a supposedly conclusive piece of evidence. But several days later, Breton's *Manifesto of Surrealism* came out in book form from Editions du Sagittaire and settled the debate in his favor.

The short of it is, Breton simply out wrote them. In place of the stolid, cerebral disquisition one might expect for such a rarefied subject, his manifesto uses a combination of bold statements, engaging (if acerbic) humor, appeals to the reader's self-interest, and, always, a firm eye on the human dimension, expressed through the author's example or that of his friends. From start to finish, and with a verve that would do any Madison Avenue executive proud, he presents an exciting new roadmap for "man, that inveterate dreamer" to follow—and, along the way, convincingly dismisses the Goll-Dermée version as the pale Apollinairian retread it was.

Indeed, at times Breton seems to take on the fiery rhetoric of a televangelist, preaching an anti-gospel of earthly marvels: "The time is coming when [poetry] decrees the end of money and by itself will break the bread of heaven for the earth!" And: "I believe in the future resolution of these two states, dream and reality, which are seemingly so contradictory, into a kind of absolute reality, a *surreality*." And again: "There is every reason to believe that [Surrealism] acts on the mind very much as drugs do; like drugs, it creates a certain state of need and can push man to frightful revolts." And finally: "Let us not mince words: the marvelous is always beautiful, anything marvelous is beautiful, in fact only the marvelous is beautiful." Though still young, Breton here demonstrates real mastery: by peppering his text with startling pronouncements (and there are others), he keeps his reader hooked, eager to hear more about this mad but alluring program. "Note how this madness has taken shape, and endured."

Using bold or lapidary statements in a manifesto is hardly new, of course, and in this regard Breton had learned from some excellent teachers. The danger is that, because they are so much a part of the genre, they are also the most easily devalued. Anyone, given a modicum of belief in his subject, can chance upon a provocative phrase—even Goll or Dermée.

What the earnest post-Cubists did not seem to have, on the other hand, and what immediately lifts Breton's statement above theirs, is his wicked sense of humor. Breton had absorbed, very attentively, the sometimes hilarious Dada screeds by his brother-enemy Tzara: no matter that the two were currently on the outs, there are certain lessons you don't forget. (Though in this regard, the Romanian's manic shriek seems to echo less loudly than Marx's sardonic snicker.) Surreality is heady stuff, and even though Breton, like any good pitchman, aimed to put it "within the reach of everyone," he knew that his particular blend of tonic might be especially hard to swallow. But how can we fail to be charmed by such humorous sweeteners as his pun about living on Rue Fontaine but not drinking from its water, or his "secret" recipes for "writing false novels" and "catching the eye of a woman you pass in the street"—the latter followed by five lines of dots?[1]

1. These dots encapsulate the entire Surrealist sense of humor, and convey Breton's point much more effectively than the original draft, which recommends walking past the woman in front of a music store and offering her a cigarette from a holster.

These recipes, under the heading "Secrets of the Magical Surrealist Art," form one of the centerpieces of the *Manifesto*. Along with the famous dictionary and encyclopedia definitions of the term (a direct snub at Goll and Dermée) and the list of "Surrealist in" ("Swift is Surrealist in malice," etc.), it acts as both a philosophical signpost and a flashy effect, a way of re-sparking the reader's attention should it threaten to flag—and of providing critics with easy "sound bites" for their articles.

In fact, Breton has understood a fundamental truth of both writing and advertising: that it is first and foremost a process of seduction. We humans are egocentric animals. When reading about someone or something else, we are really looking to read about ourselves. And just as an advertisement makes its heavy-handed appeals to our sense of want, so a writer (presumably with a bit more subtlety) will pinpoint the intersection of his desire and ours. There are few things more tedious than reading someone's hermetic inner monologue or listening to another person's dream—think how few of the Surrealist dream narratives, painstakingly detailed in their magazines, still hold up. One remarkable feature of Breton's writing, in the *Manifesto* and elsewhere, is the author's ability to weave a mystique around his life and then to draw the reader into his—apparent—intimacy, to lay open his world like the proverbial book, to give at least the illusion of uniquely privileged access. Like all good advertisements, the *Manifesto* promises a sense of belonging, membership in an exclusive club: "Surrealism will usher you into death, which is a secret society."

"One evening, before I fell asleep...": the tone, the sense of confidences made, secrets shared, immediately pulls us near, makes us listen closer. Despite Breton's diatribe against the novel (a "false genre," said Ducasse) as expressed several pages earlier, it is almost as if we have left the realm of philosophy or politics, the rightful terrain of the manifesto, and entered the domain of, if not fiction, then at least personal memoir. And the tale is worth the telling, for it evokes marvels called forth from within, the mysterious voice of our long-forgotten selves, our "inner child," as it were. Marx promised the worker singing tomorrows. Tzara showed the poet how to elude the tedium of composition and sense. Breton offers his reader, that inveterate dreamer, a glimpse into the unknown within himself. The *Manifesto* is an invitation to the voyage, to an adventure that appeals to our most buried, most ardent, most universal impulses. As the early slogan put it, "If you like LOVE, you'll love SURREALISM."

In fostering this apparent intimacy, Breton does not hesitate to name names. His writings are littered with mentions of the friends surrounding him at any given moment, cited with an authority and an assurance that confer on a bunch of young tyros a virtual fame (which, partly because of this, eventually became actual fame). In Breton's written world, these unknown, untried, often unpublished writers and artists take on a grandeur, an aura brighter than some Anatole France or Pierre Loti or other now-eclipsed luminary—and history has proven him right. "There is Louis Aragon leaving; he only has time enough to say hello; Philippe Soupault gets up with the stars, and Paul Eluard, our great Eluard, has not yet come home..." And so on for the rest of the page, name after unfamiliar name, usually followed by some sort of personal-sounding remark. These are not simply in-jokes: by refusing to draw a distinction between private and public facts, Breton endows this ragtag band of fellow travelers with mythic life, daring us to admit that we don't know who they are, to look away in complacency or disinterest. He even practices a little advertisement for himself, discussing *The Magnetic Fields*, his essay "The Mediums Enter," his poem "Black Forest" as if they were already anthology pieces.

And now a word from our sponsor. The names cited in the *Manifesto* are not only those of Breton's friends and associates but, just as important, those whose endorsement of Surrealism he is tacitly seeking, even implying. Primary among these is Freud, with whom he was "completely occupied at that time"; Freud, whose discoveries will allow the "human explorer...to carry his investigations much further" in the direction Breton is here laying out; Freud, who, despite his polite dismissal of *The Magnetic Fields*, is cited almost as a kind of guarantor of the Surrealist enterprise. And Freud is hardly alone, for the text is sprinkled with leading references to, among others, Poe, Rimbaud, Taine, Apollinaire (despite everything), Reverdy, Matthew G. Lewis, Nerval, Ducasse (present not only by name, but in such *Poésies*-inspired deviations as "Man proposes and disposes"), Dante and Shakespeare—not to mention the above-mentioned list of figures who showed "Surrealist" tendencies before the fact, a list that ranges from Sade and Hugo to Baudelaire, Jarry, Mallarmé and Raymond Roussel. The pedigree here seems endless: look at all the satisfied customers who have tried our method at one time or other. If you like Chateaubriand, you'll love Surrealism.

This is not the whole story, of course. But part of the *Manifesto's* effectiveness at the time, as well as its impact today—and this alongside, not despite, its enduring, undeniable philosophical import—derives from Breton's remarkable savvy in the ways of publicity-speak. Like an avant-garde Charles Atlas, he points at the problem, then holds up the miracle solution. Feeling old, tired, worn out by life? "The mind which plunges into Surrealism relives with glowing excitement the best part of its childhood...Thanks to Surrealism, it seems that opportunity knocks a second time." Ignored by your fellow men? Speak Surrealist and you "will be truly elected, and women will love [you] with an all-consuming passion." Hounded by feelings of persecution? "Surrealism asserts our complete *nonconformism* clearly enough so that there can be no question of translating it, at the trial of the real world, as evidence for the defense." Wish you could just put an end to it all? "Surrealism will usher you into death..."

This last is a fine, desperate claim, but something of an anomaly. For the *Manifesto* is about not death but life, "*real* life, that is"; and about destiny, with which we are daily more discontent; and madness, which conquers new lands; and dreams, especially dreams, a primary weapon against "the reign of logic," an indispensable tool "in solving the fundamental questions of life." It is about the marvelous, and fantasies to be handed free rein, and language, "given to man so that he may make Surrealist use of it," and phrases that knock at the window. It is about "the pure Surrealist joy of the man who, forewarned that all others before him have failed, refuses to admit defeat." It is about being and ceasing to be, which as the poet said are imaginary solutions. Existence is elsewhere, and it's on sale now.

Raphael Rubinstein

SELECTIONS FROM
*IN SEARCH OF THE MIRACULOUS:*
*50 EPISODES FROM THE ANNALS OF*
*CONTEMPORARY ART*

1.

Deaf since childhood, an artist begins to save the notes he must ask people to write out when he can't read their lips. Many of these scraps of impromptu writing consist of proper names—the hardest kind of enunciation for him to visually comprehend—but they also include all kinds of odd phrases that he is unable to lip-read for one reason or another. Often his interlocutors grow tired of having to repeat their words until he is able to recognize them. For everyone involved, these translations from the aural to the visual can be exhausting. The notes which result from these "conversations with the hearing," as he later comes to call them, are written on cocktail napkins, matchbook covers, cash register receipts, gallery announcements, pages torn from notebooks, business cards, pieces of brown paper bags, postcards and Post-its, in short, on every kind of paper imaginable.

One day, this deaf man, who until now has been trying to express himself through painting, decides to exhibit some of these scribbled texts in conjunction with his canvases. To reconstruct the original context for viewers, he writes up short paragraphs which are printed and hung in black frames next to the note (or notes) they comment upon. As well as giving the background to each note's creation, his accompanying texts address the socio-linguistic and psychological implications of his exchanges. As a result of this show, the public, or at least a small, but influential, portion of it, becomes as fascinated as the artist with these traces of communication between the deaf and the hearing. Critics begin to devote laudatory reviews to his note-and-commentary groupings, collectors begin to buy his work. It's not long before he stops making paintings in order to devote himself completely to the new art form that has been born out of his exploration of his disability.

As his artistic career blossoms and his circle of acquaintances widens, he begins to accumulate an ever greater number of notes. He starts to classify them, sometimes paying attention to the content of the message, sometimes to its provenance, sometimes to the color or shape of the paper. In certain cases a single word is accompanied by a long, anecdotal text. For instance, in one piece a scrawled three-letter word is flanked by an account of his visit to an upscale liquor store where, as he was buying a bottle of wine, he noticed two women employees engaged in an animated conversation. He couldn't resist asking them the subject of their conversation, which one of them wrote out for him: "sex." In another, less light-hearted work he presents the attempts of a semi-literate panhandler to write a request for money. In the panhandler's incomplete and crossed-out words the artist is able to read the man's tragic life.

As he probes ever more deeply into the afterlife of his daily exchanges, he increasingly chooses to simply exhibit groups of notes by themselves, without any explicatory text. After a while, he becomes interested in recreating the circumstances in which the notes were written, such as a table in a Parisian restaurant or an Italian hotel room (he now travels the world from one exhibition to another). Although he now thinks little about his earlier involvement with painting, these recreations clearly relate to the history of still-life painting.

## 2.

One day in 1962, a slim, dark-haired young man is sitting at a table in his cheap Latin Quarter hotel room. Although he has with him neither paint nor canvas nor any of the traditional studio accoutrements, he is about to begin his next work of art. Before this he has been a ballet dancer, the editor of a magazine devoted to concrete poetry, and a sculptor. His father, an Eastern European Jew, died in the Holocaust, despite the fact that he had converted to Christianity. He was rescued from a similar fate by a non-Jewish maternal uncle whose name he adopted. In the years to follow, his life will take him to a Greek island where, for 12 months, he will keep a detailed record of his meals, the recipes they involve and the lives of those around him as they relate to eating; he will open a restaurant in Germany where, at the end of each day, he will glue the remnants of selected meals (plates, glasses, silverware, chicken bones, cigarette butts, etc.) to the tables and sell them to an art dealer who will display the table tops, shorn of legs, on the walls of his prestigious gallery. Today, however, such extensive projects lie in the future. All he aims to accomplish now is the complete cataloging of every object on the table before him.

It will take more than 200 pages to account for the 80 entries, which will range from #1 "Piece of bread with a bite taken out of it" to #80 "A Cigarette Burn." As the entries range through plastic wine stoppers, shirt buttons, screws, obscure mementos and even the ballpoint pen with which he is writing, they offer not only descriptions of the objects but information about how they were acquired, what they have been used for and any anecdotes associated with them. For instance, he records where he bought the bread, who was visiting him when he sliced it, who took the bite of it. In this way, he gradually describes the important people in his life, the shops and cafes of his neighborhood, the living conditions in his cheap hotel.

Eventually the material will appear in a book titled *An Anecdoted Topography of Chance*, which will include footnotes, several indexes, cross references, drawings of each object and a map showing their placement around the table. Some of the footnotes stretch for pages, wandering into reminiscences, esthetic statements and etymology. By the end, the objects on the table will have provided an occasion for a self-portrait of the artist and a quasi-archeological record of his milieu and era.

3.

A 28-year-old Italian artist seals samples of his own feces in small tin cans. He produces 90 such cans whose labels give the title and description of the work in several languages. As in standard food packaging, the label also gives the weight of the contents (30 grams) and the month and year of its production (May 1961). The price of each can is equal to how much it would cost to buy 30 grams of gold.

Within two years the artist is dead. Later, rumors abound that the market is saturated with forgeries of *Artist's Shit*, as the edition is called. It is also suggested, in some quarters, that the artist only pretended to have put his shit in the cans. Despite the purported forgeries, the 2 by 2 1/2 inch containers have become so valuable that, like extremely old bottles of grand cru wine, hardly anyone dares to open them.

4.

One of the best-known works by this artist consists of hundreds of pieces of hard candy, each wrapped in cellophane. Following the artist's instructions, the candies are piled in the corner of the gallery or museum. Visitors are free to help themselves, although there is no sign authorizing this.

Inculcated with the maxim "Don't touch the works of art," most members of the art-viewing public would not dare to take a candy. What usually happens when the work is exhibited is that someone familiar with the unusual protocols of this artist's work, or simply smart and independent enough to figure out that the candy is there for the eating, takes a piece. Other visitors notice this and, seeing that no museum guard leaps on the candy taker, they begin to grab pieces for themselves. This starts a chain of candy snatching which continues until there is a gap in visitors witnessing others successfully grabbing candy. The process then starts over.

The amount of candy, which is replenished as necessary, is determined in a simple way: its combined weight must equal the combined weight of the artist and his deceased lover: 350 pounds.

5.

An artist who, a couple of years earlier, made a bonfire of all his extant canvases, conceives of a plan to produce paintings without actually having to paint them. The process begins with him paying a series of visits to amateur art exhibitions in the Southern Californian community where he lives. Wandering around these fairs, he eventually finds 14 Sunday painters who agree to execute the commissions he has in mind. Each of these painters receives about a dozen slides from which he or she is asked to select one image to copy onto a 59 by 45 inch canvas provided by the artist. Each painter is instructed to keep the copied image to a certain size and place it at a certain point on the canvas. When each painting is completed and returned, the artist then takes it to a sign painter who is paid to paint, underneath each image, the words "A Painting By" followed by the name of the amateur painter who was the author of that particular image.

6.

At a New York gallery, an artist presents three sets of autobiographical drawings. Although they are ostensibly dealing with self-portraiture, not a single one of the drawings has been executed by the artist.

In one set of drawings, viewers see studies made by participants in a life drawing class for which the artist posed nude.

The second consists of about a dozen portraits of the artist by police sketch artists working from verbal descriptions of the artist supplied by her friends.

In the last part, a courtroom artist has drawn scenes of the artist's daily life which he was invited (and paid) to witness. These include sketches of her working out at a gym, getting her hair done, having a studio visit, reading in bed with her boyfriend. One drawing even shows her modeling for the drawing class that will later provide the nude sketches hanging nearby.

7.

One day a rich man sets about learning how to make watercolors, a medium for which he has no apparent talent. He takes daily lessons for 10 years, at the end of which he has acquired sufficient skill in the medium to carry out his artistic plan, which is to travel the world for 20 years painting watercolors of port scenes at the rate of one every two weeks. The finished watercolors are sent back to Paris, the city from which he started out, where a specialist glues each of them onto a thin wooden board which he then cuts into a jigsaw puzzle. The puzzles are subsequently disassembled and each is placed in its own labeled box.

At the end of his 20-year voyage, the man returns to Paris to begin reassembling the watercolor puzzles in the same sequence that he painted them. There's an additional twist in that after being completed, each watercolor puzzle is submitted to a "retexturizing" process that restores the paper to wholeness, as if it had never been cut into pieces. This allows the paper to be separated from the board and bleached so that nothing will remain of the image. This final stage is also scheduled to take 20 years (the man has calculated that his private fortune will be sufficient to see him through completion of his life's project). His hope is that, at the end of his 50-year scheme, nothing will remain but a stack of 500 blank sheets of paper.

8.

In a moment of boredom a young artist who is feeling rather dispirited about his lack of artistic progress as a sculptor picks up a pen and draws little circles on the fingers and thumb of his left hand. Later that night he goes to a party where there is a buffet table of cold cuts. As he is reaching with his left hand to pick up a slice of salami he is struck by the similarity between the ink circles on his skin and the black rings around sliced peppercorns embedded in the salami. He rushes back home with the salami, sets up his camera and photographs his hand picking up a piece of the cured meat. After developing the negative and making a signed print, the artist realizes that he can use photography as a means of making work rather than merely documenting it. It is 1970. This same year he buys a Weimaraner puppy which he begins to photograph in all kinds of wry and humorous poses. These shots of his cavorting dog, who he has named after a famous Surrealist, eventually lead to great success and critical recognition.

9.

In 1992, an Italian artist raises money to create a foundation the sole purpose of which is to pay another artist to neither create nor exhibit art for an entire year. The organization is named the Oblomov Foundation, in honor of the lethargic hero of Ivan Alexandrovitch Goncharov's 1858 novel, *Oblomov*.

The following year, the same artist is included in the prestigious "Aperto" show at the Venice Biennale. Instead of making work for the exhibition, he rents out the space that has been assigned to him to a perfume company which puts up a big poster advertising their product.

For his next project he takes advantage of the architectural similarity of two Parisian galleries located next to each other on the rue Louise Weiss by recreating, in one gallery, a carbon copy of an exhibition by another artist then on view at the second gallery. Visitors were thus presented with a pair of identical shows in a pair of adjoining, identical spaces.

## 10.

One sunny Southern California day in 1970, an artist takes with him to the beach a camera (a friend to operate it) and an old book on a military subject. He slips out of his shirt and stretches out on the sand on his back. Across his chest he places the open copy of *Tactics*, as the book is titled, with the cover facing up. He remains lying on the beach long enough to receive a second-degree burn.

The work created by this event consists of two photographs. One shows the shirtless artist at the beginning of the process with the copy of *Tactics* on his chest. The other has been taken several hours later. The book has been removed to reveal on his bare chest a rectangle of pale, unburned skin.

## 11.

In 1965, at the age of 34, a Polish painter begins a project that he intends to continue for the rest of his life. He begins by drawing a small white numeral 1 in the upper left hand corner of a black canvas. He follows this with a 2, then a 3 and so forth. By 1977, he has painted some 70 canvases and reached the number 2,500,000. Twenty years later, he is still at it.

While the counting process does not alter through all these years, he introduces a subtle change in the series by making the background of each subsequent canvas exactly 1 percent whiter than the previous painting. This means that as he reaches ever higher numbers, they become ever more difficult to see, their whiteness gradually matched by the whiteness of the increasingly pale background. He also gives the individual paintings a similar compositional rhythm by dipping his brush into the white paint at regular intervals so that the sequence of numerals is constantly modulating from bright to dull.

While he works, the artist recites into a tape recorder each number as he paints it. Presumably, when the white numbers become wholly indistinguishable from their white background, this Polish litany of spoken numbers will become the chief evidence of the artist's late work.

12.

A child growing up in New Jersey in the 1950s develops an obsession with postage stamps. At first he is content with collecting (he eventually amasses some 100,000 stamps), but after a while he begins to produce his own stamps, using pencil, ink and watercolor. Trying to make his stamps as realistic as possible, he uses the period key on an old typewriter to imitate perforated edges. Rather than copy existing stamps from his collection, he draws on his own imagination, inventing not merely the tiny images but also fictive countries from which the stamps have supposedly been issued. By the age of 15, when he ceases his philatelic activities (he has apparently "grown out" of them), he has created some 1,000 fake stamps.

A few years later he develops an interest in art. After some half-hearted attempts at becoming an abstract painter, he bows to family pressure and takes a degree in architecture. After university, he moves to New York and gets a job at an up-and-coming architecture firm. A couple of years later he shows a few close friends the stamps he made as a child. One of these friends exhibits some of the tiny watercolors in his loft alongside miniature works by other artists. Encouraged by this interest, the now 27-year-old struggling architect begins to paint stamps again. The following year, using the proceeds from the sale of his stamp collection (the real one), he quits his architecture job and travels to Holland. There, while staying with friends, he begins to paint stamps in earnest. Executed at actual scale and usually carrying cancellation marks, the stamps evoke imaginary countries with names such as Jantar, Iles des Sourds, Adjudani and Nadopr. For each nation, he invents a history, a geography and a system of currency. The watercolor stamps, although small, are highly detailed. Sometimes they celebrate important events in the imagined nation's history or depict its leaders, landmarks or flora and fauna. He also incorporates aspects of his own life, inserting allusions to his friends, his family and his travels.

Before long, galleries began to show and sell his work. By the time of his death in a fire at the age of 31, he has become an internationally successful artist with an oeuvre which consists of about 4,000 exquisitely hand-painted stamps, assigned to 42 completely fictive countries.

13.

For an entire year, from one 4th of July to the next, a pair of artists, one male and one female, go about their lives in New York City while tied together by an eight-foot length of rope. One end is lashed around his waist, the other around hers. The brutal fact of being roped together 24 hours a day for 12 months is complicated by another aspect of this lengthy performance: they have forbidden themselves to touch each other.

In the beginning they speak together for hour after hour, but at a certain point they talk themselves out and resort to communicating by yanking on the rope. This method provokes anger and they replace the impatient yanks with gestures. For example, when one of them needs to go to the toilet or get something to eat, he or she simply points to the appropriate room. This gestural phase is succeeded by a long period when they communicate solely with grunts and moans. In the spring, about two-and-a-half months before the end of their year together, they begin to emerge from this regressive, nonverbal state, gradually reassuming the habits of normal (i.e. unroped together) people. As they approach the 4th of July and the conclusion of their project, the woman tells an interviewer that she's sad they won't be doing an 80-year piece together. For his part, the man feels they will be psychologically "all tied up" until the day they die.

1. Joseph Grigely 2. Daniel Spoerri 3. Piero Manzoni 4. Felix Gonzalez Torres 5. John Baldessari 6. Kerri Scharlin 7. Percival Bartlebooth/Georges Perec 8. William Wegman 9. Maurizio Cattelan 10. Dennis Oppenheim 11. Roman Opalka 12. Donald Evans 13. Linda Montano & Tehching Hsieh

# Ron Morosan

# LOUIS EILSHEMIUS DRAWINGS

These drawings by Louis Eilshemius on his own letterhead paper (with the address 118 East 57th Street) were created after 1921, when he had more or less given up painting due to overwhelming discouragement (the exception being a 1937 painting of the Hindenburg disaster, now in the New Jersey State Museum).

Though small in scale, they are nevertheless densely filled with themes and ideas that were the focus of many of his major paintings in previous years, particularly those painted after 1910.

The drawings, therefore, can be regarded as his major works from the last years of his life. The "cartouche" or "badge" format is in keeping with what he called his "invented frame," the border that he painted around the edge of his paintings after about 1910. The use of this badge or official frame may suggest something that would be in keeping with Eilshemius' penchant for self-obsessed promotion: the presentation of an award to himself. Most of the drawings are inscribed at the bottom with an official title, as if he was awarding this particular scene a citation.

The subjects or "scenes" within the badges conjure an image of Eilshemius in the process of recalling—i.e. in inventory fashion—the memories and accomplishments of his youth. In the drawing *Who iss Itt?* we see a nude girl bathing in a landscape with a stream. This composition is similar to the paintings *Bathers* of 1918, or *Two Women Bathing* of 1920. The subject, a favorite of his, recalls the myth of Actaeon surprising Artemis at her bath, and clearly indicates the remoteness of vision, or spy perspective, that generated in part the peculiar personal visions of artists like Eilshemius.

In the drawing titled *Where Is It?* he evokes a memoir of his family home in North Arlington, New Jersey, a manor house with cupola and wrap-around porch. In the yard, tiny figures play in a manner recalling scenes from the pleasantries of his youth.

*Somewhere* is a drawing not only mysterious but to some extent troubling. It depicts two tiny stick-like figures, one walking up a road while the other lies hidden behind a fence aiming what appears to be a rifle. It suggests an ambush. This subject is also used in a painting from 1901, titled *American Tragedy, Revenge*, where a male figure hidden behind a hedge shoots a female as she crosses a bridge.

In one of the most curious and abstract scenes, *lines, lines,* where the tiny figure of a man walks through a vortex of swirling lines, Eilshemius conveys a sense of extreme isolation, recalling his numerous paintings of a single boat with a tiny, lone figure at the helm. This recurring image suggests the isolation and exile that haunted him throughout his life.

In his October 15, 1920 lecture to the Societé Anonyme, he revealed the intensity of the private world he was creating, one where collective spirit and personal longing meet: "The real object of art is to represent on canvas the real soul of things, of persons and landscapes. The other thing is just painting."

Eilshemius' life as an artist underlines the tragic fate of the eccentric personality in American society, and presents the image of the artist as outcast and loner. This popular image may be acceptable in a Henry Darger, where eccentric means "whacky" or "disturbed," but Eilshemius was neither of these. He was simply dedicated to the poetry of what he considered "soul work," or art that reveals a window to the soul. Alas, to the American mind this window to the soul is only acceptable if the window-shade remains pulled down, with the soul exposed occasionally by peeking in at the edge of the shade.

LOUIS M. EILSHEMIUS
118 EAST 57TH STREET
NEW YORK

## LOUIS M. EILSHEMIUS
### 118 EAST 57TH STREET
### NEW YORK

## LOUIS M. EILSHEMIUS
### 118 EAST 57TH STREET
### NEW YORK

**LOUIS M. EILSHEMIUS, M. A.**
118 EAST 57TH STREET
NEW YORK

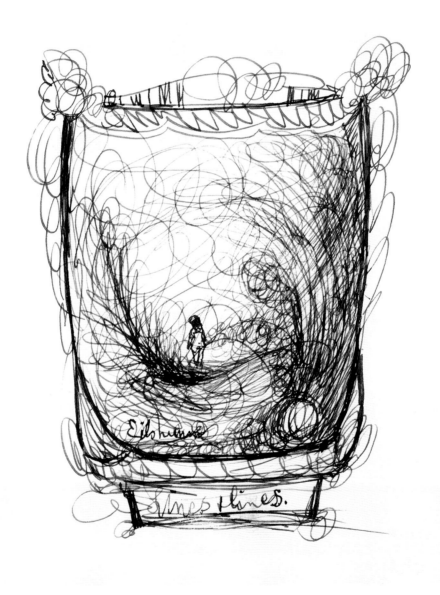

**LOUIS M. EILSHEMIUS, M. A.**
118 EAST 57TH STREET
NEW YORK

Wild Mt. Scenes

172

Coast-View.

## THE MONKEY

What would you think of one who spent his time, his energy, and all his hopes on the project of teaching a monkey to talk? There he is, tearing at his hair, muttering to himself, looking deep into the monkey's eyes, scanning its face for signs that would justify the optimism he knows he will soon begin to feel, whatever he sees in the monkey's eyes or face or abrupt but graceful gestures. His optimism is reliable, for he loves the monkey. It is reliable, though he hates the monkey. He hates himself. He wonders if his hatred or some weariness or occasional light-headedness is what stands in the way of the monkey's speech. He suffers reveries of the monkey's first word. He sleeps, exhausted, and dreams that the monkey is speaking, but in some unintelligible language. He awakens wearily. A gorgeous light is at the window, severely gray, a harsh light, yet subtly, soothingly pink. He heaves himself up in bed, wondering if indeed the light has precisely this tinge. He sees the objects in his bedroom with a clarity that is new to him. The peculiar sharpness of his vision gives the moment a convincing weight. He loves the light. He loves the faculty of vision for having delivered this moment to him. Then he wonders if he did truly love the moment, the light of the moment that now is gone. Of course it's gone. That's obvious, but no more obvious in this dreary light than the truth that he no longer loves the moment, or any moment, not of his life, anyway, and he wonders if his treacherous infatuation with that gaudy, fleeting, delusive moment, that moment that never really occurred, he is now convinced, has so effectively deadened his feelings for the monkey that, now, in this moment of grainy gray despair there is no longer any point in hoping that someday the creature will talk.

## SNAKE EYES ARE BLIND

Steering suckers to fat cat Bertram Sullivan's clip joint, smalltime hustler Billy Williams dreams of bigger things. He wants to be a major promoter, a maker and breaker of careers. Ignoring the advice of his big-hearted girlfriend, Jean Jones, he embarks on a series of shady adventures, always in the hope of finding his way around the next corner in the nocturnal labyrinth of the major metropolis where he plays out the frantic scenario of a desperate life. Always suave, sometimes sinister, Billy is a mixture of wised-up hustler and naïve dreamer. Whether he is pulling strings to fix a summons, as a favor to his boss, Mr. Sullivan, or acting as a go-between in a drug deal always threatening to go bad, or cozying up to a chanteuse who might, just maybe, be his ticket to the big time, Billy Williams is a riveting presence, an embodiment of all that has enthralled us ever since night fell and we realized that we, too, are creatures of the darkness.


## THE ARCHITECTURE OF YOUR TIMES

A year ago you thought you had it knocked. Your theory about Adam's house in paradise was watertight. The house, of course, was not. Who cared? Paradise was a juicy, labyrinthine thriller. No beginning, no end, but it kept you on the edge of your seat. In Adam's house in paradise, comfort was not a consideration. The body no more fit the furniture than the house fit its site, and when your paradisiacal digs fell off the edge of the map you just drew another map. You were big in paradise. Then paradise got small and you were forced out.

Still lashed by storms, you are looking for the architecture of your times. You'd better find it. Before it finds you and makes you live in it. As of course you do but not the way it wants. Never like that, ever since you realized they aren't as phony as you thought—those emblems of people that dot our models of the buildings that couldn't care less about Adam's house in paradise. People really are that flat, or almost, and definitely that small. That's why the architecture of your times is trying to track you down. It wants you to be that small.

All of which made sense no more than twenty-four hours ago, but that was then and this is now, and there is one thing I can't figure. Who found the body? Was it the architecture of your times, meaning this is you stretched out on the floor, your form reduced to a function of the small black hole in your forehead? Or was it you who found the body? Meaning the small black hole in the forehead is all that is left of the grid that supplied the architecture of your times with its logic, the logic that perfected paradise and had no room for you.

Marie Chaix　　　　THE SUMMER OF THE ELDER TREE
(excerpt)

## INTERPLAY OF LIKENESSES

Last summer we took some friends who were passing on a tour of the house in Lans. In one nook of the huge granary that Harry uses for an office there are only a few photographs on the wall. One romantic oval frames a serious-looking, long-haired young woman. The pale low-necked blouse she's wearing makes it clear that the portrait is fairly recent, despite its intentional sepia tint.

"What a lovely picture!" the woman exclaims. "I've seen that person before. Which one of your daughters is she?"

"It's only me," I say with a laugh. "At thirty-two."

In her embarrassment the woman apologizes profusely.

"Why? I'm delighted to be taken for one of my daughters. They're a lot more beautiful than I am."

In fact, I could have half-jokingly gone on, that sepia girl (she'd appeared in '74 on the back cover of my first book) isn't half bad after all! It's hard to refer to her as "me." Is she still me? I've been separated from her, too—with regret, obviously.

"The funny thing is," my friend said appeasingly, "your daughters don't look like one another, but each still has something of you."

No need to say, that was music to my ears.


## PASSING THINGS ALONG?

More than once I've been told, "You're lucky, you have a good relationship with your daughters, and that's no accident: you got on well with your mother."

No doubt it's true. Among my childhood paraphernalia there weren't only sorrows but a multitude of tiny items passed along to me, trifles that are shining treasures that never burn out, whatever advanced age one reaches. What are these treasures if not childhood itself, broken into pieces that are glued back together with words, colors, beach pebbles, whatever comes to hand… On condition that something new is made of them? Assembling small memories—decals and scraps of all kinds, a medley of jingles…

Chocolate bar between two slices of bread—time for your afternoon snack?

Garden, elder tree, sheets shaken out at a window, the house has been sold—the pink horse-chestnut flowers with it?

Velvety skin, cheek smelling of fruit, maternal breath when she comes home, train at night delight.

Intimate scent of scarves, silk and muslin, snitched the length of an absence.

Rings, jacquard knitting, how slow your weariness climbing Mont Valérien.

Chopin waltzes, the Moonlight Sonata and the German language never shall I forget it.

Molyneux No. 5, compact snapping shut (powder mist), and your voice in church, so pure, so other and beautiful I'm almost ashamed of it.

Smoke rings, Lucky Strike, blue whorls, black coffee…

My mother, you've disappeared and yet you walk in silence at the edge of my dreams.

Thus the "good relationship" takes shape, and it keeps moving on like a ball passed along from player to player, from mother to daughter. Love and trust—if that sounds old-fashioned, too bad—those were for us our infallible code of transmission. It hasn't always been a smooth ride—sometimes the motor races or stalls—it is, I repeat, a question of improvisation, dependent on humor more than on principles, at least I think it is. Love, trust and every shade of laughter: I stick obstinately to a maternal space where you can navigate by sight.

I was lucky: the legacy was weighty but the passers had a light touch—thanks to them I finally published it for all to see. If you believe that not everything can be told in a book, words know how to find their own way and, left to themselves, decide where to land.

Love and trust kept flowing between me and the two lovely links I had for daughters. It happened effortlessly on my side: the child of the '40s must have remembered the air she'd breathed, the atmosphere of pure love that enveloped her in spite of the folly of adults who had escaped disaster.

It wasn't always perfect. We had our rough moments, malignant episodes of adolescence, we fell somewhat out of touch and "conflicts" abounded, very different at the interval of five years between my very dissimilar daughters. Precocious loves and shudders of anxiety. Insomniac dawns waiting for news. And Léonore's punk years! Sound and fury, tortured sulks, Technicolor hair-dos. The faces our bourgeois neighbors made! And my own face when I had to plead her case at meetings of the parent-teacher association! Today we giggle helplessly when we talk about those things or see the two of them in snapshots of their dissolute youth.

Now when I look at them, one and the other, I'm dazzled by their beauty, their drollness, their independence, and by the thousand and one unvarnished truths we've uttered without killing each other. I wonder how they managed it; since after all what else have I passed on to them besides life, on a first and second of September? They're the ones I'll have to ask, a long time from now. Who they are—what I can see in them today—is their own doing. The transferal was something they grasped in the awareness of a moment not to be missed if they wanted to remain in contention in the great common place into which I'd released them. They've stayed the distance with no help from me. Am I saying they "managed" with what I passed on to them, the thoroughly tangled skein taken from a trunk in my family attic? That is still my version. Up to them to go on asking.

Judging by the complaints I heard, it can't have always been rosy with a mother around who—much too often for their liking—was waving her handkerchief from a train window or at the porthole of an airplane. They'll have to write their own version of desertion. For my part, I love them. Wherever I may be and without limit.

If that isn't enough (and haven't we heard all too often that "love isn't enough"?), let them find something else and come tell me about it when I am old and gray and full of sleep...

You ask, what about the father in all this? That is my weak point. It's no use: where I'm concerned, fathers play a thankless part.

## HANDKERCHIEF AT A TRAIN WINDOW

You're right: I did leave you often. You can't imagine how guilty and torn I felt among my suitcases. It wasn't to get away from you, my lovelies; I would have liked to put you each in a pocket and take you with me, never break up our threesome, and go on babbling with you above the clouds.

I admit that more than once, following where love led me, I tore myself away from you and put you in homes where you say our separation used to make you weep. The memory of those homes still haunts you: I swear that you must have transformed them—they were only inoffensive refuges with kindly families. But you were alone there, far from your divided parents, far from your itinerant mother who left you to the protection of forests and snowbound roads, clinging as she was to the wings of a migrating bird, pursuing her dream of being loved by a man and hearing him tell her so in every hue of the rainbow, and at last believing him.

We remember departures better than returns, don't we? There's more poetry in the lyricism of abandonment than in daily contentment. And we forget the gayest parts. Later we try to reconstitute the past: that hurts, and we look for help elsewhere.

What do we pass along other than songs that have vanished in the night, scents fluttering in the wake of laughter, blurred images, fragments of a story that even for two beings who have shared them will never be the same? Memories are longings that are rewritten and passed along on the current of words that reinvent them; and so it goes...

An unseasonably summery evening in springtime Vermont; a white house on the campus of Bennington College, a typically American house of painted wood. Nightfall is barely in sight. The babysitter is busy in the kitchen. We're going out to dinner. Harry waits for me at the wheel of our pale metallic-green Buick, the motor running. I'm coming! Just one last kiss for my two hoppingly happy ones, damp and soft after their evening bath. I break away from them and find myself on the porch steps, beyond the screen door that has shut to a squeal of laughter.

Freeze frame: a mother, breeze in her hair, earrings tinkling, her long billowing dress of Indian cotton printed with roses and mallows that glitter with fragile spangles, fragrance of musk or sandalwood. On the other side of the screen, four little hands as still as startled squirrels, my two household elves, the blonde and the brunette, openmouthed, two pairs of eyes raised in wonder: "Maman, you're beautiful!" Did they say it, did I even hear it, astonished to find myself the icon of such an outburst of love? The horn honks; I hustle off. There's a rush of laughing that fades away within the white house.

An indelible snapshot of absolute happiness. I've described it to them in every detail. Neither one has the slightest recollection of it.

*Translated from the French by Harry Mathews*

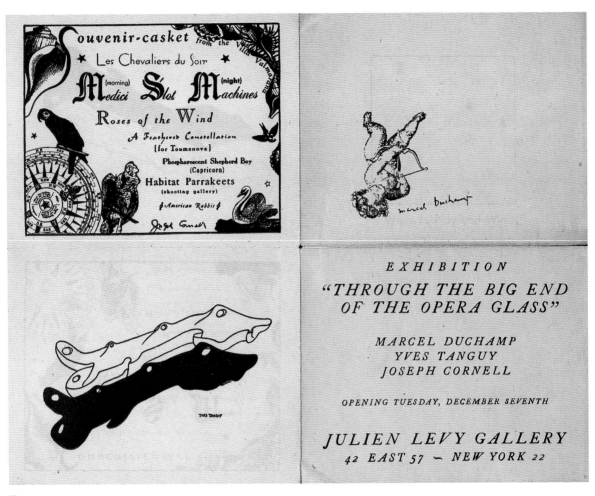

Fig. 1

In 1943, Marcel Duchamp was asked by the gallery owner Julien Levy to design the announcement for an exhibition to be called "Through the Big End of the Opera Glass."[1] As the title implies (adapted, as it was, from Lewis Carroll's *Through the Looking Glass*), the show was to feature unusually small-scale work. Years later, Levy explained that the idea for the exhibition came from having seen an example of Duchamp's *valise*, in which the artist had packed miniature reproductions of his work into a portable suitcase.[2] The show was to include not only work by Duchamp, but by two other artists as well: the French Surrealist painter Yves Tanguy, and the American collage and assemblage artist, Joseph Cornell. Within the announcement (Fig. 1), Duchamp reproduced a black-and-white layout by Cornell featuring the titles of Cornell's work printed in a variety of expressive type faces surrounded by a collage of images referring to them, while Tanguy was represented by a drawing of one of his characteristically biomorphic three-dimensional shapes, accompanied, in this particular instance, by an opaque black shadow that curiously overlaps it.

For his own contribution, on the back cover of the announcement Duchamp provided the image of a cupid with a stretched bow and arrow in his hands, but the figure is inexplicably reproduced upside down, for the artist's signature—which is oriented legibly—streams off to one side at the level of the cupid's head. At first glance, knowing that Duchamp often appropriated imagery for whatever purpose was required—in the fashion of culling images readymade—one might easily conclude that the cupid was clipped from some printed source and collaged into this position. However, the original layout for this announcement was recently discovered among the effects of Julien Levy, and it is now known that Duchamp painstakingly drew the cupid himself in pen and ink (Fig. 2). It is likely that he took the time to render this image because he could not find the reproduction of a cupid fixing his arrow in this precise direction, a detail that, as we shall soon learn, is critical to his intent, for the significance of the cupid's aim can only be understood when the announcement is unfolded and fully opened.

The paper stock Duchamp selected for this ephemeral publication was a translucent sheet folded in quadrants, forming a booklet. The first thing the

Fig. 2

White to Play and Win

Look through from other side against light

Fig. 3

recipient would have seen upon removing the announcement from its envelope was the title page, providing the name of the exhibition, its dates and its location. Upon opening the booklet, he would find Cornell's layout opposite Tanguy's drawing, and, on the back cover, Duchamp's cupid. Closer examination of the cupid would reveal that something is printed on the opposite side of the paper: below Duchamp's signature, in red ink, one can faintly read the words: "White to Play and Win" (Fig. 3). To chess enthusiasts, this phrase can mean only one thing: one is being presented with a chess problem to solve in which white is instructed to move first and eventually go on to win the game. Indeed, just above it, one can discern the faint outline of a chess board with pieces in various positions, printed, like the writing below it, on the opposite side of the sheet. If, at this point, someone is compelled to unfold the sheet and examine the opposite side, Duchamp provided additional instructions: "Look through from other side against light."

For those already familiar with Duchamp's work, these words might well bring to mind the elaborate title that he gave to a work on glass from 1918: *To Be Looked at (from the Other Side of the Glass) with One Eye, Close to, for Almost an Hour* (The Museum of Modern Art, New York). The comparison may not have been a simple coincidence of wording, for if an attempt were made to solve the chess problem, even grand masters would likely need more than an hour to solve it. If we follow Duchamp's instructions and "look through from the other side against light," we will see the layout of a chessboard from the proper position (with a white square in the lower right corner), each player with a king, a pair of pawns, and a single rook. We will also see the cupid he drew on the other side, the arrow from its bow pointing down the white knight's file (or "B" file in algebraic notation), suggesting that the next best possible move for White would be to advance its pawn. One who studies this endgame problem at any length, however, would determine that this move would not attain a win for white. Indeed, virtually any move by white seems to result in a draw, even though there are a few compelling scenarios that—until properly analyzed—give the false impression that white has a chance to win (see analysis in boxed insert).

# AN ANALYSIS OF DUCHAMP'S ENDGAME PROBLEM
# AN EXCHANGE WITH LARRY EVANS

At first glance, the endgame chess problem that Duchamp devised (see Diagram A) gives the impression that White could play and win, for White has a pawn on the seventh rank and a quick promotion would seem inevitable. Black has two isolated pawns that could also advance, but they are farther from promotion and look as though they could easily be attacked by White's rook. The following scenario seems plausible, as was suggested to me thirty years ago by international grandmaster Larry Evans:[I]

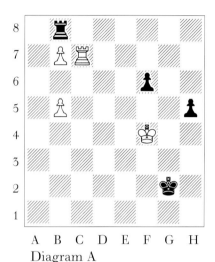

A B C D E F G H
Diagram A

|     | White | Black |
| --- | --- | --- |
| 1. | Ke4! | h4 |
| 2. | Kd5 | h3 |
| 3. | Kc6 | h2 |
| 4. | Rg7+ | Kf3 |
| 5. | Rh7 | Kg2 |
| 6. | Kc7 | Rxb7+ |
| 7. | Kxb7 | h1=Q |
| 8. | Rxh1 | Kxh1 |
| 9. | Kc6 | f5 |
| 10. | Kd5 and wins (see Diagram B) | |

This variation, however, misses a possible move for Black, one that would not only extend play, but would eventually result in a draw.[II] After the white king moves to c7 (the sixth move), the pieces are in the position and shown in Diagram C.

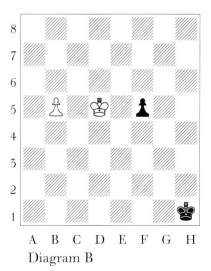

A B C D E F G H
Diagram B

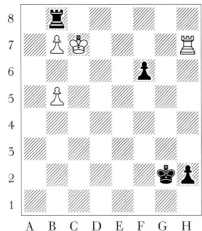

Diagram C

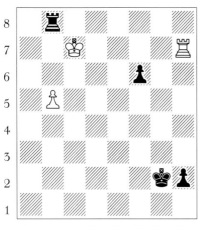

Diagram D

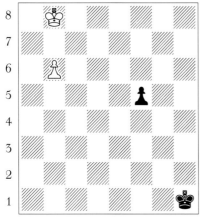

Diagram E

At this point, Black is forced to move his rook (otherwise, the white king will capture it on its next move). If he captures the white pawn and checks white's king at the same time, the result will be a win for White (as Evans demonstrated above). But if Black moves his rook to g8 (6. ... Rg8), he is in a far better position. There, if White promotes on the next move, he can capture the promoted piece (as indicated in Diagram D).

On the very next move, the white king will capture the black rook. The white rook will then capture the black pawn when it promotes, and the black king will, in turn, take the white rook, leaving a pair of kings and isolated pawns on each side of the board, a position that results in a draw.

There is another scenario that would allow White to continue play even further. After 6. ... Rg8, if White does not promote his pawn on the 7th move, but, rather, advances his other pawn one square forward (7. b6, in the direction indicated by the Cupid's arrow), play would continue as follows:

| 7. | ... | h1=Q |
| 8. | Rxh1 | Kxh1 |
| 9. | b8=Q | Rxb8 |
| 10. | Kxb8 | f5 draws |

In this position, it may appear that White will win, since his pawn seems closer to promotion. When played out, however, this leads to Diagram G (discussed below), resulting in another book draw. A number of other possible scenarios were later suggested by Larry Evans. In the initial position, he strongly encouraged investigation of moving the white king to e3, or advancing the trailing pawn to b6 (as suggested in Duchamp's design by the direction of the Cupid's arrow).[III] This latter suggestion (1. b6) eventually transposes to Diagram E. Following the strategy that I had proposed—of Black moving his rook to g8—Evans also suggested that White promote right away on b8, followed by a black rook capture (thereby eliminating White's pawn that was threatening to promote). White's king would then capture the black rook on b8, followed by the promotion of Black's pawn, which would, in turn, be captured by the white rook. The black king would then capture the white rook, leaving the position found in Diagram F. If we compare the final positions in Diagrams E and F, we discover that they are very similar and transpose into each other. They both lead to Diagram G, which ends in a classic draw (as explained below). In position F only, the white pawn would queen, leaving the black king protecting a pawn that is about to promote (see Diagram G). The position leads to perpetual check, or stalemate.

The way a stalemate is achieved (from Diagram G) is that White starts a series of checks leading to the following position: White Kc7, Qg4 (check); Black: Kg2, f2. Then after … Kh1, Qf3+ Kg1, Qg3+, Black does not protect his pawn with … Kf1 (because then the white King steps back up the board, followed by a series of checks and King moves again, leading to eventual mating position), but instead plays … Kh1! Then if the white Queen takes the pawn with Qxf2, it is a stalemate; but meanwhile, Black is threatening to promote. So White has to give perpetual check or allow stalemate.[IV]

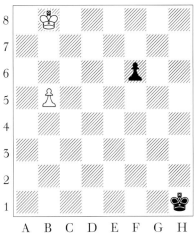

Diagram F

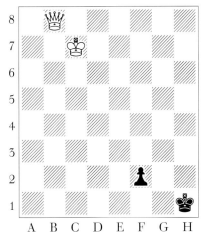

Diagram G

(Fig. 4)

Larry Evans—who had played chess with Duchamp on more than one occasion (Fig. 4)—was sufficiently intrigued by this problem that he graciously accepted my request to publish it in his monthly column in *Chess Life & Review*.[V] At the time, I offered a $15 reward for its solution, not realizing that I would be inundated with responses, a number of which came from prison inmates who demanded immediate payment of the reward. Phone calls from several of these individuals were all the intimidation I needed to send checks, even though none of their solutions were actually convincing. The most thoughtful and detailed responses came from regular readers of *Chess Life & Review*, specialists in endgame strategy who proposed a variety of intriguing possibilities, all hoping that theirs was the ultimate solution (although I do not believe that any of them actually were). I have since subjected this problem to the most powerful computer programs available to me, and no solution has yet been found. I am now all the more convinced that this is a problem that cannot be solved. Duchamp has given us, in effect, a problem with no solution.[VI]

I. In an effort to solve this problem, I wrote to E. B. Edmondson, then executive director of the American Chess Federation. He passed on my inquiry to Larry Evans, who responded to me in a letter dated June 2, 1976.

II. I presented these alternatives to Mr. Evans in a letter dated June 4, 1976.

III. Letter from Evans to the author, June 5, 1976.

IV. The analysis of this final position was generously provided by Allan G. Savage, author of *Reconciling Chess: a Marcel Duchamp Sampler* (Davenport: Thinkers' Press, 1998), and who is in the process of writing the fourth volume of the series published by Moravian Chess, *The Chess Biography of Marcel Duchamp (1887-1968)*, which is scheduled for publication in 2008.

V. "Larry Evans on Chess," *Chess Life & Review* (October 1976), p. 580.

VI. I have provided copies of the present analysis to several experienced chess players: Jennifer Shahade, Ralph Kaminsky, Allen G. Savage and Malcolm H. Wiener. These individuals are familiar with standard chess analyses and, although they agree with my general conclusion (that the problem has no solution), they believe my analysis to be redundant and—in comparison to professional analyses—somewhat amateurish. Nevertheless, I am grateful to all of them for having taken the time to review my text, and for having provided various recommendations for its improvement.

The rigor and intensity of this endgame problem stands in sharp contrast to the means by which Duchamp presents us with a hint of its solution: a cupid aiming his arrow toward the ground (or into the sky, if we consider that the cupid is presented upside-down). Cupid is, of course, the mythological god of love, and his arrow is usually aimed in the direction of an amorous target; a direct hit can cause the recipient to fall deeply and blindly in love. Knowing this, and knowing that when Duchamp designed this brochure he had recently met and fallen in love with Maria Martins— a Brazilian sculptor, married with three children, and in almost every respect, unattainable—one is tempted to speculate that Duchamp might have had a personal situation in mind when he decided that a cupid should indicate the path to follow in pursuing a solution to this vexing problem. Duchamp was well known for having said: "There is no solution, because there is no problem."[3] In the end, the problem that he faced with Maria Martins was insurmountable, demonstrating that in both chess and life— and perhaps in art as well—there are, indeed, problems without solutions.

1. The date of this exhibition has been given variously, as either 1943 or 1948. Julien Levy consistently gave the date as 1943 (see his autobiography, *Memoir of an Art Gallery* [New York: G.P. Putnam's Sons, 1977], p. 309, as well as the reference contained in the following note). For reasons that are unclear, however, in all editions of his otherwise reliable catalogue raisonné of work by Marcel Duchamp, Arturo Schwarz gives the date as 1948 (see *The Complete Works of Marcel Duchamp* [New York: Harry N. Abrams, 1969], cat. no. 329, page 523; revised and expanded edition [New York: Delano Greenidge Editions, 1997], cat. no. 530, p. 793, and descriptive bibliography 71, page 904). The date of 1943 cannot be challenged, however, for the show was reviewed in *The New York Times* on December 12, 1943 (I am grateful to Ingrid Shaffner for bringing this citation to my attention).

2. See the statement provided by Julien Levy for a brochure published on the occasion of "Through the Big End of the Opera Glass II," a recreation of the original 1943 show at the Joan Washburn Gallery, New York, February 15 - March 12, 1977 (the brochure contained a facsimile reprint of the original fold-out catalogue).

3. This comment seems to have been quoted for the first time in Harriet and Sidney Janis, "Marcel Duchamp: Anti-Artist," *View*, series V, no. 1 (March 1945), p. 24; it is repeated again in Winthrop Sargeant, "Dada's Daddy," *Life*, vol. 32, no. 17 (April 28, 1952), p. 111.

## ADVICE

1
Suppose the dreams are
getting advices, what does
"advice" mean. Suppose it
means I want you to read this, and
hope very much that you are
able to do so.

2
Jason lassos Medea
and winter piles up, distinguished
by its rich inner life from
thieving sunset. Bring it
in a little? Would Scarr and
Sue please mug more directly—not *more*—
into the camera? Bulk as
waywardness, waywardness under the romance

of whatever branches it chooses,
in most of the constructions.


## ENTER GHOST

And what do you think of an inference that gobbles up differences,
right or wrong, or
anything that smacks of interpretation.

> The restless palaver: restlessness
> plus circummuring. A bench-warmer
> on the side of meaning well (despite being
> dangerously over-determined).

Suspected that the faces inside are equal to or greater than
what you see from the vantage of your divided life.

## NEIGE DOLOROSA

Cut it out! All it is,
formulated and not, as the pre-existing
head thinks in any meaningful way

> I mean flush as head and heart
> in the deposition category. Blueberries

are immortal, not so unstinting care.
One of the things you see over a city piled high with freight
the clouds recuse themselves. Please extend the representation

to include you shooting beyond the undesirable
but reasonable idea, push/pull in doing so
but no regeneration. So neige dolorosa.


## PRINCIPALS

Plus — a genuinely freelance position with
repetitive selves, a saw horse,
an old-fashioned pipe uncomplaining, since
error is a natural feature like shoulders,
the setting for a wearer and not merely
largesse of the trial of "incremental
vision" plush as truth and buzzing
with underpinnings, nor should it be
mistaken for corporate accommodation as
pastness, since beyond fueling drift
snatches of the melody incrementally and not
because the defiance gains, blogger to
atmospheres featuring the light of day
through error and impossible waylay.


## CLOSEUP

At long last, which would be
called exile if
not for a charmed life shimmering, specifically
the light that bolted

plus a red face to go with it
bigger than life. From that point on
an administrator to some, partial to new developments
in an unfriendly world. But you get rid of the underworld.

# A DRAGON-FREE ENVIRONMENT

Along with breathing's
disregard, I'd say
for nuances.

By the time the suspension bridge
reaches the other side, time is
the extreme case if not upwards
of pure space — ya mug, whaddaya

say to a cat-fur beer along
with the questions that fly across the switchboard?
Specially wide and colorful

paths they wear out
by the light of the moon.


# DEONTOLOGY

and the Belmonts.
All the same, you don't consider unexpressed desires
comparable to expressed ones. The sun
has no unexpressed desires save the satin ruse
that has picked up the filters and saved them, favorites
long past, things leveled

and moved to the thesis box
in semblable grace, like the stars
no one really likes, horsehair und tinder,
smudges of time's *noir*.

The pawky dream shelf is next to what's best,
talking about the binges of Nextville

but in a higher plane.

Nick Carbó     THE ABSENCE OF ATMOSPHERE

A three-dimensional poem
Materials you will need for construction of the poem:

3 — three-foot-long thin but sturdy sticks
1 — any kind of glue
15 — any kind of thread cut into two feet lengths
2 — printed color copies of the 3-D poem

Instructions for use:
cut out the spheres from page one in a vertical fashion.

Cut in this order:

| (stick # 1) | (stick # 2) | (stick # 3) |
|-------------|-------------|-------------|
| touch       | the         | lusty       |
| the         | undertow    | room        |
| bouncing    | legs        | removed     |
| to          | leave       | ululations  |

Place the spheres on a flat surface with the words facing down (white side up) in the same order as above. Space the spheres evenly apart. Do the same for all three rows of words. Place one length of thread over the spheres going down. Keep at least four inches of thread slack above the first word (touch) in order to tie it to the stick so the spheres will hang. Cut out the second copy of the poem spheres and glue the words to the same words so you will have a two-sided disk with a thread running through it. Glue "touch" to "touch," "the" to "the" and so on. The same word should appear front and back of the sphere. When you finish gluing a row, you will have four spheres with words connected to each other with a thread. Hang this first row on one end of the three-foot long sticks.

Go on to page two and do the same process of cutting, gluing, stringing and hanging. Be sure to keep the order of the words and spheres intact in their proper rows. Repeat the same process for pages three, four and five. You will hang five evenly spaced rows on the stick. Do the same with the second and third sticks.

When you are finished assembling the poem you should have three sticks with five rows of hanging spheres and each row should have four spheres on it. Now you must attach two long strings to the ends of each stick to hang them from the ceiling. Hang all three sticks at least three feet apart and make sure all the spheres are aligned horizontally and vertically. The poem should make a floating cube-like shape with spheres: 4 (height) x 5 (width) x 3 (depth).

To "read" the poem one must walk around and through the piece and follow the predetermined color scheme to follow the order of the words. Each color represents a line of the poem. There are eight lines in this poem and eight colors to follow. Each line begins with the word "the" except for the last line which starts with "this."

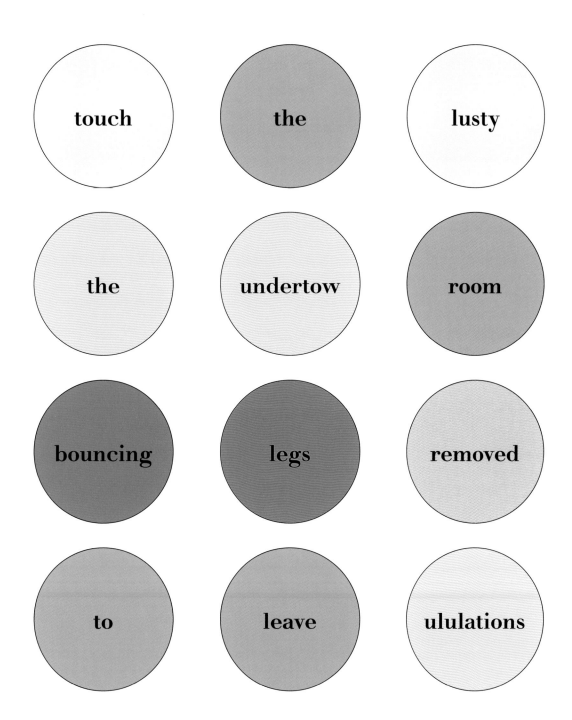

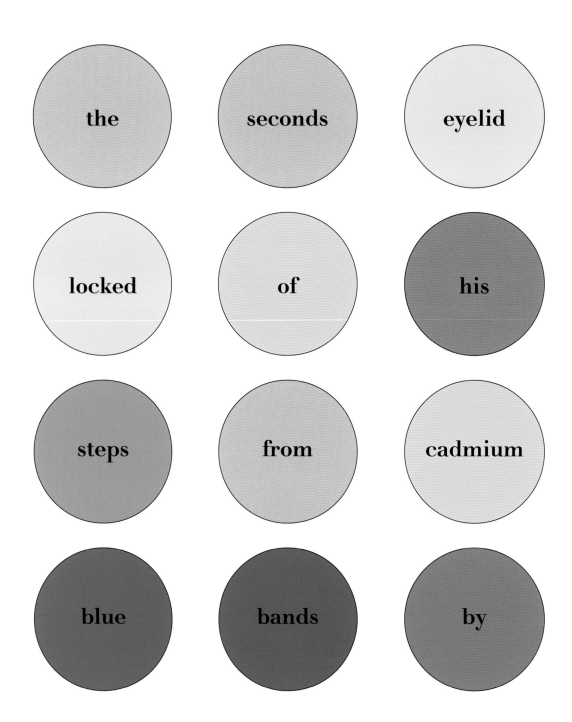

the    seconds    eyelid

locked    of    his

steps    from    cadmium

blue    bands    by

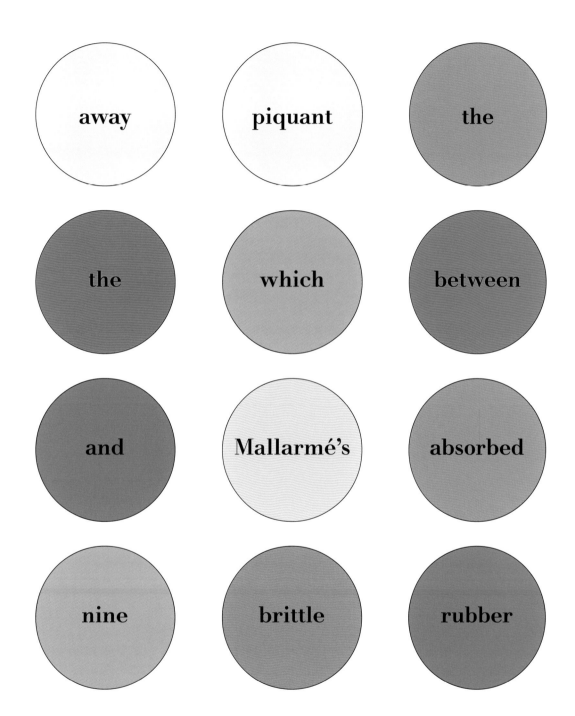

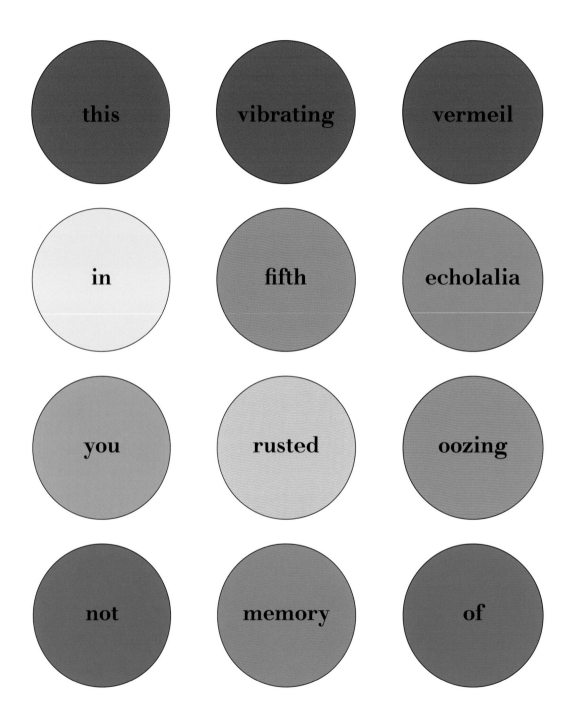

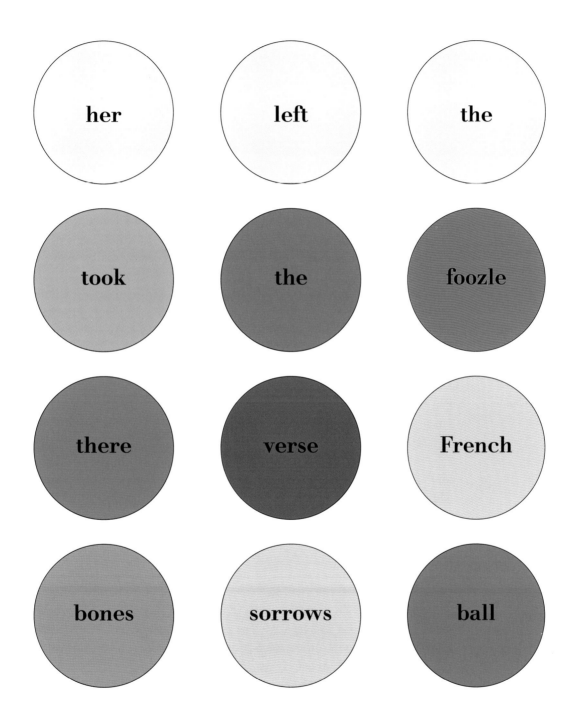

Kreg Hasegawa                    THE NEW CRUSTACEAN

I looked at the new crustacean one more time. It lay in the palm of my hand. My fingers were dark and crooked, fingers of an old hag. The crustacean's little black eyes glared at me. I had named it after myself. I felt entitled. I had discovered it, though I concede I hadn't researched others of its class. Documentation no longer interests me.

If I told you about myself, you'd never be further from the truth. Not that I exist only in the imagination—most certainly not. On that score my resolve has strengthened. I also do not mean that I am a sort of reasoning lie. That would imply that I am also conscious of the truth. No, I am determined entirely by context. Here I am a father, a brother, a lover, a friend, and now, an enemy. All this has become quite clear to me.

I was on the train to Portland, to visit my sister. The sunshine and the clicking of the rails lulled me into a comfortable half-sleep. Houses flew by. A lumber yard. Huge smoke stacks. Fences. A forest. Later, I was eating a cucumber sandwich and drinking a cold can of seltzer. A little girl climbed into the seat next to me. She reached out and touched my arm. Her fingers were soft and warm. She looked at me. Her eyes were green. Her mother appeared and took her by the sleeve. Leave the nice man alone. I was alone again.

The rails stretched on and I opened the newspaper. It was the anniversary of the bombing of Nagasaki. There was a profile on the employees at Hanford, who produced the plutonium that went into the making of Fat Man. They were proud to be part of something larger than themselves. I didn't understand that. I always wanted to be part of something small.

The conductor announced the name of the next town but it came out garbled. Unintelligible, OR. The train stopped. I got off to stretch my legs. At least that's what I say now that it's convenient. It was a small town, hardly worth the stop. I realized I had been here before, when I was a boy. There was a national park five miles outside of town where my family had camped. A large lake was its main attraction. We swam in it, and my father and I did some fishing. The women, as my father would refer to my mother and sister, went to town to shop.

The town had one large store. I bought a jar of peanut butter, cheddar cheese, crackers, a canteen, a flashlight, a pocket knife, a fishing pole, hooks and an army jacket. Carl rang up my items. He asked me if I was going to the lake. I nodded. He stepped from behind the counter and said, "If you are, you'll need these," and pointed to an assortment of objects I'd never seen before. I asked him what they were. He looked at me askance. I took one off the wall. His face was stony. I took three more. He sucked on his teeth and we walked briskly back to the counter.

On the hike to the lake two things happened. I wasn't yet a mile out of town when a pickup truck stopped. A fat man wanted to give me a ride. I waved him on. He asked me how far I was going, and then he told me how fast he could get me there. His choice of words was troubling. I declined the offer, and he grew angry. I apologized as insincerely as I could. What was there to say that could explain it? He stepped out of the truck and threatened me, called me no good, asked me if I was too good for a ride, but ultimately he grew exasperated and drove off.

The second thing that happened is difficult to describe. Almost abstract. I began to feel that I shouldn't be here, that I should still be on the train to visit my sister. This was no crisis of conscience. I knew that feeling. This had a keener edge to it. It was something original. I had broken a rule I had not known was there, a rule I am unable to describe. I felt compelled to pick up my pace, to run, even, to flee whatever it was that was coming at me. Instead, gritting my teeth, I walked slower, then fell onto my hands and knees to crawl. I was overcome by nausea, as though I had been punched in the stomach. It dissipated slowly, and only after awhile was I able to stand again, wipe my mouth, and continue to the lake.

A man, standing on an aluminum ladder, was hammering nails into the side of one of the cabins. They had fallen into disrepair. I approached him and asked if any were available to rent. The man was rail thin and his face had the look of someone who had spent the greater part of his life squinting. He nodded, spat, climbed down the ladder, and walked away. The lake seemed smaller than I remembered it. I went down to the shore and onto a rickety pier. The water undulated gently. The sun disappeared behind the trees. I began to feel hungry. I walked back to the cabins, but there was no trace of the handyman, even his ladder had been removed. All the windows of the cabins were boarded up. I tried a couple of doors. Locked tight.

The temperature dropped. I put on the army jacket and ate the cheese and crackers. I turned on the flashlight. My footsteps crunched the dry pine needles. Everything shied away from me. My thoughts. . . How long had I been waiting for this moment? Now that it was finally upon me, I panicked. I pounded on the office door and on the walls of the cabins. I searched for other dwellings, for people. I heard an owl hoot. My eyes widened. I was trying to believe in something old fashioned. A revolution to die for. Or a romance. But what was there left worth salvaging? My flashlight dimmed and then went out.

I woke up in the morning, shivering in a patch of damp grass. My pant leg was ripped open and my thigh was exposed, clotted with blood. There on the rocks, next to my broken fishing pole, was a small crustacean, unlike any I'd seen before. I picked it up. Its tiny legs wiggled in the air. I heard voices nearby and then footsteps. I put the crustacean in my jacket pocket, ran to the woods and hid behind a large, fallen log, overgrown with moss. A young couple and a small boy came into view. The boy chattered wildly. He wore a navy and red striped shirt. The colors were vivid and they made me giddy. I wanted a family. My hand suddenly hurt and I gasped.

The three people turned toward me. The man said:

"Don't move."

"Come here, honey," the woman said to the boy.

"Who *is* that?" he asked. It was a simple question.

"Let's go back to the car," said the man.

"Now." The woman said.

Three elk bounded over a barbed wire fence and crashed through the brush. I've always felt an affinity for flight. I hollered and it came out presumptive. I leaned forward, listening. The air rushed around me. My ears were raw. When I was a boy, I thought of the kinds of men I could become. My teeth stuck out.

Working with my pocket knife, I poked holes in the lid of the now empty peanut butter jar and put the crustacean in it. It opened and closed its claws like it was explaining a difficult thing to me. Periodically, I would unscrew the lid, add a little lake water and something I thought it would like to eat. I wanted to understand it, so I gave it my name. The logic of this didn't interest me.

An army truck was stopped in the middle of the road. A specialist was working the tire jack. A sergeant grumbled:

"I think it goes under there."

"Where?"

"There. Did you get out the yield signs?"

The specialist shook his head.

"We should do that. What if a semi buzzes us? That'd piss me off!"

"I *said* watch out for that pile of nails."

"Shuddap! You really think it was a trap?"

"A trap for fools."

"Well, I'm sorry to waste your fucking time, Jackson. Do you believe me when I say, 'I'm sorry for wasting your fucking time?' Because we're supposed to be back at eighteen hundred and if we're not, it's *my* ass. Do you have that whiskey?"

"What?"

"The flask of whiskey."

"There's only a little left."

"That's fine, Jackson." The sergeant took one swallow and then another. I caught his eye.

"What the fuck?"

"I know," I said. "I had a bit of an accident."

They stood up to take a look. There was a pause.

"Should we take him to town, sir?" asked Specialist Jackson.

"We're not here," said the sergeant.

I knew that feeling from somewhere.

"He's pretty messed up."

"*You're* going to be messed up if you don't change that damn tire, Jackson."

Telling a story is always a risk, a minimal one in light of current events, but even so, it has its own hazards. One usually underestimates the stakes, and by the end of the story it is too late. The specialist jacked up the truck and changed the tire. He released it and helped me climb into the cab. The engine made a severe sound and then turned over. My gut hurt. I looked at myself in the rearview and laughed. The sergeant grunted. The truck strained up a steep hill into the sky, which had the consistency of heavy cream. I was ready to serve.

*Untitled*, 2006
oil on paper
10 1/2 x 13 1/2 inches

In October 2000, I traveled to Egypt to write an essay about the pyramids for *Modern Painters*. The following are excerpts from postcards and a letter I wrote to my wife, the painter Evelyn Twitchell.

## Postcard 1

First night * October 13 * 7:00 PM * Pyramid Time * ^^^*
Dear Evy—My Love—I am here. Cannot believe it! Everything pretty okay as far as trip/travel is concerned. I was whisked through customs—treated like (and told that) I was a VIP. In the morning I meet my driver and guide and go to the pyramids ^^^s. I can see the ^^^s from my hotel window, as well as the hotel pool—beautiful blue tile sloping from shallow to deep end. Palm trees surround our courtyard (poverty and a strong military presence just over the wall). I miss you❤—wish you could see *this* light!!!! Unique and spectacular—as always. I arrived at sunset (not as dramatic as on this postcard) but beautiful just the same. The ^^^s appeared to be transparent in the dusty, yellow-orange light. Camels, donkeys, goats—men who sit like pyramids!—can you believe it? This place is *so* old—everything crumbling around me. City seems to be shedding one skin after another. You could do so much in Egypt with the color-range here: sand, cream, ochre, tan, yellow, dust, dust, dust, haze and more dust. The sun seems to be tethered to the ^^^s—as is all time. You can feel the cycle of ages here—magic—extreme calm. The sun is smaller than the pyramids ^^^s. Don't you just love this stamp? These Egyptians love to smoke. Local beer is good. Traffic here is crazy! You will smell the pyramid ^^^ dust on me soooo soon. From the Pyramid capital of the world ^^^ love you—miss you. Wish you were here, Lance

## Postcard 2

Day 2—Pyramids Today—October 14, 2000
Egyptian Art my new love. Dear Evy —The ^^^s are beyond description. What will *I* say? Light, color, camels' humps rising out of the sand. I went inside the big one—King's chamber, Queen's chamber, etc. Steep, hot, haunting! It rained while I was looking at the Sphinx—one of the *greats* as far as sculpture goes!!! Even though missing its nose. The gaze penetrates ➤ beyond this world. It can see through you to New York ➤ and beyond ➤

probably knows your dreams. The Sphinx looked so far beyond me ➹ through me, through the sun ➹ through this time ➹ through all time. And it rises slightly on its haunches—as if it were going to strike—but as if for all time! I ❤ Egypt. The ^^^s are the most impervious, beyond, most self-effacing architecture ever built. I have not looked death in the face, but the Sphinx looks through death—is a portal into and beyond it. Dust. Death. Every color of sand flashes every color of fire. I don't know if the pyramids envelop the light or the light envelops the ^^^s—but something is going on here. I'm on the case! Tomorrow: Egyptian, Islamic and Coptic Museums. I saw some spectacular sculpture—at sunset in the rain—looking at the Sphinx!—Rilke is right: "A face in which a god and a star stood in total communion" (or something like that)—Rilke is always right. ❤ Love, Lance

## Postcard 3

Day 3—October 15, 2000—Dear Evy, Full moon two days ago. Pyramids by full moon! Who can stand it!—Mummified monkeys, kings and queens. Relief sculpture. Cairo's Egyptian Museum: crowded, great stuff in corners and overlooked. Death, Death, Death, King Tut—sculptures that won't stop [...] Indiana Jones-crates, machineguns, dust, tourists, guides, more tourists and guides. My guide kept trying to convince me that 5 hours in the museum was stupid—HA! [...]

## Postcard 4

Dear Evy—I am on the Nile!!! (October 17, 2000) This is one of the most calming places on earth. Faluka sailboats everywhere. Distant rocky cliffs of light gray and tan—pure blue skies, water. This morning I watched, just after sunrise, the pure, bright white sun in the haze [...] a pearly, rippling wonder. The islands—a dusty gray-green. The palm trees—milky silhouettes (like the cutouts in a children's book)—And the moon [...] Small stucco and mud brick homes line the banks [...]—goats walk slowly along and turn toward us. Children wave. The sky weighs down upon us, pushing the hills, trees and river downward. Pure magic this place. Today my guide and I—I have a personal guide on the boat, too—went to a temple. Fantastic late-Egyptian carving. "Temple of Horus" yesterday. So much we saw—(I tried to write you a letter but there are no envelopes onboard the boat). I also saw "Isis Temple" yesterday. We move too fast really to see the sculptures well. Iconography is all to the guides— ❤ Lance

Letter

Lance Esplund
Land of the Pyramids
Somewhere on the Nile
Land of Secrets Never Revealed
Egypt

(October 17, 2000)
Dear Evy—They do have envelopes onboard. I tried to buy them earlier. I did not think to ask for them. They are free. I just had to write you a proper letter. This place is so inspiring and calming—it makes for perfect creative balance. What one does with this is another question. A long, dirty-silver train is passing by near the coastline. I just finished writing you two postcards—I am still on the upper-most deck of my boat. The train creeps along like our boat: steadily, calmly, as if we had all time to reach our destinations; in fact here destinations mean so little. That is why it is a perfect place to work or just to be. Palm trees, water, a herdsman, the desert cliffs, the sky—a sky like no other, a sky that rightly so deserves a god. All is honored here. Yesterday I visited a temple for the crocodile: "Kom Ombo Temple," with mummified crocodile remains in cases—sarcophagi. The art is as still as anything—like the landscape [...]. There is pure harmony, totally unglorified and unpretentious, in the art here. The tensions are all about eternal stillness—held in the plane—not in the round. One experiences all the architecture and sculpture and painting and carving in clearly defined transitions from frontal to profile views, all submerged in the constant plane—life. Each contour edge defines a body with the clarity and insistence of the Nile cutting through the desert. The landscape, the art and life are in total harmony—like the seasonal floods (now obliterated because of the Aswan dam)—but so apparent in the time of the ancients. Sad that so many tourists rush through here—as gods and goddesses are pointed out to them—and leave. But even then I think that it is possible to absorb part of the eternal power of this place in conjunction with the art. [...] I want to draw you a picture, my love, of a palm tree. They are everywhere along the Nile banks:

The fronds are tiny when they meet the trunk, so that they appear to be suspended away from the tree. The trunks, so long and leaning, seem to be suspended above the ground. The fronds, needle-like at their bases—the sky suspended above the trees—everything suspended, just as the oasis of the Nile is suspended in the desert—(suspension of life to the grand desert—death). [...]

—•—

We are approaching a large mound made up of sandstone hills—a large piece of sand overhanging a village. So many of the temples were half-covered with water—floods from the Nile—or with sand from the desert. The people were constantly struggling against the desert and working with the annual flooding of the Nile. What it must be like to feel the power and cycle of the earth—to work with it. [...]

———•◆•———

I am so sad that you are not here with me. This is a must-see, must-feel, must-comprehend—and must-not comprehend—experience. I need to share this with you. The extreme simplicity is beyond description. How does one describe the desert, the pyramids [...] or the Nile? [...] The thing is that one feels the energy of the Nile's current and length but its breadth is compressed by the desert. There is something about this combination of extremes. The pure elegance of extremes: oasis vs. desert; bright lime-green vs. dirt and barren sand; the height of the pyramids vs. the desert's flatness; the verticality of the pyramids vs. the stretch of the Nile. And the colors—the ochre homes reflected yellow in the crystal-blue Nile—flickering like gold. (King Tut's Death Mask is not ostentatious or glitzy at all.) [...] What a culture Egypt must have been! To see the pyramids covered in bright white limestone flashing in the sun—pulling you upward, pulling you across, and pulling you inward [...] The pure unadulterated sky and lime-green of the papyrus, all at once. My god! Who could stand it? Not I.

———•◆•———

And now the light is hazy. The not-too-distant cliffs appear like apparitions [...] White birds break up the blues in silver flashes—so much horizon here. The desert is so still yet so alive, endlessly changing—so broad in every direction. The Nile feels like a comforting womb. (I know this all sounds corny but I cannot help it.) Where is the clarity of Chardin when I need it? I need Marquet! Egypt needs Marquet.

———•◆•———

My boat is a little cheesy, like the cheap hotels in France. But the view out my picture window is fantastic. I like my guide—but he pushed me out onto the dance floor for a game with the Germans and French—not my bag. I bought a galabea (sp?) in white cotton, for the party last night. I went to bed early, as I was surviving on little sleep—3-4 hours per night up until now. I bought a picture of my table guests and guide for you to see. Everyone is selling something here. The people are pushy in a friendly way or friendly in a pushy way: "Where are you from? England? Are you Dutch...Oh! I love the Americans! I am a maker of 'such-and-such'—good price." The stuff I have seen is all cheesy and the guides always have a store owned by a cousin to take you to. Rugs, papyrus, perfume, glassware, trinkets, carvings. […] The man is banging the pan—Lunchtime now—I will write later. ❤ Lance

———•◆•———

That was not lunch, but another stop "Esna," for another temple, a temple in honor of "Khnum," "God who makes men, fashions them out of the wet clay of the Nile"—like Adam. The sun is so strong here. Dogs lie in the shade—as still as death. Every time I see a sleeping dog, I assume it is dead. It will be lunchtime soon. I will write more to you later, my love. ❤

———•◆•———

We just went through a lock. We went down 25 feet or so. I am sitting at the front of the boat near the horn—the worst thing about this trip, I suppose. Whenever we meet a boat, the boats honk at each other. Ours sounds like a big Buick and blasts three times. We are coming up on a wide, tall rock-face—rose-colored and the shadows are blue-violet. The lower sand dunes, which rise up to the rocks, have a light-Bellini-green cast to them. It is all set-off against a light-blue sky. Children are playing kick ball on the grass next to the shore, and some are swimming, surrounded by row-boats—red and violet and a pale, worn turquoise. The children wave and yell to us. We are passing another village of crumbling, mud-brick buildings with open holes for windows. […] Today, when we went to the temple, we walked through a bazaar—basically a street lined with open shops selling brightly colored junk—but the streets are covered with brightly colored blankets to shade the tourists and the sellers. The experience is unusual. An explosion of color. We were driven to the temple by horse-drawn carriage, painted red and purple and curved like a buggy.

———•◆•———

I always want to draw from the carvings but we never have enough time. I could tell my guide to leave me alone but he always has another cartouche or offering to Horus to show me. The name of my boat is "Nile Bride." Others are called "King Tut II," "Diamond Host," "Cosmos-M/S Flash." Tonight we have a belly dancer for entertainment. My table mates are a young Spanish couple from Barcelona, economists. They are on their honeymoon and are not pleased with the boat. I offered them my room, which is a little nicer than theirs, but it was not worth the move to them. They have their own guide, like I do. We all sit at the same table, six of us, surrounded by the Germans and French, 120 in all. The whole cruise thing would be sleazy if it weren't for the Nile and the sites. We are right next to the rocks I mentioned earlier. They really are rose and green. I don't know how. It is 3:45. Teatime is at 4:00. I will leave you soon for a cup of coffee and a piece of cake. Then I will watch the beautiful sunset. I am afraid the wind will blow my letter away. I am holding it down with my hand. There is smoke up ahead on the shore. They make sugar along the Nile—could be that, or maybe it is a real fire. More boats approach—more horn honking: the sound of a police siren. An island covered with cows. It is like I am in the Arizona desert, Nebraska, the tropics, and God-knows-where. An island is perfect—cows don't swim—I think, so no fence is needed. [...]

---

Today is Wednesday the 18th. I saw three tombs in the Valley of the Kings, in Luxor. Amazing carving and painting. I also saw the Temple of Queen Hatshepsut, an unbelievable site. I had no idea before how varied the flat surfaces of the carvings actually are. A lion's nose may bulge at the bridge or snout, and the surface across a body or face may waver a little—swelling here and there. The sun is fierce. 9:00 AM is stronger than high-noon anywhere else. It is not that I feel so much heat, but the force—the strength—of the sun is never absent, even in shade. [...]. Hatshepsut is huge—built into the wall of a cliff. They are restoring it, carving and cutting each paving stone with chisels and a wet handsaw. Slow, slow work—all by hand. Don't know, but I imagine it is the money more than the principle—either way, it gives the place a more authentic feel.

---

Also, I had a fight with my guide—he told me I could have only 12 minutes at Hatshepsut. (It takes ten minutes alone to travel up the ramp.) I walked all the way up, looked at everything that was open and stayed 1 1/2 hours, while he sat and smoked in the shade. He was furious. We talked about my job vs. his job. We eventually made up. The guides and tourists and Egyptian hangers-on at the sites are annoying. Men stand around and point out the shade to you; want to tell you information; sell you the right to touch the art; ask you where you are from. Can you imagine—you are trying to experience a great carving, finding the best position, feeling the rhythms of hunters' legs—fantastic!!! And then: "You like the cartouche? No? Is much better over here in this corner in the shade." Never have I been so annoyed by a culture that looks at its art from the safety of the shade. [...] No one—the guides—say anything of any importance: "This god is 'so-and-so.'" "Here is the beautiful, original color. See. See." "This 'so' high—'such-and-such' meters and weighs 'such-and-such' tons." "Blah, blah, blah." Same shit, different language. And they are everywhere. Ahhhhhh—but the views—the ART!!!!! It is all worth it!

---

I am going to the museum here this afternoon—by myself—and the Temple of Luxor. Both are open late. Tomorrow: Temple of Karnak. There are as many monuments here, seemingly, as in all of Greece. It would take at least two weeks to do one temple any justice. I just had lunch. I will take a short nap and then—off to the museum. I so wish you were here. I need to talk to someone who appreciates this stuff. I feel as if I am trapped, mute and deaf, and yet I have so much to tell you (and if you were here you would have so much to say). […] I am looking forward to, and I am also afraid of, Giza—hope I can find the courage really to open up to the pyramids. I feel as if so far I have only been introduced to them, and now I must do the work. […] Wish me luck. I can't wait until we come back here together. I will mail this now. We are docked, and the boat sends out its letters while at port. Want you to get this before Xmas. We must go cruisin' on the Nile with each other soon—as all the Egyptian gods intended!

———◆•◆———

There is one other thing I wanted to tell you about: SUNSET ON THE NILE. The sun is huge, a perfectly circular ball—strong but you can stare at it. Close, so that you feel you can touch it […] And then the sun hits the blue of the water—water that is spreading out behind our boat in a reverse pyramid—a triangle—rolling outward, swelling and growing; and the Nile is bright orange where the sun hits it and bright blue in shadow, so that the boat seems to be churning out rich, ever-changing, alternating stripes of blue/orange/blue/orange/blue. The best moment is when the sun stands almost precariously, or wobbling a little, on the palm-treed horizon. It sits there but only for an instant, and then it begins to descend below the trees—what beauty! And then the rich range of orange and violet and yellow and blue fill the sky for the longest time, as darkness falls and brings with it an infinite range of grays in the sky, trees, islands and water. […] The distant sandstone hills to the South are rose-colored, blanketed in gray-violet, with pockets of shadow that seem slowly to envelop the earth; and in the farther distance another range of sandstone hills shines almost milky white—a white tinged with green or yellow in places—with rose-colored shadows. These hills spread out just above the lime-green vegetation along the Nile's silhouetted gray-green palms—storybook magic I tell you…Impossible views! Impossible. Impossible. Un-believable! Nothing like it. Nothing. Oh, Egypt!…And all of this under a pure blue sky—boatmen rowing and lifting nets, children waving, animals grazing, birds swooping, tour boats passing. Come. Come away with me to the mysterious land of secrets, the land of the pyramids, the origin of the world, the life-vein of civilization. Please? Please? My Love, ❤ Lance

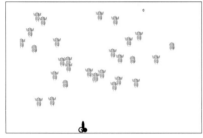

German Atari rockers *Bodenstandig 2000* at Deitch Projects, NYC, 2005

Akiko Sakaizumi, *Get Your Head* custom game, 2004, vertexList Gallery, NYC (screenshot)

*8 BIT* was born in the East Village bar Open Air, which used to host Share, a monthly gathering of computer musicians, geeks by choice, and people interested in computer art in general. At that time, I was really into chiptune music, curating performances at vertexList, and trying to check out all the related events happening in the city. Chiptunes are musical pieces created with old computers or game decks with internal sound synthesizers. For example, Commodore 64, Atari, Nintendo Entertainment System (NES) and Game Boy, all mostly created using 8 bit. As I became more and more familiar with this little scene of musicians, demo people, and hackers of all kinds, I realized that there was a huge cultural potential in games, both old and new. Affected by too many cocktails, I decided to make a documentary.

Of course nobody took my claim seriously, since I am known to make grandiose alcoholic statements that often translate into nothing much at all. But this time I was firm in my intentions. The phenomenon was genuinely exciting and unique, and I quickly realized that the folks using Game Boys to compose/perform music were so exotic that to just show them playing music, without a deeper investigation, wouldn't do much good. I had to get into cracking games, the demo scene, original chiptunes and many other things I didn't even anticipate.

One discovery led to another until the scope of the project grew and changed. The final topic of the project was music and art influenced by video games. Suddenly the visual arts became as much a part of the equation as music, which was only a natural progression: demos were both visual and sound pieces.

———◆•◆———

I started out with the music people: Bit Shifter, Bubblyfish, Glomag, Nullsleep, and Bodenstandig 2000 (who, luckily for me, came to play at Deitch Projects in Soho, NYC). Later I managed to talk to Role Model (aka Johan Kotlinski from Stockholm, the author of Little Sound DJ, a tracker software for making music on Game Boys), Teamtendo from Paris (two guys dressed in animal costumes who love to assault camera men), the Treewave duo from Dallas and Gameboyz Orchestra from Poland. The music content naturally divided itself into three chapters: Demo Scene, Chiptunes and Game Boy.

*Demo scene* is the root of many of today's new media ideas. It started in the early '80s in Europe, with teenage game crackers who replaced the 64 Kb used for the disc copy protection with their own custom animation and sound. These demos soon became quite sophisticated, and hackers pitted their productions against one another. *Chiptune* is the sound accompanying a demo: It is music made through an internal 8 bit sound chip. In fact, all early video game music was chiptunes. It was only in 1999 when the first chiptune records came out: "Maxi German Rave Hits 3" by Bodenstandig 2000 in Germany and "8-Bit Construction Set" by Beige Records (Cory Arcangel) here in the US. *Game Boy* music is a form of chiptune but for less computer-savvy musicians. The platform was made accessible by Johan Kotlinski's LSDJ in 2000 and Oliver Witchoff's Nanoloop (2000). Ever since then, musicians have been rocking out to their Game Boys all over the world, especially in Vienna, Stockholm, NYC and Tokyo.

———◆·◆·◆———

The second wave of production efforts involved talking to visual artists who dealt with game content in their work. Cory Arcangel was a perfect bridge between two worlds because he co-founded the seminal Beige records, and later became well known for his modified Mario Brothers cartridges and other gallery based post-game work. He is a great example of the DIY approach to art, and his work is as much about breaking in and explaining how to do it to others, as it is about the image and subject matter.

It soon became clear that there were several very distinct approaches artists used in treating game material. Some artists came from demo culture and hacking, and were interested in opening up existing codes, exposing weak points of commercial software and re-purposing commercial gear. In this category of structural game works are Cory Arcangel, Jody, Alex Galloway and all the good folks who worked on hacking Game Boys and NES.

Another huge field directly related to the gaming world and only sometimes crossing over to the art field was machinima. Machinima is a trendy term describing pieces of linear animation created with game engines. Many multiplayer games like Halo, Quake or The World of Warcraft allow modification of characters, weapons, backdrops and recording of live action. Artists like Eddo Stern and Brody Condon used this capacity to convey social and political commentaries; others used the game environment to stage live online shows and interview the avatars of online guests (This Spartan Life).

Carlo Zanni,
*Average Shoveler*,
custom online game,
2005 (screenshot)

Johan Kotlinski (aka rolemodel), the author of Little Sound DJ software for Game Boy playing live at vertexList, 2005

Many digital artists went beyond using existing games and created their own, sometimes functional, sometimes highly abstract, interactive environments based on game behavior patterns. John Klima and Carlo Zanni used live internet data input to animate their complex and optically stunning game environments; Mary Flanagan and Akiko Sakaizumi built simple game levels around personal narratives, gender issues and social criticism. In some cases game works move beyond software into the realm of installation. Paul Johnson's game consoles covered in hand-formed plastic endlessly play each other, while Joe McKay forces the viewers to use their bodies and voices in order to interact with his Audio Pong and a garage version of Dance Dance Revolution.

Artist and blogger Tom Moody in his studio

Eddo Stern, *Sheik Attack*, art machinima piece, 1999/2000 (screenshot)

I was stunned by the richness and complexity of this clandestine domain of art making. I also couldn't help but notice that it introduced some fresh models of thinking, mostly related to the semiotics of a game situation, so different from being a passive beholder of art. Interactivity, often problematic in an installation context, became the key element of vocabulary, opening up metaphors and activating content.

To help clarify the theoretical and historical aspect of my exponentially growing documentary I turned to people who wrote about new media and could help forge the discussion about art after video games. Ed Halter, the media critic from *The Village Voice* provided a short history of video games and compared the explosion of game works to independent cinema after WWII. A curatorial perspective and a who's-who map of the digital art world came from Christiane Paul, Whitney curator and the author of *History of Digital Art*. Finally the artist/blogger Tom Moody added his critical voice, placing the 8 bit scene in the art-historical context and pointing out the vital problems of new media.

————◆•◆•◆————

The making of *8 BIT* exposed some very interesting intellectual issues concerning videogames and their place in the discourses of contemporary art and music. The fun began when I tried to place the artists I interviewed into the context of a modernist/postmodernist practice. In some cases the task was easy: Cory Arcangel declared himself a cyber-minimalist; Alex Galloway compared his own approach to Nam June Paik's; Eddo Stern and Mary Flanagan placed themselves in the political/activist discourse of postmodern art. All that made perfect sense: Structural game works are about taking games, code and gear apart, showing the nuts and bolts of the medium being used. This interest in purism and delineating the limits of a particular method of making is typical for modernism in it's classical, Greenbergian form. And in fact I would risk the statement that the structural game works we see today may be the last bastions of modernism. Machinima, based on pre-existing game models, is a postmodern medium par-excellence. The statements made by the artist exist within the language that is pre-authored, and they need to subvert it's own language in order to become significant. The content conveyed in those significant statements is a social commentary, an attempt at deconstructing the dominant power hierarchy, a statement of disobedience against the system.

Glomag (Chris Burke) playing Game Boy at Cythea, Paris

Cory Arcangel, *Don't Touch My Computer*, Thadeus Ropac Gallery, Paris

In some cases however, the modernist terminology was flatly rejected. Carlo Zanni stated that his work is not about the process but about the project and control, and the element of quotation is just a tool in building his fully functional micro-universes. Paul Johnson and John Klima both mention the necessity of building coherent, controllable environments. Akiko Sakaizumi simply recognized the game format to be the next logical progression of media escaping cinematic linearity and embracing algorithims.

As I went through the footage I found the word "control" in every single artist's interview. It seems the element of control is a very present, if not central, element in the discourse of game works, found anywhere from Cory Arcangel hacking the Mario chip himself and taking control of the technology, through Eddo Stern controlling the game to the point where it would let him generate meaning, to Carlo Zanni who wants to make little worlds which he fully understands—and controls.

Are we witnessing a paradigm shift? Is the open structure of Deleuze's rhizome giving way to something more organized, stratified and centralized? Do we, as artists, feel controlled, responding with a compulsory need to control? Could this be a manifestation of our current social-political ambiance? Are we searching for stable, safe limits of expansion?

I guess we are going to see the answer in some twenty years. Until then, I found one metaphor in the world of computer media that I think might be the competition for rhizome: object oriented. The Object Oriented Paradigm (OOP) is a contemporary way of thinking in computer programming, based on using pre-fabricated code "machines" (objects) which can be modified and are capable of responding to events and communicating with other objects. Objects are instruments of power: they allow the programmers to liberate themselves from "command line" coding and simply shape their coded environments the way you shape Sim-City. At the same time, they remove the programmer from the position of direct communication with the machine, alienating and displacing. OOP is the way most games are written now. The metaphor behind the object-oriented game

Marcin Ramocki,
*History*, interactive
software environment,
2005, JCAL, NYC

universe is a platonic void filled with perfect virtual cyborgs, with no access to DOS shell, no going back to the black screen. It is a post-Baudrillard world, where simulation found a way of reproducing its constituents. Objects bring back the hierarchy, order, control and perfect numerical accountability.

To paraphrase Mary Flanagan: If game design is de facto social programming, we have to pay close attention to what worlds we are making out of code. The way we think about those virtual models will translate slowly into flesh, because flesh has become nothing but a step necessary to close the loop of a game algorithm.

——◆——

*8 BIT* is a hybrid of historical document, rockumentary, art-historical exposé and philosophical thriller. It is most likely guilty of idiosyncrasy, silliness, superficial treatment of some material and inconsistent directing. However, I genuinely believe this movie captured some of the most significant artistic developments of the beginning of the 21st century. This is a movie about artists, made by artists, and I certainly hope not only for artists (although this is a distinct possibility). If you like video games, electronic music and furry animals, this film is definitely for you.

USEFUL URLS:

www.ramocki.net/8bit/

www.glomag.com

www.bubblyfish.com

www.bitshifter.cc

www.8bitpeoples.com/nullsleep/

www.beigerecords.com/cory/

www.bodenstandig.de/

www.teamtendo.com/

www.littlesounddj.com

www.edhalter.com

www.digitalmediatree.com/tommoody/

www.transliteracies.english.ucsb.edu/post/conference-2005/participants/christiane-paul

www.maryflanagan.com/

www.cityarts.com/

www.eddostern.com/

www.vertexlist.net/akiko.html

www.zanni.org/

www.homepage.mac.com/joester5/art/index.html

www.mutationengine.com/

www.ramocki.net/

## HOUSE OF IMPORTS

Was there nothing else
to make silk from
thought the last spider
rather uncomfortably

The horse you are looking for
already have go. What do
these pebbles tell us Chen,
which road did it take

Anita's eliminating guesswork
Chen thinks, the eunuch
when bamboo features
a chased look

The horse felt cool
to his legs and hips. Invent enemy
space travel desirable?
Let me go for bridge

Stopped morning full rubber
Chen installed better
and Lipstick was his crooked she
(Anita) circled partly in skies

Tattooing a mean mask
with golden bits
the sun played against the side
of a falling tobacco leaf

Shots of animal colour
rotated Lipstick wet glass
perched on left-hand top shelf
the target

Target-breasted enlarged
and correlated species, types
took off, the peacock's feather
swatted a friendly face

Weak food bullets hungered
a monk appeared and dis-
robed in saffron did Chen,
the handler, appear

Made keeping elaborate hard
a nickel-plated toga
a cheap bunch of horseshoes
mint prison stripes are inside of

Safely held the disturbed rain
hat in season mixed and poured
another hand to take her
winter balm and coat essence

A tooled cistern
checks were nothing
might be all they need but
no fist had drawn breath

Her meal simply plucked Anita
fixed Lipstick, content as well
with the so-called west-
making orange

Chen cocked
Anita plucked
his outstretched baton
with credit

Admitting his price when
hills filled with
a Spanish hoard dug
the helmet's crest—fish scales on a Buddhist

Already immersed
to the tops of
gesticulating skyward, Chen dipped
his inner pilot in silence

Uncommunicative men
spelled out the words—
he captivates
ordinary swimmers

Chen sold the
palm tree sketch
his aquatic sculptures
followed

Amid a salad of
wilder capable sunsets
and a toothpick
fashioned into darkness

Patch buoy spared
leak die toss
one upset oar
came tap-tapping, thirsty

Out ripe hunger
got a free throw
but mistook the sea-chance,
and green-throated a segment

Totally tropical
a drank summer thing
galloped needing
no brakes, for coffee

And stashed a fair balance
under the overhang
a stiff headpiece
dis-treed, a roof joist

Anita coughed
she didn't sneeze
but patted flower droppings to show
she'd port-holed a signal

Chen sleeps,
nice cover
such that he drew his own
blood with six Lipsticks

Two were stuck with cloves
Chen switched off his nose
and parked between blows
his refills out for Anita

The sneak tidal rose
eight feet
in length, like a sacred
prosthetic fin

His Lipstick, Anita
astride the anima
they'll feel the dark build
across tepid windows
first thing

## TARGETS/WASH

some wing chance fifty hatch
amid alone dice deals fold
choice not affirmative cast
it wax some tot been
simply & perfidy candidly
exquisite milk skin
start him tery
lacks takes nota mal
sheds roofs tips
and not and part
sets up fate winds
clear canvas coats clear
stops checks
under amid about traces
amid contain
out shakes out
fashion craze stiff white fashion craze
nail fans shut

slap which rocks simply tears blue

armchairs is rocks

bids

him that chairs lay

place foam hollow holds

that that wave that at it's

very there by climbs cloud

dips

reaches

mist makes listless skies

blots out bid

decks

signaled didn't captive eats to

pecks wreckage

sleeper when tight

pleat

most makes

tint

clots pink

pleats filed edges

compline compline

must importance

under sky postage

customs

reveals swans

hat flock

don't paint fifty flock

crease crease & stems

a

cap

bird

seat upon reflects

primes

is glazed gold

cajole senile empty conch

shot shot to blasted vague

a tag

ice bags feather closeted mean cold

wipes

or dims

spotless hair

of poured

neat drop clad still

scrapes of and cups

work study act lies

counter?

skirt god crime scent

sport is a light base

base

under until sparks for

scantily lace

total crystallised

arse flute

silver gas

amid a set pipe and then

word leak

rib show

teats flower

winds chaste amid

twist over

footprint

were all toques peaked

subdivide

by colour induced

colour stand to safe

egg strike

mock instrument

flake

not the at gild

clamped

toss

minds stand at makes

combs a test

song sign paper shoe

earthward the a cube trims board

ticket ing void

same detach board

painted cube

stock pipe grease

fifty head

bushes

paint

seek bloom

calm very leaf horn

emptily by sails

locks she she

is rusty dawn

on the I lap

nail colour

ready rose only

map brushes

pear gel!

bers

tet whore

lip shade

sleeping shore

bans

and sity doors

potence

reed

ives

masts

fo

quet

dian

gers

cut in front as a square is for a square a

Paul Etienne Lincoln

# THE LURE AND DRAW OF HONEY'S METAPHORIC ENERGY TRANSFER

*A description of "The Battersea Bee Station," and "Indicator for Burg Vischering."*

**The Lure and Draw of Honey's Metaphoric Energy Transfer** investigates two unrealized proposals: "The Battersea Bee Station," 1983 and "Indicator for Burg Vischering," 1998-9. Although conceived almost fifteen years apart, both centrally manipulate honey's role as a metaphor for cultural wealth.

The bee is one of the oldest forms of animal life. In existence since the Neolithic Age, bees predate human civilization on earth by ten to twenty million years. This delicate, complex creature has procured for humanity honey, propolis, royal jelly, beeswax and, most important of all, the fertilization of many of our crop-bearing plants. According to Greek mythology, the infant Zeus, out of gratitude for the honey that sustained him, gave the honeybee its sting for defense. Because the bee abused this power, Zeus later decreed that whenever the sting was administered the unfortunate bee must die. Ironically, humans have developed the means to milk *Isopentyl acetate* from bees and to use this substance as a treatment for bee venom hypersensitivity and for the relief of arthritic individuals.

Honey has been readily associated with cultural wealth by writers and philosophers throughout history, the hive being a recurring analogy for human civilization. Bernard Mandeville (1670-1733), a Dutch Doctor of Medicine specializing in *Hypochondriack* and *Hysterick Passions*, moved to England and penned the poem "The Grumbling Hive" and a series of essays arguing the necessity of vice as the foundation of the emerging capitalist economy. Ridiculed and condemned as a "Public Nuisance," Mandeville's *The Fable of the Bees*, as the collection became known, describes a flourishing beehive resembling England, even to the unique advantage of being happily governed by a limited monarchy. The most noticeable characteristic of this beehive or nation is its addiction to vice, especially to fraud, luxury and pride. As described by Mandeville, the committing of crime, for example, is responsible for keeping whole multitudes at work: lawyers, gaolers, turnkeys, sergeants, bailiffs, tipstaffs and locksmiths.

1. Bernard Mandeville, "The Grumbling Hive or Knaves Turn'd Honest," *The Fable of the Bees, Public Vices, Public Benefits* (London, near the Oxford Arms in Warwick Lane: J. Roberts, 1714).

*Then on a cloud the Hood-winke'd fair*
*Justice her self was push'd by Air:*
*About her chariot, and behind,*
*Were sergeants, Bums of every kind,*
*Tip-staffs, and all those Officers,*
*That squeeze a living out of Tears.*[1]

As for the vices of luxury, avarice, prodigality, pride, envy and vanity displayed by the more respectable members of society, these promote trade by creating wants, which can only be satisfied by merchants, tradesmen and manufacturers of supply. Under ordinary circumstances we might expect that the wicked bees, in spite of temporary prosperity, would ultimately come to grief as a result of their numerous sins. But while misfortune does become their lot, this reversal comes about only when the knaves are suddenly turned honest. With the ensuing absence of the crimes that created employment and the vices that fostered trade, the professions decay, commerce dwindles, thousands of unemployed emigrate and the hives' prosperity comes to an end.[2]

## APICULTURE

Five species, named by Carolus Linnaeus, dominate apiculture: *Apis mellifera* (common honeybee), *Apis dorsata*, *Apis laboriosa* (giant honeybee), *Apis cerana* (Indian honeybee) and *Apis florae* (dwarf honeybee). Three types of individuals or castes control the colony: the queen (fertile female), workers (infertile females) and drones (males). Only one egg-laying queen is allowed in the hive at a time.

drone

queen

worker

The majority of the colony is composed of workers who build and repair the combs, search for nectar and pollen, produce wax and honey, feed the young and protect the hive against enemies. Blossoms' pollen is transported to the hives in a special pouch inside the worker's body called a "honey stomach." Fermenting in their stomachs, the sugar and nectar are broken down—by a process called inversion—into the simple sugars levulose and dextrose. This nectar mixture may contain as much as 70% water and after the honeybees have deposited the nectar in the hive, they fan the honey cells with their wings to aid evaporation, reducing the water content and thereby increasing viscosity. The honeybees also add enzymes that enhance the flavor. A special gland in the abdomen of the young worker produces beeswax. It is interesting that the honeycomb walls, only 1/80 inch thick, can support thirty times their own weight. Royal jelly, a creamy substance rich in vitamins and proteins, is secreted from a gland in the head of the young worker bee. The length of time that grubs receive royal jelly determines whether the female grub will develop into a queen or a worker.

All female bees, both queens and workers, have the *diploid* complement of chromosomes whereas the males, drones, have *haploid*. Drones develop from unfertilized eggs, their only function being to mate with a young queen. Her Highness takes six to twelve fine drones to fill her *spermatheca* sac and for this valuable privilege they forfeit their lives. In autumn, when the honey flow is over, the workers allow the remaining drones to starve to death, saving the precious stocks of honey for the winter months.

2. See Phillip Harth, Preface Notes to *The Fable of the Bees* (London: Penguin Books, 1970).

Madame de Pompadour à sa toilette *by Francois Boucher, 1758, Fogg Art Museum, Harvard University, Cambridge, MA*

3. See Karl Von Frish, *The Dancing Bees* (New York: Harcourt, Brace & Co., 1955).

4. Battersea power station was designed by Sir Giles Gilbert Scott (1880-1960) in 1928. Scott was already famous for designing Liverpool Cathedral and for creating one of London's most cherished icons, the pillarbox-red telephone box. From the start, the power station was criticized by many important luminaries for its location and for the inevitable health hazards that it was imagined would ensue. As a result, the London Power Company (LPC) pioneered a gas washing system that proved effective in removing more than 90% of the sulphur from the chimney gases, and which helped the LPC to achieve a world thermal efficiency record in 1935.

The integrity of the colony is maintained by chemical secretions called pheromones. Workers secrete pheromones from the *Nasanov gland* at the tip of their abdomens when they cluster, enter a new nesting site or identify a source of nectar or water. The colony scent is recognizable by members of the same colony because of its unique combination of components derived from the colony's particular collections of nectar and pollen.

When queens fly to mate, a *mandibular-gland* pheromone attracts the drones. The same gland produces another pheromone, called *queen substance*, which workers lick from the queen's body and pass along as they exchange food with one another. The ingested pheromone inhibits the ovaries of workers.

Dance plays an important role in communicating direction and distance of nectar sources. In 1973, Karl von Frish received a Nobel prize for deciphering the language of bees.[3] This language consists of two basic dances: a dance in a circle, for indicating sources without reference to specific distance or direction, and a tail-wagging dance in which the exact distance is indicated by a number of straight runs with abdominal wagging—the fewer runs per minute, the farther away the source. The direction, or azimuth, to the food source is indicated by the angle of the wagging dance to the sun. Bees use the Sun as a compass, orienting the dance angle to the plane of polarization of the sunlight.

## BATTERSEA BEE STATION

Designed in 1983 in response to a competition for possible uses of Sir Giles Gilbert Scott's original Power Station in London,[4] "Battersea Bee Station" was intended to be viewed in the context of another recently completed project, "In Tribute to Madame de Pompadour and the Court of Louis XV" 1983-4.[5]

"In Tribute to Madame de Pompadour and the Court of Louis XV," is an elaborate machine evoking a celebration of the enlightenment in eighteenth century France, focusing on Madame de Pompadour's relationship to King Louis XV and his various courtiers. When in operation, live bees and snails run the machine's main conical structure. The bees produce the cultural wealth (honey) of the society and the snails (courtiers) devour this wealth and distribute it to various symbolic and practical uses. The machine was an intricate model of a society whose system was hopelessly inadequate for growing and sustaining itself, floundering in a metaphoric illusion of a thwarted paradise.

Madame de Pompadour is depicted as neither a bee nor a snail. She is an enigma, an artificial vacuum, invisible. One is only aware of her presence through an olfactory trace in the form of a specially prepared perfume, reputed to have been her favorite, emanating from the "Hyacinths" chamber, in the main piston mechanism of the Court. King Louis XV (a snail) controls water to the Court and one of his duties is to water a series of vats on which the Court rests. These vats are carefully packed with crushed snail shells that have been prepared with carbon to form calcium carbide. The action of the King's water on this substance causes a vigorous reaction which releases the anesthetic, Acetylene $C_2H2$. This gas is piped into the main piston mechanism where it creates a vacuum in the top of the glass chamber. Madame de Pompadour is thus artificially created by King Louis. She, in turn, invisibly controls—through her vacuum—the entire honey chambers of all fourteen courtiers, and, as a result, wafts her perfume into the hive inciting the worker bees to venture out of the court and forage for

*In tribute to Madame de Pompadour and the Court of Louis XV.*
*Installation view of the first performance in London, 1984.*

Battersea power station began producing electricity in 1933 when section (A) comprising just two of the familiar chimneystacks was competed. Ten years later an additional pair was added, giving the structure its four-tower form. In 1975 the first section was closed down and in 1983 section (B) was finally closed, sealing its fate. In 1980 the Secretary of State for the Environment listed it as "a building of special architectural and historic interest" and, shortly after its closure in 1983, a competition was held to see what possible uses the structure could be converted into. Ten entries were finally judged by Sir Hugh Casson and a consortium of advisors.

5. See Paul Etienne Lincoln, *In Tribute to Madame de Pompadour and the the Court of Louis XV*, Atlas Anthology III (London: Atlas Press, 1985); and Paul Etienne Lincoln, broadsheet *Explication: In Tribute to Madame de Pompadour and the Court of Louis XV*, (New York: Christine Burgin, 1990).

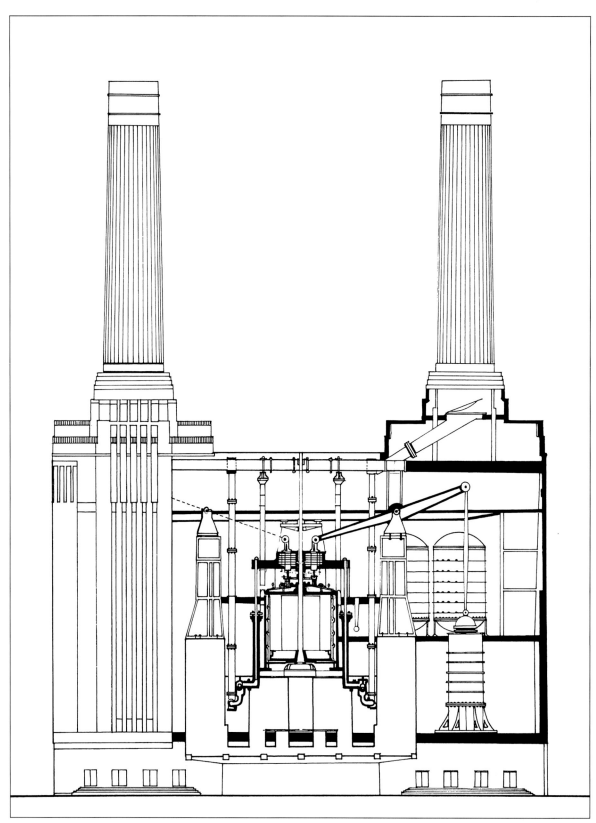

*Cut-away drawing of the large Cornish Steam Engine for pumping mead, situated in the south wing of Battersea Bee Station.*

226

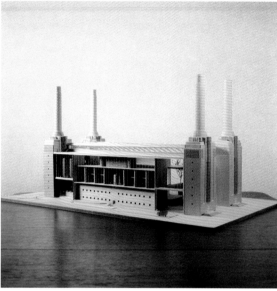

*Model of Battersea Bee Station:*
*left, east wing; right, west wing*
*Scale 1 to 333, 1983.*

fresh nectar and pollen, leading to the inevitable possibility of swarming and abandoning the hive.

"In Tribute to Madame de Pompadour and the Court of Louis XV" would be installed as part of the "Battersea Bee Station" in a shrine together with seven large vitrines explaining the workings of the machine and the inevitable demise of such a political structure, one perhaps not to be upheld.

The idea of taking a real power station and replacing its generators with centrifugal extraction machinery for the production of honey was, it seemed, a perfect transformation of its use. The "Battersea Bee Station" proposal stipulated that the whole of South London's parkland and the verges between opposing roads be planted with lavender, reinstating Lavender Hill as a true anachronism.[6] An accompanying proposal for a government tax allowance would have encouraged people to develop their gardens and to cultivate new species of plants to help augment the bees' diet.

As outlined in the "Battersea Bee Station" proposal, the Main Turbine hall of the station, once clad in Italian marble, would house an enormous ground glass prism, a "Fool's Paradise"[7] placed at the north entrance foyer. There, a series of mirror reflectors would channel light into the east wing where it would be refracted into the full color spectrum. Spectrums produced by refraction through glass were common phenomena during the eighteenth century.[8] Isaac Newton's experiments with refracted light were key in advancing his conclusion that white light could be decomposed into several colors. Yet Newton was also making a subtly different and much bolder corresponding statement: that different colors of light, when combined, create white light and that white light should therefore be viewed as a compound or a mixed color. In "Battersea Bee Station" each individual color refracted from this grand prism would be separated and refracted

6. Prior to the railway age, pre-1838, the hill east of Clapham Junction Railway Station in South London was called Lavender Hill, on account of this rural area growing lavender to be used in the production of perfume.

7. Christopher Merrett (1614-1695) one of the founder members of the Royal College of Physicians, and Keeper of its Harveian Libary and Museum, makes refrence to the Fool's Paradise in relation to the prism in his translation (1662) of Antonio Neri's L'Arte Vetraria (Art of Glass), first published in Florence in 1612.

8. An experiment with a prism had appeared in Giambattista della Porta's *De refractione*, published in Naples in 1558. The

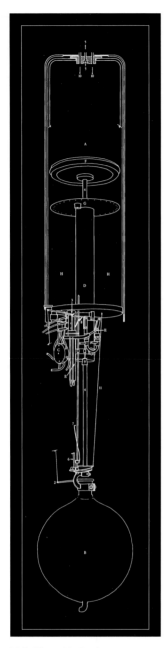

**Main Piston Mechanism
(Madame de Pompadour)**

The main piston mechanism is the piston arrangement which creates Madame de Pompadour, allegorized as an artificial vacuum in the top of vacuum flask A

Piston D is fed gas from the King's Bellows which raises Piston F. Gravity caused by the reservoir of accumulated resources, B, causes a vacuum to form in chamber A; it also pushes air through grill G into hyacinth (perfume) chamber H which is released into the Court.

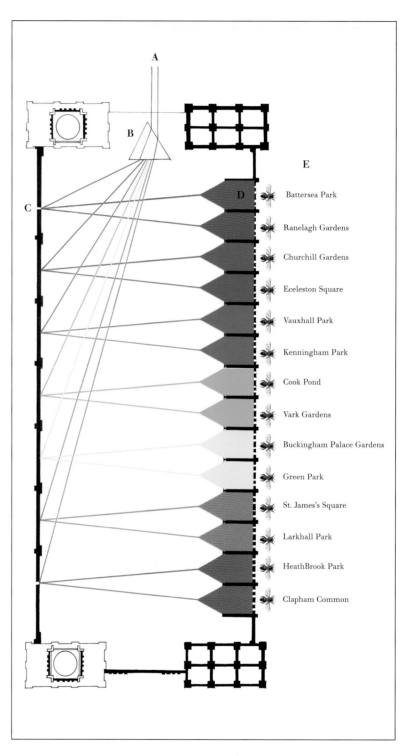

**Diagram of the Fool's Paradise (Prism)
and its refraction into the fourteen hive chambers**
A (white light) enters prism **B and** gets refracted off lense C into individual hive chambers, **D,** each holding up to three hundred hives. **E:** possible destinations for pollen gathering.

into fifteen sequentially identical hive rooms. Each chamber would radiate a pure color which the worker bees, by color association, could identify as their zones of occupancy.[9]

The structure of "Battersea Bee Station" was intended to house an assortment of wonderful subsidiary industries and treatment clinics. A library stocked with every conceivable reference book pertinent to apiculture would reside in the two north towers. Research laboratories and education departments would service in-house medical and beauty product manufacture. Wax extraction facilities would supply such products as polishes, candles, cosmetics, leather and fabric preservatives and wax models for dentistry. A restaurant using products taken from the hives would be the only food source for the human workers. An elaborate brewery would be set up to manufacture mead from fermented honey. A centrally placed reflecting pool, running parallel to the hive rooms, would circulate water via a giant vascular system, cooling the hives and transferring their heat together with heat generated from the solar roof decking to run a giant stationary steam pump[10] placed at the opposite end of the station, facing the "Fool's Paradise." The pump's sole purpose would be to distribute mead, via a network of supply pipes, to fourteen cultural institutions throughout Greater London, among them: The Houses of Parliament, Battersea Dog Home and Atlas Press. Sir Giles Gilbert Scott's original Power Station was reputed to be the largest steel and brick structure in Europe, and with some modifications its interior would not be much diminished from its original grandeur. "Battersea Bee Station" would promise to be the largest center for apiculture in the world and the inhabitants of England the envy of every civilized nation for their clear skin and renewed health.

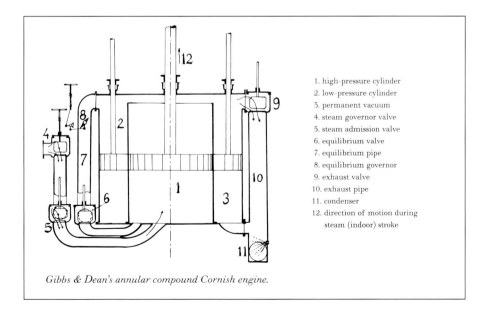

1. high-pressure cylinder
2. low-pressure cylinder
3. permanent vacuum
4. steam governor valve
5. steam admission valve
6. equilibrium valve
7. equilibrium pipe
8. equilibrium governor
9. exhaust valve
10. exhaust pipe
11. condenser
12. direction of motion during steam (indoor) stroke

*Gibbs & Dean's annular compound Cornish engine.*

phenomenon was explained in terms of the old Aristotelian concept that light is white and that colors arise through its gradual modification. Red and yellow light, the colors of fire, were said to be modified the least. Then came green, blue and violet, each "mingled" with increasing amounts of "darkness."

9. Within the allegorical structure of "In Tribute to Madame de Pompadour and the Court of Louis XV," Newton's observation was put to use in the color coding of the individual courtier's (snail's) life lines. Each snail had attached to its back a colored silk thread wound onto a bobbin with the number of windings corresponding to the number of years each individual courtier lived. The combined assembly of the courtier's silk threads ranged in color from red to indigo. This "Newtonian ring," which surrounded the vacuum chamber of Madame de Pompadour, illuminated the mistress' controlling influence over the courtiers' honey supply.

10. The Mead Pump would be based on Gibbs & Dean's annular compound Cornish engine (see diagram for key to parts).

# INDICATOR FOR BURG VISCHERING

The second proposal, "Indicator for Burg Vischering," 1998-9, involved a more ephemeral use of honey as a metaphoric reward for the viewing of an exquisite vista. "Indicator for Burg Vischering" is a project intended for the medieval moated castle of Burg Vischering in Lüdinghausen. The site comprises three distinct areas. The first is the wooden footbridge and weir gate A parallel to the main entrance. The second is a circular area B approximately one meter in diameter in the receiving pool, fed with the controlled waters from the two interconnecting moats. The third site is a small isolated pool C on the north side of the castle's moat.

At A, a telescope is positioned on the wooden footbridge, beneath which is a waterwheel operated by the waters flowing through the weir gate. At area B is a cast of a tree rising from a conical drain; upon one branch is a cast honey-guide bird. An enlarged translucent cast of a chirping linden flower floats at area C; the flower is fed with water pumped from area B.

On the wooden footbridge parallel to the entrance, a specially constructed telescope is mounted on a structural aluminum I-beam spanning the length of the bridge that provides stability to the optical apparatus. Directly below this device a stainless steel waterwheel in the shape of a ball is mounted on the face of the weir gate. This waterwheel spins as the water from the castle's moat exits the weir gate. The waterwheel has two functions: it generates electricity which powers the optical mechanism of the telescope, and it operates a self-priming pump which draws water from the linden tree drain and transports it to site.

# Map of Burg Vischering

A- Telescope and waterwheel
B- Site of cast tree
C- Site of cast linden flower
D- Burg Vischering

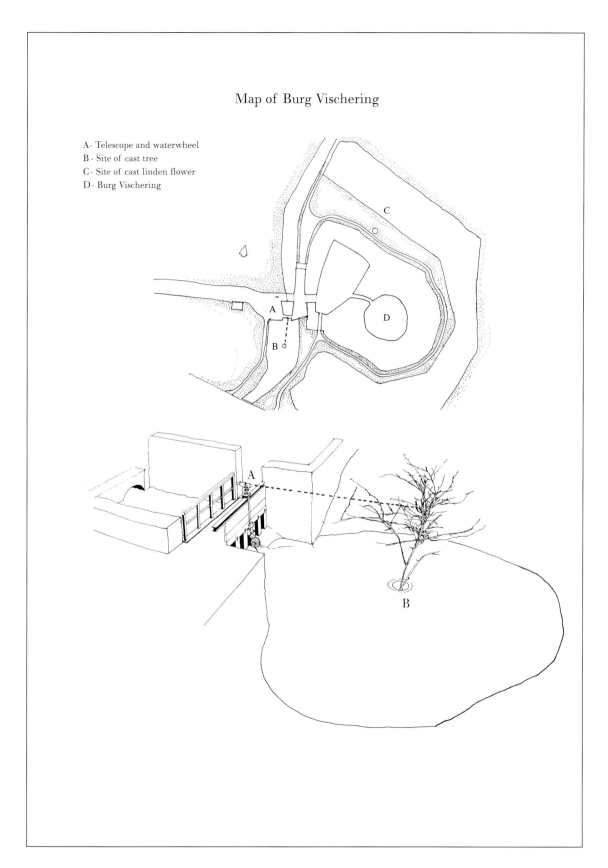

11. The silver linden, or
*Tilia tomentosa*, has been
chosen for its mythological
associations—it is a blood
purifier and a talisman
against misfortune. The
flowers of the linden tree,
although intoxicating to
bees, produce a honey
unsurpassed in flavor and
delicacy.

*Sequence of images viewed*
*through the telescope mounted*
*on the footbridge.*

In the receiving pool at B a 3-4 meters-high cast in clear resin of a silver linden tree,[11] *Tilia tomentosa*, is placed. This is positioned in a conical funnel which functions as a drain. The drain acts as an internal fountain or void: the linden tree appears to be isolated in a black hole. The water around the drain becomes smooth, producing an ideal surface to reflect the image of the tree. A pre-cast concrete ring with an embedded stainless steel tube is set in the center of the pool, then the tree and funnel lowered onto the ring. To compensate for the fluctuating water levels in the receiving pool, a float mechanism is incorporated so that the top of the drain is always parallel to the surface of the water. A flexible PVC tube is attached to the base of the funnel, running along the bottom of the pool to Pump P at the side of the pond and then to the third site. A cast of a honey-guide bird, *cuculus indicator*, is placed in the center of the linden tree. The bird is life-size, approximately 15 cm. high and cast in

rhodium. It is hardly discernible to the casual eye.

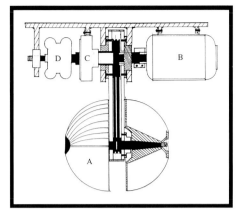

Water Wheel

A- Stainless steel waterwheel
B- Electrical generator
C- Electrical clutch
D- Transfer pump

As visitors to the castle chance upon the telescope and look through its eyepiece, an image of the transparent linden tree, reflected in the water, is visible in a circular frame. The action of the visitor's eye against the eyepiece activates a pump attached to the waterwheel, thus emptying the conical drain. The waters quickly begin to fall away around the trunk causing the tree to appear isolated in a void. The drawn water from the drain is transferred to site C via a tube, where it enters an enlarged clear resin cast of a linden flower. It is only during the telescope's operational cycle that the water flowing through the flower creates the imitated calling sound of the honey guide.[12]

After the initial contact with the eyepiece of the telescope, the lens begins to zoom slowly into the tree and onto the honey-guide; it continues zooming in on the bird's head and finally ends when the honey-guide's eye fills the frame. Appearing to be reflected onto the surface of the bird's eye is a magnificent hidden view of the castle. In fact it is not the view one would assume—the vista seen from the bird's position—but rather, the view seen from the third site C. This image is superimposed within the telescope's apparatus by a black-and-white slide mechanically shifted into the focal plane. By the same method, this idyllic black-and-white image of the castle is slowly faded into a mirror, reflecting the image of the sky and bleaching the ethereal image of Burg Vischering into a white light. The entire viewing cycle occupies sixty seconds, beginning again as the next viewer puts their eye to the telescope.

The interconnected objects and actions taking place at the three distinct areas transform the castle into a symbolic vascular system. The lifeblood of the castle is the carefully regulated water of the moats. As the water flows around the system it provides not only the physical material and force required to drive the mechanics, but also serves as a transformative medium. The castle has always relied on maintaining a precise level

12. A very distinct two-note call "*weet—eer*" repeated every few seconds. When trying to draw attention to a bees' nest they have an excited chattering cry, "*ke, ke, ke, ke, ke, ke, ke, ke.*"

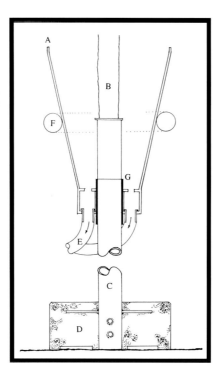

Conical Drain

A- Conical drain
B- Trunk of cast tree
C- Stainless steel shaft
D- Concrete foundation
E- Waste pipes to pump
F- Flotation device
G- Nylon bearing

of water in the two interlocking moats, not only to protect the wooden foundations but also, in the past, to protect against marauding bandits. This passage of water through the final weir gate is the castle's life-blood, the waterwheel becoming a monitor of its flow.

The situation of the telescope directly above the waterwheel is not merely a physical proximity. It is the water's flow that permits the telescope's operation and also the viewer's engagement of the eyepiece that activates the water's metaphorical functions. As the water flows, so the viewer experiences the almost cinematic image through the telescope, in a manipulated, albeit real-time, frame.

The telescope is a familiar tool for cultural observation offering improved, if distorted, possibilities for scrutiny. The telescope addresses the history of the castle, as it was in the fifteenth and sixteenth centuries that this instrument changed people's view of the world and their surroundings. Viewing through a telescope changes the viewer's perception of reality, both literally and metaphorically. This object serves as both a scientific instrument and a cultural tool; the effect of displacement encountered by the viewer on seeing the 'wrong' view of the castle is an intimation of the mutability of perception. That experience of displacement through space and time returns to the viewer when they make the perimetric walk around the castle and encounter the previously projected view.

The honey guide has an extraordinary habit, as the name implies, of guiding humans (and honey badgers, *Mellivora capensis*) to bees' nests by flying back and forth with a chattering call. Humans or badgers once led to the gilded site break the nest for honey leaving the redundant wax for the honey guides. This bird has the unusual ability to digest wax using special enzymes to break down the wax esters (*ceraphagous*)—a quite remarkable

example of mutualism. A second quality the honey guide possesses is that it is parasitic, using other birds' nests to lay its eggs in; the cuckoo is perhaps the only other bird up to this trick. Newly-hatched honey guides have a calcareous hook on the tip of their bill that they use to kill their nest mates. The honey-guide bird was chosen as a metaphor for the castle's precarious security, the honey as a symbol of cultural and physical wealth. The moated castles of Westphalia were constantly being overrun by the knights of Lüdinghausen and other ruffians, aping this familiar trait of the *Cuculus indicator.*

Here the honey guide serves as an indicator, pointing not towards honey but towards a cultural experience or vista. As the bird produces its calling sound from within the linden flower at the small pond—beckoning the curious to the site—the onlooker will recognize the view of the castle already viewed through the telescope. Visitors to the castle regularly explore its inner towers before making the final circular walk around the grounds. "Indicator for Burg Vischering" uses the same form to create a

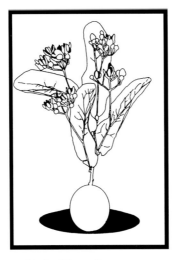

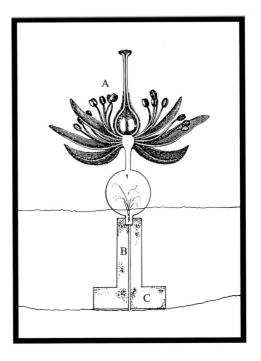

Linden Flower Cast

A - Enlarged cast of flower (section)
B - Water inlet from drain
C - Foundation

metaphorical roundelay, both of images as they are presented and of experiences as they are introduced into the spectator's regular route. "Indicator for Burg Vischering" is an ocular investigation of the eye of a *cuculus indicator* and the mnemonic trace it leaves, presenting through manipulated mythologies a rarefied view of an exquisite site.

# Joris-Karl Huysmans        A TRIP TO HOLLAND

"This is Haarlem, Monsieur," said my neighbour in the train carriage, "you can get out here." I grab my bags and jump on to the platform.

I'm heading towards an exit gate when an inscription traced on the station pediment, 'Uitgang,' stops me. I stare; nowhere is the word 'Haarlem' written on it. My heart stops; my travelling companion was mistaken. I lose my head and I shout at the train: "Stop! Stop!" Everyone turns around and laughs at the sight of this foreigner calling after a departing train. I spin round and make signs to those near me that I don't understand Dutch. I mime the hopeless despair of a man who has alighted too soon. I grimace, pointing at the inscription over the front of the station, then, with a dejected air, I repeat the word "Haarlem! Haarlem!" At which the other passengers repeat in unison, "Ja! Ja!"

What is going on? These people are very kind to be concerned about me, but their bearded faces emit only guttural noises, the meaning of which escapes me. Finally a man arrives who gabbles a little French. I recount my misadventure to him, at which he begins to shake with laughter. He ends up by telling me that I am in Haarlem, that the word 'Uitgang' isn't the name of the station, but rather the word that signifies the entrance or exit to the station, I can't remember which now.

I feel perfectly ridiculous, especially as the man describes the enormity of my blunder to those standing by and they all laugh.

I take the man by the sleeve of his jacket, and, determined to flee as quickly as possible, I say to him: "I was expected here last night by an uncle who lives in the city; but I missed the train. I can't see anyone at the station waiting for me and my suitcase is so heavy it hurts to lift it. Where could I find a cab?"

He obligingly takes me to a cabdriver, who makes ready with his harness. I give him the address 'Oude Gracht', which my rescuer corrects the pronunciation of, and so, driven by a coachman whose face is ringed by a thin beard like those of certain old monkeys, I bowl along the cobbled streets of the town.

Through the frame of the coach window I stare at the passing canals whose pistachio-coloured waters bathe the feet of step-gabled houses, their tops pierced here and there by round sky-lights encircled by ornamental dolphins, upright, heads down and tails in the air. A peal of bells rings out, followed by six chimes; the houses begin to stir; everywhere servants are washing and sweeping, big jolly women in clogs, their ample breasts constrained by corsets decorated with small flowers, and while some burnish brass door plaques or polish concealed mirrors, those spy-glasses that every good Hollander keeps in his window, others spray jets of water on to the brown bricks of the walls or scrub with big circular motions of their arms the terracotta slabs of the pavement.

The coach pulls to a halt. I get out, the door opens, and I fall into their arms. I explain why I'm late, and they take me to my room. I catch sight of myself in the mirror: I look like a hundred-year old chimney-sweep. I peel the dirt off my face and scrub, for my ears are full of coal dust and my nostrils black. Finally, I manage to repair the ravages of the journey, and go back downstairs. It's strange, all the same, the smell that houses in Holland seem to have: an elusive aroma, a vague hint of cloves and gingerbread.

And then, food is served! Steaming hot tea in cups, smoked-beef sandwiches, buttered rye-bread and a fruit loaf, all come in succession; then some finely-grated cheese in a kind of compote dish, and some red aniseed on a saucer.

I devour it, then it's: "Let's go," says my uncle; and we immediately set off across the city. We walk along canals, thread our way through narrow streets lined with old houses from the 16th century that bow and nod, each opposite the other; and all these alleyways, all these lanes that cut across one another, that run so crookedly, reflect their pompous old dowager facades, rouged with red-coloured bricks, in a looking-glass of green water; and then we come out on to the river, on to the Spaarne. Here, the women, arms bare, hail barges whose bellies are streaked with tar, and whose cabins are enlivened by leek-green shutters. All along the river masts thrust upwards, as far as the eye can see, up in to the ultramarine green of one of those Holland skies that always seem to be fleeced with reddish clouds. Everywhere on the quay, there are sailors in short, coarse trousers, old sea dogs with tanned faces and dry wiry hair; everywhere fishermen in ill-fitting jackets, with lead weights in their waistcoats and iron gaffs at their hips. And the women labour away, running about, swearing, and pulling on ropes, while others, the older ones, make their way down to the beach again, lurching arm-in-arm and leaning on their sticks, to look at these young women whose muscles bulge just like those of men. Another few steps and we reach the open countryside, that green and flat Haarlem countryside, dotted with the small mounds of windmills whose revolving blades seem to churn up the gilded froth of the clouds. On every side, kneeling women uproot potatoes, thrusting them into bags. All work in silence and in haste; only rarely does some raucous exclamation echo over the deadening noise of clogs ploughing the ground.

And so we return to the town, arriving at the large public square. To our left rises the church of Saint-Bavon; in front of us is the market, its pediment covered with carved bull's heads; then there is the town hall, the Stadhuis, which proclaims the banal motto of the municipality: *Vicit vim virtus*. It's here that the museum is housed. To be admitted, one must be more than sixteen years of age or "be accompanied by a mature person" (as stated in Article 5 of the statutes). As I was more than double the stipulated age, and as my uncle could by reason of his sixty-five years be considered a "mature person," I was authorised to see the Hals. Everything has been said about these eight canvases, which have been described over and over again by the critics. Besides, to judge them properly you need to linger over them, and it was too crowded. It seems more interesting and more original to me to mention the great unknown artists that are here, but of whom no visitor, no critic, ever speaks, so much is it agreed at Haarlem that only Hals exists! And yet Jan de Bray, born in the same town at an unknown date, and who died in December 1637, was an admirable portraitist, who painted with less freedom and enthusiasm than his rival Hals did in, say, those great paintings of guild members that have established his ineradicable glory, but who had a unique eye that saw beneath the skin and within the soul. Haarlem possesses nine canvases by this man whose name has been so unjustly swamped in the wake left by the vivacity of old Hals. Many of Bray's panels, portraits of kings and queens and orphans and lepers, are truly beautiful. Equally remarkable is Jan Verspronck, represented by a portrait of a haughty cavalier painted in silver-grey tones; and then, finally, from a comical point of view, there is Breughel the Younger, who in a canvas entitled *Flemish Proverbs*, interprets—I don't know how else to put it—the popular adage "To gamble is to lose the world" in the following manner: a trouserless peasant is playing at cards, sitting over the edge of a windowsill, and positioned below him is a terrestrial globe which topples under the weight of this…pleasantry. I know of nothing more curious.

The museum also has a collection of prints by Laurent Coster whose statue is in the square, and, amid antiquities of every kind, a certain instrument which set me thinking. It was a colossal beer tankard, which had lost its stand so it could be positioned on a table only when empty. In the middle of the glass was a wheel to force the beer out, like a waterwheel, as you drank. It seems it was necessary to down this glass in one, without pausing for breath—and it holds at least five litres! What bellies must they have had, the boozers who could swallow such draughts, and what incombustible brains they must have been endowed with. It was, in effect, a question of torture by beer rather than the age-old torture by water we've all heard about.

But, no. It wasn't prisoners who had to empty this glass in front of a judge, but honest fellows, the same jovial-faced ones that Hals has painted. Which goes to show that it wasn't the quantity, but rather the quality of the liquid that was to be feared. Perhaps if, instead of clear water, they had unloaded barrels of vintage wine into the stomachs of their torture victims, no one would have bothered to cry mercy.

Opposite the facade of the Stadhuis, on the market square, overrun by carts drawn by donkeys and driven by worthy termagents straight out of Jan Steen's paintings, stands the imposing mass of Saint-Bavon, a basilica of the 15th century whose mighty columns spring up to formidable heights beneath a colossal arch. It is enormous, but cold, lacking the mystery of stained glass, and the guilt-laden odour of a church. The only ornament, aside from the recent marble tombs dedicated to the glory of Conrad the engineer and Bilderdijk the poet, consists of a magnificent copper screen, decorated with figures and foliage, and a series of small model ships suspended from the arches. Unfortunately, these little boats are relatively modern toys (they date from the 17th century, I believe), the old ones, put up in memory of Count William who led the fifth crusade, having crumbled into dust over the centuries.

And then we flee, because a polyglot sacristan starts talking to us about the organ, beginning to enumerate for us in minute detail its stops and its keys. "Let's go and visit the Teyler Museum," my uncle says, and *voilà* he leads me into rooms piled with machines and magnets. I yawn, but he stops me and starts to explain the secrets of Herschel's reflecting telescope, of which there is a model here. Lord have mercy! Eventually we depart, leaving the city behind again so we can go to the woods.

Ah! here the scene changes. Like the woods at The Hague, those at Haarlem boast magnificent avenues of beech-trees as far as the eye can see, enormous beeches unscalably high, with trunks so large that no-one could get their arms round them. Unfortunately, skilled pruners have trimmed this forest of trees, cut back the leaves that adorn them, and shaped the bushes. It's like the Bois de Boulogne but planted with real trees, and, by a stroke of fortune that is hard to explain, without the fountains that are so dear to the public. Here and there are outdoor cafés where families have installed themselves, preparing their picnics and their teas. That's your Hollandais, for you! The waiter carries a huge iron bucket, full of hot coals, on which kettles are singing. *Papa* finishes smoking his cigar while *Mama* prepares the tea, butters the bread, and cuts smoked beef into slices as thin as lace, the taste of which is a marvel of subtlety and a rare treat, and they eat in the shade, making themselves at home, their children sitting round the table and then breaking off from time to time to go and play.

Here and there, young girls are laughing or reading thick magazines with dull, wholesome covers. Some are beautiful, but a bit unsettling. Fresh complexions, little rounded faces, clear and carefree eyes, a hint of puppy-fat around their mouths tempered by the flaming white of their teeth, dimples everywhere that deepen when they smile—and what a singular gait they have! Their waists are nearly always too heavy, necks too large and short, there's no elegance in these solid frames, like butchers' wives, even the thin ones, none of that delicate bone structure, that slender machinery, that kind of de luxe model which even the poorest people in Paris can manufacture. Added to which, when she walks there's no poise, no flow, no grace. And her clothes, however well-fitting, have something about them which betrays the ridiculous imitations of a provincial. We are far from *la*

*Parisienne*, whose slightly knowing charms would seem too affected here, next to this natural openness, this genuine bloom of youth.

I was reflecting on this while we were wandering on the edge of the forest, when, through a sieve of leaves, I caught sight of flat fields in the distance, immense fields which, in the months of April and May, are ripe with prodigious flowerbeds of pink carnations, auriculas and, above all, tulips. This is indeed the great garden of Europe, a worldly marketplace where florists from every country provision themselves, though it's a long time since a tulip bulb was valued, as the *Semper Augustus* was, at 13,000 florins! Today, the bulbs are the same but they are sold at reasonable prices, according to the going rate.

"Let's go. We must get back because it's four o'clock and dinner is ready."

And so, tired out, on the way back to the house, I asked my uncle if Haarlem, celebrated for its Hals, for its tulips, and for its organ, equally merited the reputation it had for its laundries.

But I learned that this fourth jewel in its crown was made of paste. Whether in Paris or London, in Boston or Suez, laundries now use chlorine, they mangle and mislay your household linen, they leave their order books behind and don't come on time—they even try to hide scorch marks by audacious folding.

Was I satisfied? But how could I be? Besides, what good would it have done to complain in front of that hunch-backed hotelier? Yesterday, I had arrived feverish, sweating, in the good city of Amsterdam, and, furnished with earnest and useless recommendations, I presented myself at the Haas Hotel (of Lievre). They had immediately shown me to a vast room, and apprehensively, I looked at a bed that was almost as high as the ceiling. As soon as I was alone and undressed, I went up to a chair and, with a vigorous spring, I leapt on to the bed. It was terrible. Having fallen from ceiling to the floor through an abyss of feathers, I sank into a crevass as walls of lukewarm fluff closed over me. I longed for a Belgian bed, those hard flat mattresses stuffed with beans, and napkins in lieu of sheets. Of course it's not pleasant to wear out one's back on those lumps, or, as soon as you've got into bed, to see the sheets riding up and leaving you naked, but at the end of the day that's better than being interred in a duvet tomb, the walls of which give off a humid heat like a warming pan.

What's more that evening I had the set menu, and they served me a stew with meatballs and purslane. After that a waiter, dressed in black, the gravity of which imposed itself on me, placed a turbot enveloped in a bed of red-currant jelly on my plate. This unexpected mixture of jam and fish dismayed me. Taken separately, the turbot was excellent, and the red-currant jelly, to be sure, smelled of the fields. But together they gave off a horrible smell, like a dish that had gone off and been disguised by pepper. I was beginning to have my doubts about this hotel when the patron himself came up and eagerly served me, as if it was some kind of rare dish, something muddy and purplish, like the dregs of a congealed wine. Fear gripped me. I asked the man, who spoke French, the name of the dish. He smiled and leaning over whispered: "Red lettuce stuffed with honey." Ugh! I tasted it and leapt from my chair. A stream of yellow grease, incredibly sweet, oozed from the belly of the lettuce. My stomach heaved, I excused myself saying I had another engagement and left.

Once outside, I inhaled a breath of air and rolled a cigarette. Night was falling, and all around me was the noise of the city and the musty smell of mud. I tried to orientate myself, guiding myself by the monuments which line the Dam, the large central square of the town. I wandered along interminable canals, crossed drawbridges, retraced my steps, circled back on myself, and found myself, stupefied, back at the Dam.

All the streets being roughly concentric, you walk for hours and end up back at the place you started.

Weary of this merry-go-round, I go down the Kalverstraat, the most magnificent street in Amsterdam, and, tired of walking in circles, I decide to walk, and to keep on walking, in a straight line. Then, I get lost. At last I come out at a large canal, full of barges. Before me stands a façade of balconies, beneath them, a sheet of still water. The place is deserted. I take a few more steps and then a strange monument rises up before me, an old brick building, flanked by five towers topped with candle-snuffer roofs and pierced with ogival windows. If I wasn't mistaken I'd arrived in front of Saint-Anthonieswaag in the new market, an old fortress which in the Middle Ages served as a defensive gate to the city, and which now houses, I believe, the public weights and measures office.

It made a strange impression on me. Among the silent barges sleeping on a bed of still water, these towers were not out of place; they naturally drew you back across centuries gone by, leading you to epochs that live only in the reader's imagination. This was the authentic Middle Ages, and the silence of the town, the monk-like shadows which passed, solitary and slow, recalled the melancholy of the curfew bell, the forbidden nocturnal life of ancient times.

All of a sudden, a peal of bells rings out, a poor, thin peal, playing one of those lightweight popular tunes, a childish and uncouth melody that strikes a false note, and this gives way to the slow, heavy strokes that signal the hour. Truly, one is a long way from Paris; in another country, another century. I retrace my steps and finish up, after repeatedly wandering along the banks of the canals, back at the Dam.

I'm worn out. I notice a café, and ask for a cup of tea because, despite my hurried journeying, that dreadful red cabbage I had tasted still oppressed me. But I was completely in the dark. How customs differ! In France, the cafés are celebrated for their light. Everywhere is gilt and mirrors, waiters jostling plates and glasses, juggling with carafes, responding with a yelled '*Voilà*!' to customers they've just served. Here, there was not a single lamp, not a sound. You are separated from the body of the dimly lit café by an impenetrable screen that blocks out every gleam. On tip-toe, as if he had come into a sick-room, the waiter advances, and in the obscurity which surrounds us, it's only with difficultly that you can make out the shapes of other people sitting down and drinking. You grope for your cup, and stupidly scald your fingers. Every now and then, amid this gloom speckled with the red dots of glowing cigarette ends, you can make out, when your neighbour puffs more intently, the edge of a nose, the end of a mustache, a portion of forehead, a little corner of a mouth, a glimpse of an eye.

The peacefulness of this scene on eye and ear didn't displease me. I mulled over in my mind the day's events. What an expedition! What marvels I had come across in these museums. I had at last seen Rembrandt's *The Night Watch*, so-called, even though the scene takes place in full daylight. And what strange sensations you experience in front of this canvas. First, amazement, then a vague feeling of disappointment, and finally, an admiration which suppresses criticism of specific details: the awkwardness of the man with a long body and short legs who is speaking to Captain Cocq, the vast sprawl of the subject, the hurly-burly of the canvas, the strange apparition of that small wizened child, that bizarre fairy, that dwarf Morgana who looks like Rembrandt—because it's a fact that hasn't been noticed before by any of the numerous writers desperate to explain the mystery behind this work, that this delightful little monster has the features, the nose, and the wrinkled eyes of the painter. Rembrandt has created in this painting a spiritual daughter, drawn in his own image, as pompously dressed as himself, magnificent and barbarous, the daughter of a rajah, a Hollandaise born in the Orient and brought up in a synagogue by the side of the Rhine. This painting of his is perhaps the one in which fantasy is most intimately blended with reality, an admirably mad, divinely precise work of art.

And then a procession of canvases parades through my over-tired mind. But the strange thing was, it wasn't the works of art so vaunted by the Museum—Van der Helst's *The Banquet of the Civic Guard*, the Steens and the Rembrandts—that came back to me, but works by unknown artists: paintings of churches by Hendrik Van Vliet and Delft, portraits by Moreelse, landscapes by Jodocus and Momper—and a disconcerting painting by Adriaen van de Venne and Jan Brueghel, *Fishing for Souls*. Imagine a blue landscape, vanishing into the distance, like those painted by Brueghel, and a river which, as it spreads out, sinks below the horizon. There are boats everywhere; to the right, in a barge, is a bishop in a red mitre surrounded by priests holding a fishing net full of holy objects and men, who wriggle like fish in a kreel; to the left, in the foreground, in another barge, are the Protestant clergy, all in black, reading the Bible; they too are casting their nets and fishing for men. What does this scene signify? And what about that unexpected bluebottle painted on the canvas, in *trompe l'oeil?*—there are no explanations in the catalogue—nothing on this picture which has been almost wholly ignored by art critics.

And I think back now to a marvelous seascape, the best perhaps that the Holland school ever produced, *A Storm on the River Meuse*, by Klaatz Zorgh, a livid green sea leaping up almost to the black clouds louring on the fearful horizon. And so I left the Museum, the Trippenhuis as they call it, and I went as far as the old pensioners' hospice where the Van der Hoope Museum is now installed. Ah! the two splendid Ruysdaels and that formidable Jan Steen! Hazily, I saw again that huge woman lying on a bank, drunk, and smoking a pipe. Hazily, I was back in front of Ruysdael's windmill, beating the black smoke of the clouds with its cross sails, but everything became confused and then faded as my eyes closed.

I pulled myself together. I decided that it was better to go and sleep than to drift like this on a chair. Besides, I had, thanks to the tea, defeated the fabled red lettuce, and so I returned to my hotel, where I fell straight to the bottom of the ditch in the bed, between two banks of feathers.

The next day, I rose early and strode across the city. Everywhere, there were tall houses, pitched gables stepped like stairs, and pierced with skylights like large eyes. Behind them was a forest of masts the tops of which rose up even higher, streaking the sky with the shrill colours of their ensigns. All the streets are liquid, the thoroughfares being filled with water, and bordered by pavements onto which the doors of the houses open directly. And these almost identical houses, all tall, with their narrow patchwork facades, white mortar in between the red bricks, checkered by gaudy signs. Here, a wooden Turk's head denotes a pharmacy; there, a crown of dried corn, plaited with tatters of old silk, dotted with wisps of straw, advertises a fresh herring merchant, and amid the monotony of almost identical streets, such images succeed each other, amusing the eye like Epinal images, the sight of which inevitably evokes memories of childhood, its great sorrows and lively joys. It's strange, but the impression this immense city gives me, at first sight, is that of a city for children, of a city smelling of cinnamon cakes, aniseed, milky coffee and warm bread. God knows, however, whether the opulent ship-owners of the port bother themselves with such idle speculations, or if they are obsessed by such puerile joys. Everywhere, boats are loading and unloading, everywhere, the whole length of the street, one sees brass plaques, signs, and men wandering round with quill-pens behind their ears or in their mouths. Ah no, there's no laughing here during the day, apart from in the morning when the maids are out. Here they are, squawking and laughing, chatting with the women who work in cellars that open out onto the pavement and from which they can buy hot water for tea and smouldering turf for foot-warmers.

I turn back towards the port, where a crowd of people, many dressed in bizarre costumes, is growing. Officers pass by, squeezed in to their beautiful blue uniforms trimmed with orange; children from the public orphanage sport the town's colours, black and red, on their jackets; a few women from the countryside mingle in the crowd with their silver or gold ceremonial helmets, on which—how stupid can you get—they had put awful straw hats decorated with sprouts and purple ribbons! I stare at people embarking on a steamer leaving for Jakarta; no heart-rending quayside scenes like the ones you see in France. Here, they set out for the Pacific or for Asia as easily as a Parisian takes the train to Marseilles. They think of the colonies overseas simply as provinces, and will go there on the slightest pretext.

This procession of travellers amused me. Some were truly comical: I can still remember a pudgy man, with a red face and blue eyes, his mouth stuffed with a cigar as big as a tree trunk, and carrying an unbelievable amount of packages. He was rolling along on his short legs, sweating and puffing, enveloped in an enormous overcoat and with a tiny bowler hat on his head. He carried expandable suitcases and trunks, had satchels strapped to his body, and dragged bags behind him; he waddled like a duck, and put his things down every now and then to wipe his brow and emit a throaty sigh that recalled the squeal of a rusty door hinge. May the journey of this jolly and blustering fellow-traveller be short!

Seeing these people embarking, I was possessed by the idea of taking a long voyage, stirred by a desire for the nomadic life. Really, it was now or never to see the world. The embarcation point for boats to Zuyder Zee was two steps away; a head of steam and we're off. I took a 45-cent ticket to Zaandam, which my uncle had warmly recommended me to visit. My 'long voyage' would take an hour. My God, this was a fine beginning to a journey! We threaded through a forest of masts, then the dykes began, those dykes of pasturages of a soft green, under a pale blue sky. All along the route, black and white cows lifted up their snouts, watching us; we crossed fishing boats, often manned by a lone fisherwoman. They would hail us, shout their hellos, signal to us with their hands, all the while suckling babies already bronzed by the spray. What beautiful pieces of machinery they were, solid and broad-backed, equipped with biceps of steel and hams of iron. Here and there, seagulls passed above us, and immense dunes appeared, then great white poles sticking up out of the water, beacons intended to signal the shallows.

Then at last the windmills began to appear, masses of windmills sawing wood, husking barley, grinding dyes, draining land, gigantic windmills whose circular movements give the illusion that the sky itself is spinning; and the town, with its houses painted yellow and green, and its glazed tile roofs, was like a town in a comic opera, as bright as a penny, properly looked-after and freshly painted. We disembarked and clouds of people threw themselves at me: invalids and polyglot beggars who offered, in French, English, German and Russian, to conduct me to the "House of Tsar Peter." It's the marvel of Zaandam. I found a wooden shed wedged into a larger stone shed, like those Japannese boxes which fit one inside the other. I went into this place of pilgrimage composed of two rooms and a bed, and then I left, because, to tell you the truth, the interior contained nothing of any worth. The story which has it that the Tsar lived in this dog-kennel to supervise the building of ships in Calf's building-yard is completely apocryphal. He spent at the very most just eight days in Zaandam. This relic is a simple tourist trap which I advise my compatriots to avoid. But if "Peter's House," as they call it here, is of no interest, the town itself is as charming as the scene in the last act of a play, with its canals lined with houses and trees, and its light wooden bridges which connect the two banks. One almost expects to see Nemorin appear in sea-green silk, and Estelle in her dove-grey and purple finery; and instead of Madame Pompadours in shepherdess costumes, there are honest, fat old women who salute you, stout women as velvety as fish, as plump as quails, as happy as chaffinches, who love a little tipple, applying their blusher from the inside, their faces stained red by voluminous bumpers of pure Dutch gin. As a change of scene, I returned by the Alkmaar boat, which took me through an infinity of canals, weirs and locks, a strange passage it was, full of toll-gates through which only the smallest barge could pass, toll-gates on the top of which stood an old man in cap and clogs, who dangled a clog at the end of a fishing line, like fish bait, in which sailors deposited a few centimes for the right to pass through.

And by dinner time I found myself back at the Dam, standing in front of a metal cross, a monument commemorating the campaigns of 1830, represented by a yellow sandstone statue of Concorde on a pedestal ornamented by jets of water.

Certainly, I prefer the few vestiges of old houses that can still be found in certain streets in Amsterdam to these modern monuments, and it was these that I went to see before returning to dine, where the patron continues to bow as he serves me the most unusual dishes. The man has, however, taken my observations into account; he has procured me a fairly hard straw mattress, which should exorcise the softness of the feather-bed. The trial I made that evening was enchanting. The blades of dry straw in the mattress cracked whenever you touched them. I played a game with myself, imagining that it was the noise of canal locks. I saw myself in a cabin, navigating a boat, I dreamed of Java, of Batavia, of the Sonde Islands, Asia, and the Pacific, all the while snoring like a contented dormouse. This was proper travelling this was: no danger, no time-wasting, and, what's more, it was free.

*Translated from the French by Brendan King*

# NOTES ON THE CONTRIBUTORS

JOHN ASHBERY's most recent book of poems was *Where Shall I Wander*. His next, *A Wordly Country*, will be published this winter. He is a Leo, born the same day as Marcel Duchamp and Gerard Manley Hopkins, as well as film comedian Joe E. Brown. The collages reproduced in the current issue were all executed in the early 1970s. For more information go to: www.flowchartfoundation.org.arc

JACK BARTH is an artist who lives in New York. His work can be found in a number of public collections, including the Museum of Modern Art and the New York Public Library.

BILL BERKSON's latest publications include an online chapbook, *Same Here*, from www.bigbridge.org (#11); a collaboration with Bernadette Mayer entitled *What's Your Idea of a Good Time?: Letter & Interviews 1977-1985* (Tuumba Press, 2006), and a special issue of Fell Swoop magazine, *Parts of the Body: A 1970s/80s Scrapbook*. He is the Distinguished Mellon Lecturer at the Skowhegan School of Art for 2006.

NICK CARBÓ is the author of three books of poetry, the latest being *Andalusian Dawn* (2004). He has edited three anthologies of Filipino writing, including *Pinoy Poetics* (2004). His visual poems have been exibited at the "Infinity" show at Harvard, the Studio Alternative, and the Museum of Contemporary Art in North Miami.

DAVID CARBONE is a painter and writer living in New York City. He has exhibited widely, including the Boston Museum, the Aldrich Museum of Contemporary Art, the Institute of Contemporary Art, Boston, the National Academy of Design and Phyllis Kind Gallery, Chicago. He has published criticism and essays on painters in *Antaeus*, *Arts Magazine*, *Art and Antiques* and *Modern Painters*, and can occasionally be heard on National Public Radio.

MARIE CHAIX, born in Lyons and raised in Paris, is the author of nine books, seven of them autobiographical, two of them novels. She is best known for *The Laurels of Lake Constance*, which retraces the life of her collaborationist father and that of her family during the postwar years. *The Summer of the Elder Tree*, a memoir and meditation on the theme of separation, was published in Paris in 2005, her first book to appear in fourteen years.

MILES CHAMPION's books include *Compositional Bonbons Placate*, *Sore Models* and *Three Bell Zero*. His recent poems were published as issues of *I Saw Johnny Yesterday* and *Tolling Elves*. A chapbook, *Six of One*, is in the works from A Rest Press, and a new collection is forthcoming from Adventures in Poetry in 2007.

WILLIAM CORBETT is a poet living in Boston's South End and teaching at MIT. Among his books are *Philip Guston's Late Work: A Memoir*. He has edited *The Letters of James Schuyler to Frank O'Hara*.

EDWIN DENBY (1903-1983), though principally known as a dance critic (his legendary *Dance Writings* were published in 1986), was also a semi-secret poet whose work proved to be a major influence on the second generation of New York School

Poets (see *The Complete Poems*, 1986). The present poem commemorates an accident which befell his young friend Thomas Burckhardt, and dates from the early 1970s.

DENISE DUHAMEL's most recent poetry titles are *Two and Two* (University of Pittsburgh Press, 2005), *Mille et un Sentiments* (Firewheel, 2005) and *Queen for a Day: Selected and New Poems* (Pittsburgh, 2001). A winner of a National Endowment Fellowship in Poetry, she teaches poetry at Florida International University in Miami.

CHRIS EDGAR is the author of the collection *At Port Royal* (Adventures in Poetry, 2003), and was formerly Publications Director of Teachers & Writers Collaborative in New York. Since February 2006, he has been a resident of Geneva, Switzerland.

LANCE ESPLUND is the chief art critic of *The New York Sun* and serves on the editorial board of *Modern Painters*. He has taught at the Parsons School of Design, Queens College/CUNY and Rider University. His essays have appeared in *Harper's*, *Art in America*, *Modern Painters*, *The Yale Review*, *The Threepenny Review* and *The New Republic*.

THOMAS EVANS edits *Tolling Elves*, a monthly magazine printing one author and one artist (see: http://www.onedit.net/tollingelves/contents.html). He is also editing a *Collected Poems of Jess*. Five *'emblems'* can seen at www.onedit.net.

LARRY FAGIN, a New York City native, is the author or co-author of fifteen collections of poems. He co-edits *Adventures in Poetry* books and teaches at the New School.

JANE HAMMOND has had 28 solo exhibitions. Her work is in the collections of 40 major museums, including the Museum of Modern Art, the Metropolitan Museum of Art and the Whitney Museum of American Art. A traveling museum exhibition of her works on paper commences in late 2006. She lives in New York City where she is represented by Galerie Lelong.

KREG HASEGAWA lives in Seattle. He has co-edited *Monkey Puzzle*, a literary magazine, and has curated a reading series at the now defunct 1506 Projects Art Gallery. His work has appeared in *Sal Mimeo*, *The News*, *Spring Formal* and *Greetings*. He is currently working on a degree in Library Science. A chapbook is due out this winter.

JORIS-KARL HUYSMANS (1848-1907) first published his Decadent masterpiece *A Rebours (Against Nature)* in 1884. Robert Baldick's unsurpassed English translation is available from Penguin. The present Dutch travelogue was originally published in two issues of the *Revue illustrée*, no. 25 and no. 27 (December 1886 and January 1887). Brendan King maintains an excellent Huysmans website (http://www.huysmans.org) and has also translated Huysmans' *La Bas, Parisian Sketches*, *Marthe* and a revised and annotated re-edition of Baldick's *The Life of J.-K. Huysmans*. The excellent Societé J.-K. Huysmans may be reached at Centre de recherche sur la litterature française de XlXe siécle, Université Paris-Sorbonne, 1 rue Victor Cousin, 75230 Paris.

SHIRLEY JAFFE is an American painter who has lived and worked in Paris since 1949. The artist is represented by Galerie Nathalie Obadia in Paris, and Tibor de Nagy Gallery in New York, which presented an exhibition of her recent paintings in 2005.

JESS (1923-2004) was a painter, collagist, and poet. Born Burgess Collins, he trained as a chemist, then studied at The California School of Fine Arts with Clifford Still, David Park and Elmer Bischoff in 1949. With his partner Robert Duncan and the painter Harry Jacobus he ran the King Ubu Gallery in San Francisco. Among his best-known works are 'Tricky Cad' (paste-ups of Dick Tracy cartoons), the 'Translations' series, and the large-scale paste-up 'Narkissos.' A touring exhibition of his book-related paintings, drawings and collages will open in 2007.

DON JOINT is an artist who lives in New York City and Milton, PA. He is represented by Francis M. Naumann Fine Art in NYC and Craig Flinner Contemporary in Baltimore, MD. His work has been favorably reviewed in *Art in America, The New York Times* and the *New York Observer*, and is in the collections of the Oklahoma Museum of Art, the Cleveland Museum of Art and the Erie Museum of Art.

PAUL ETIENNE LINCOLN creates elaborate installations and allegorical machines that investigate circumstances. Projects include a study of Madame de Pompadour's effect on the Court of Louis XV, and the technological infrastructure of New York City. Recent books are *A Violet Somnambulist Spiriting the Fugacious Bloom, The Metropolis of Metaphorical Intimations* and, most recently, *Sinfonia Torinese*, and *The Velocity of Thought*.

HARRY MATHEWS is the author of six novels and several collections of poetry, his most recent books being *Sainte Catherine*, a novella written in French (Éditions P.O.L, 2000), *The Human Country: the Collected Short Stories* (Dalkey Archive Press, 2002), *The Case of the Persevering Maltese: Collected Essays* (Dalkey Archive Press, 2003), *Oulipo Compendium* (co-edited with Alastair Brotchie; Atlas Press and Make Now Press, 2005) and *My Life in CIA: A Chronicle of 1973* (Dalkey Archive Press, 2005).

RON MOROSAN is a painter who lives and works in New York City. He exhibits his work nationally and internationally.

FRANCIS M. NAUMANN is an independent scholar, curator and art dealer, specializing in the art of the Dada and Surrealist periods. He is author of numerous articles and exhibition catalogues, including *New York Dada 1915-25* (Harry N. Abrams, 1994), *Marcel Duchamp: The Art of Making Art in the Age of Mechanical Reproduction* (Harry N. Abrams, 1999), *Wallace Putnam* (Harry N. Abrams, 2002) and, most recently, *Conversion to Modernism: The Early Work of Man Ray* (Rutgers University Press, 2002). In 1996, he organized "Making Mischief: Dada Invades New York" for the Whitney Museum of American Art, and in 1997, "Beatrice Wood: A Centennial Tribute" for the American Craft Museum in New York. He is preparing for publication a selection of his essays on Marcel Duchamp, and currently owns and operates his own gallery in New York City.

MARIO NAVES is an artist, teacher and critic. Naves' collages are shown at the Elizabeth Harris Gallery in New York and Allyn Gallup Contemporary Art in

Sarasota, FL. He has taught at Pratt Institute, the New York Studio School and The Ringling School of Art. Naves' column on the visual arts, "Currently Hanging," has appeared weekly in *The New York Observer* since 1999.

CHARLES NORTH's most recent books are *The Nearness of the Way You Look Tonight* (Adventures in Poetry, 2001) and *Tulips* (collaborations with Trevor Winkfield; Phylum Press, 2004). His new book of poems, *Cadenza*, is forthcoming from Hanging Loose Press in March 2007.

RON PADGETT's most recent books include a collection of poems, *You Never Know*, and two memoirs, *Oklahoma Tough: My Father, King of the Tulsa Bootleggers* and *Joe: A Memoir of Joe Brainard*. He is the editor of *The Handbook of Poetic Forms* and *World Poets: An Encyclopedia for Students*, as well as the translator of Blaise Cendrars' *Complete Poems*. His poetry has received awards from the American Academy of Arts and Letters and the Guggenheim Foundation, and the French government named him an Officer in the Order of Arts and Letters. More can be found at www.ronpadgett.com.

MARK POLIZZOTTI is the author of *Revolution of the Mind: The Life of André Breton*, and has translated works by Breton, René Daumal, Jean Echenoz, Maurice Roche, Marguerite Duras and others. His other books include *Lautréamont Nomad, The New Life: Poems*, the collaborative novel *S.*, and a study of Luis Buñuel's *Los Olvidados* for the British Film Institute. A monograph on Bob Dylan's *Highway 61 Revisited* will be published later this year.

MARCIN RAMOCKI is a new media artist and curator based in Williamsburg, Brooklyn. His work involves software art projects, generative and interactive media installations as well as web-based projects. He is a founder of vertexList space in Brooklyn and an instructor of new media arts at the New Jersey City University. Marcin's first feature-length documentary *8 BIT* will premiere at MoMA in October 2006. For more info on his work please visit www.ramocki.net.

CARTER RATCLIFF's books of poetry include *Fever Coast* and *Give Me Tomorrow*. *Arrivederci, Modernismo* will be published by Libellum Press later this year. A contributing editor of *Art in America*, he writes frequently about American and European art.

RAPHAEL RUBINSTEIN's books include a collection of poems (*The Basement of the Café Rilke*, 1997), a selection of autobiographical prose (*Postcards from Alphaville*, 2000) and a volume of art writing (*Polychrome Profusion: Selected Art Critcism 1990-2002*), all from Hard Press Editions. A French translation by Marcel Cohen of *In Search of the Miraculous* was published in 2004 (Editions Grèges Montpelier). He is a Senior Editor at *Art in America*.

ALAN SHOCKLEY has held residencies at the MacDowell Colony, the Atlantic Center for the Arts, and the Centro Studi Ligure. Recent performances include *candlepin bowling deadwood* by the California EAR Unit and *cold springs branch, 10 p.m.* by pianist Guy Livingston. In 2005 his orchestral work *the night copies me in all its stars* was released on CD in a recording by the Kiev Philharmonic. His current preoccupations include experiments in musical form, misplaced or frustrated grooves, and toys. He recently acquired a theremin and a fretless banjo.

JUDITH E. STEIN, former curator at the Pennsylvania Academy of Fine Arts, organized the exhibitions *Red Grooms: A Retrospective*, *The Figurative Fifties: New York School Figurative Expressionism*, and *I Tell My Heart: The Art of Horace Pippin*. A recipient of the Pew Fellowship in the Arts for her writings on art, she is working on a biography of the late art dealer Richard Bellamy. "Bonds of Steel: Mark di Suvero and Richard Bellamy" (*Art in America*, November 2005) draws on this research, as does the present text.

ADRIAN STOKES (1902-1972) was an English art theorist, painter, poet and the author of over twenty books, of which *Michelangelo* (Routledge Classics, 2002) and *The Quattro Cento/Stones of Rimini* (University of Pennsylvania Press, 2002) are presently in print.

EVELYN TWITCHELL is a painter who lives and works in Brooklyn, NY and Milton, PA. She has had three solo exhibitions at the Prince Street Gallery in New York. She has taught at Marymount College, New York City College of Technology and Rider University.

TREVOR WINKFIELD exhibits his paintings at Tibor de Nagy Gallery in New York City. *Trevor Winkfield's Drawings* was recently published by Bamberger Books. The present text on Sassetta is the first part of a book in progress. For more information go to trevorwinkfield.com.

*Acknowledgements*: "The Body-Emblem and Art" © Estate of Adrian Stokes. "Osap's Faebles" © Jess Collins Trust. Thanks to Sharon and Thurston Twigg-Smith, Hilde and David Burton, Christopher Wagstaff and Ida Hodes for assistance with its transcription. Nadleman's *Standing Male Nude*, courtesy Private Collection, New York, NY. *Standing Male Nude* photo credit: David Carbone. Louis Eilshemius drawings courtesy Private Collections, New York, NY. John Ashbery Postcard Collages courtesy Flow Chart Foundation. Thanks to Eric Brown and Andy Arnot of Tibor de Nagy Gallery for their assistance with Shirley Jaffe's images. Special thanks to Don Joint.